THE PRIMARY SCHOOL IN
CHANGING TIMES

Educational management series
Series editor: Cyril Poster

Recent titles in this series include:

THE PRIMARY SCHOOL IN CHANGING TIMES

The Australian experience

Edited by Tony Townsend

London and New York

First published 1998
by Routledge
11 New Fetter Lane, London EC4P 4EE

Selection and editorial matter © 1998 Tony Townsend; individual chapters the
contributors

Typeset in Times by Routledge
Printed and bound in Great Britain by
Page Bros (Norwich) Ltd

British Library Cataloguing in Publication Data
A catalogue record for this book is available from the British Library

Library of Congress Cataloging in Publication Data
The primary school in changing times: the Australian experience / edited by Tony
Townsend
p. cm. – (Educational management series)
Includes bibliographical references and index.
1. Elementary schools – Australia 2. Education, Elementary – Australia. 3.
Educational change – Australia. I. Townsend, Tony. II. Series.
LA2104. A97 1998
372.994 – dc21 97–43238
CIP

ISBN 0–415–14656–9

To my parents,
Elsie and Colin Townsend,
who provided the love, support
and direction required to assist their
child in his quest for a
successful primary-school education.
I wish that all children could
have been so fortunate.

CONTENTS

CONTENTS

CONTENTS

CONTENTS

ILLUSTRATIONS

TABLES

FIGURES

xi

NOTES ON CONTRIBUTORS

John Ainley is an Associate Director of the Australian Council for Educational Research and Head of its Policy Research Division. He is a Fellow of the Australian College of Education. Dr Ainley has undertaken a number of policy-oriented research studies for Commonwealth and state education authorities, and is the author of many research reports and journal articles. Among studies concerned with aspects of secondary schooling which he has directed are two national studies of subject choice in the senior secondary years (*Subject Choice in Senior Secondary School*, Australian Government Publishing Service, 1990), a study of students and their secondary schools in Victoria (*School Organisation and the Quality of Schooling*, Australian Council for Educational Research (ACER), 1986), an investigation of socio-economic status and school education in Australia and a four-year longitudinal study of the progress of students through the senior secondary years in New South Wales (*Progress Through High School*, ACER, 1992). He has also conducted research on the achievements and attitudes to school of students in the primary-school years (*Primary Schooling in Victoria*, ACER, 1990) and has maintained a continuing involvement in research on factors which influence the quality of school life for students. In 1982 he was a visiting scholar at the Far West Laboratory for Educational Research in San Francisco, where he worked on the Instructional Management Project, a study of the ways in which elementary-school principals influence learning processes and outcomes in classrooms. In 1991 he was a visiting scholar at the Ontario Institute for Studies in Education, where he worked on an evaluation of the transition-years initiatives of the Ontario Ministry of Education and had responsibility for investigating the views of parents about educational issues in those years.

Hedley Beare is Professor Emeritus in Education at the University of Melbourne, where he specialises in Educational Administration and Policy. He is currently a part-time Senior Associate in the Centre for Applied Educational Research, an educational consultant and a freelance writer. He has degrees from Adelaide, Melbourne and Harvard Universities, has been a visiting scholar at the Universities of Oregon, Stanford, Bristol, Penn State, Harvard and London, was a Harkness Fellow from 1967 to 1970 and a senior Fulbright Scholar in 1979. He has been awarded the Gold Medals from the Australian College of Education and the Australian Council for Educational Administration, and has been President of the International Congress for School Effectiveness and Improvement. He helped to found the only two public-school systems established in Australia this century (Northern Territory and the Australian Capital Territory) and was the foundation chief executive officer (CEO) for both systems. He speaks and writes on the topics of the future of schooling and the professionalisation of teaching, and is a well-known public commentator on education policy. Recent publications have included *Education for the Third Millennium: Planning for School Futures in the Context of Global Developments* (Incorporated Association of Registered Teachers of Australia (IARTV), 1996) and *Education for the Twenty-first Century*, with Richard Slaughter (Routledge, 1993).

Len Cairns is an Associate Professor in the Faculty of Education at Monash University. He has been a prominent teacher educator in Australia for many years and has been significantly involved in the introduction of such innovations as micro-teaching, clinical supervision and aspects of school-based teacher education into pre-service courses at the University of Sydney and at the former Gippsland Institute of Advanced Education (now part of Monash). A successful primary teacher, Len has also taught adult literacy classes and has been a student counsellor in the New South Wales technical and further education (TAFE) system. Len has published extensively in the areas of teacher education, psychology and multiculturalism. He currently co-edits *The Journal of Teaching Practice* and serves on the editorial advisory boards of two international education journals. Recent publications include entries in the *International Encyclopaedia of Teaching and Teacher Education* (Pergamon, 1995) and the *Handbook of Communication Skills*, (Routledge, 1996). Len is currently working on the interface between education and industry with the Australian Capability Network and teaches at undergraduate, teacher upgrading and higher-degree levels at Monash. He is also actively involved in professional development for primary teachers. Len was honoured as a Fellow of the Australian Teacher Education Association in 1991.

Brian J. Caldwell is Professor of Education and Head of the Department of Education Policy and Management at the University of Melbourne. He was a member of the research team in the Cooperative Research Project, which sought the views of principals in the landmark reform in the state of Victoria known as Schools of the Future, with key findings reported in this book. His main interests lie in leadership, policy, resource allocation and the management of change, especially where significant responsibility, authority and accountability are decentralised to schools. His co-authored books (with Jim Spinks) on this theme – *The Self-managing School* (Falmer, 1988) and *Leading the Self-managing School* (Falmer, 1992) – have helped shape developments in a number of countries, with *Beyond the Self-managing School* (Falmer, 1998, with Jim Spinks) and *The Future of Schools* (Falmer, 1998, with Don Hayward) proposing further development to achieve lasting school reform in the early years of the third millennium.

Janine Collier has been a teacher since the 1970s, and has worked in a number of government secondary colleges in Melbourne and Geelong; she has also worked as a humanities and general curriculum consultant to both primary and secondary schools in the western region of Melbourne. During the early 1990s she worked for several years as a Research Assistant at the Faculty of Education, Deakin University, Geelong, before returning to teaching in 1996.

Lindsay Fitzclarence has been teaching at Deakin University since 1977, prior to which he taught as a physical education teacher. His postgraduate background is in the study of curriculum and contemporary cultural change. Dr Fitzclarence currently teaches in a range of education and curriculum studies programmes at both undergraduate and postgraduate levels. Recently he has been involved in a number of research projects that have studied the relationship between education and popular culture. He is currently involved in an action research project designed to explore the learning which occurs within the subculture of a junior-aged football team.

Maurice Galton is Professor of Primary Education and Dean of the School of Education, University of Leicester, UK. His first book (with Brian Simon and Paul Croll), entitled *Inside the Primary Classroom* (Routledge & Kegan Paul, 1980), reported the Observational Research and Classroom teaching (ORACLE) project, which was the first large-scale classroom observation study in Britain. Since the ORACLE project he has published eight books and over thirty articles on all aspects of primary education. He has served as a consultant on primary education to the Council of Europe and has conducted research for the Council in several European states.

Anne Kennedy is a lecturer in the Faculty of Education at Monash University, Melbourne. She has taught in junior schools and pre-schools, and has been a director of a University childcare centre. She is co-author of the *Review of Quality Indicators in Services for Children 0–12 Years* and recently collaborated in the development of a curriculum framework for school-age childcare services in Victoria entitled One Arena for Childhood. She is a moderator for the National Child Care Accreditation Council and serves on the executive of both the Kindergarten Association of Victoria and the Victorian Early Years Foundation. She has been a visiting professor at the University of Linköping in Sweden. Her research into transition-to-school issues for children, families and teachers has been presented at conferences in Australia and the United States. Her doctoral research is in the area of early childhood teachers' socialisation.

Jane Kenway is a Professor of Educational Administration at Deakin University. Her strengths are in research, research leadership and research-based teaching. She has published widely in international and national refereed journals, in books and in journals for the education profession. She has written or edited five books, including *Marketing Education: Some Critical Issues* (edited; Deakin University Press, 1995), *Economising Education: The Post-Fordist Directions* (edited; Deakin University Press, 1994) and *Gender Matters in Educational Administration and Policy: A Feminist Introduction* (edited with Jill Blackmore; Falmer Press, 1993). She also has a successful record of building cross-institutional and state research teams, and regularly provides consultancy services to governments.

Colin Marsh is Dean of Academic Studies at the Australian Institute of University Studies at the Joondalup Campus of Curtain University. He has had extensive experience as an educator and administrator, having worked in primary and secondary schools, as a chief executive officer (CEO) in the public service and as a university professor. He has published twenty books on curriculum and teaching. Recent publications include *Key Concepts for Understanding Curriculum* (2nd edn, Falmer, 1997), *Producing a National Curriculum: Plans and Paranoia* (Allen and Unwin, 1994) and *Handbook for Beginning Teachers* (Longman, 1996).

Geoff Romeo is a Senior Lecturer in the Faculty of Education at Monash University, Melbourne. His research interests include the use of computers in education to improve teaching and learning, the development of primary curriculum and action research. He spent fifteen years in the primary classroom, including twelve months as an International Teaching Fellow in Arizona, USA. He is also active in delivering and organising professional development for schools, community organisations and teachers. He is a state councillor for the Computing in Education Group of Victoria. He has written a number of articles related to the computer as a learning tool in primary schools, and has presented conference papers and workshops in various Australian states and the United Kingdom.

Tony Townsend is an Associate Professor in the Faculty of Education and, from 1988 to 1997, the Director of the South Pacific Centre for School and Community Development at Monash University in Melbourne. He has brought the research interests of community education and school effectiveness together in his work for the International Community Education Association (where he was the elected Director of the Pacific Region between 1987 and 1996) and the International Congress for School Effectiveness and Improvement (ICSEI) (where he serves on the editorial board of the journal *School Effectiveness and School Improvement* and was conference manager for ICSEI's 1994 conference in Melbourne). He has published widely in school management and community education journals, and is the author of *Effective Schooling for the Community: Core Plus Education* (Routledge, 1994) and the editor of the recent publication *Restructuring and Quality: Issues for Tomorrow's Schools* (Routledge, 1997). He has conducted workshops and seminars for principals, teachers, parents and community members in over twenty countries in the Pacific, Asia, North America and Europe.

Ian Walker is a principal lecturer in the Faculty of Education at Monash University, Melbourne. His two research interests are children's literacy and parental involvement. He has presented papers on aspects of these areas, including literacy in crisis families and parental involvement at a number of international conferences. Recently he was funded by the Swedish Council to contribute to programmes at the University of Linköping. Ian has recently completed a PhD in the area of parental involvement in children's literacy.

John Williamson is Professor of Education and Head of Department at the University of Tasmania. He is a graduate of universities in Australia and the United Kingdom. He has published in the areas of curriculum implementation and evaluation, teaching studies, including classroom processes and teachers' work lives, teacher education, and vocational education and training. During 1993–5 John was a consultant to the Organisation for Economic Cooperation and Development (OECD) on a sixteen-country study of teacher quality and in 1994–6 directed the Australian contribution to the OECD twenty-two-country study of science, mathematics and technology education innovation. He is a Fellow of the Australian Teacher Education Association.

PREFACE: CHANGING TIMES, CHANGING WAYS

Over the past few years Australian primary schools have had to respond to the claims that primary schools seem to be much the same places in the mid-1990s as they were in the mid-1960s. The buildings still look much the same; there is still a teacher whose task it is to guide a group of around thirty students through the year; there are specialist teachers in some areas but much of the work being done is still a combination of 'chalk and talk' (although this is now perhaps 'whiteboard and marker') and individual or group task completion. Principals, teachers and parents are all involved in various ways in the education of the children.

Comments such as 'Schools are still modelled on a curious mix of the factory, the asylum and the prison' and 'We are glad to see the end of the traditional factory; why should we expect the school modelled on it to be welcome to children?' (Hargreaves 1994: 43) suggest that change is necessary, even overdue: 'no other institution faces challenges as radical as those that which will transform the school' (Drucker 1993: 209). This has led to the perception that schools have been largely protected from the types of changes that other institutions in our society have recently undergone:

> this one most vital area of our national life – public education – has not undergone the process of revitalising change. In our economic and social life we expect change, but in the public schools we have clung tenaciously to the ideas and techniques of earlier decades and even previous centuries.
>
> (Gerstner *et al.* 1994: 3)

However, in many ways the primary school of the mid-1990s is hardly recognisable when compared to one of twenty or so years ago. The international trend towards devolution of many of the decisions and responsibilities for managing schools to the school itself – with the end-point being self-managing or self-governing public schools – has been perhaps the most powerful influence changing the understanding of the management of education over the past two decades. Instances can be seen in Canada, where the

Edmonton School District pioneered many of the features we see today; in the United Kingdom, with grant-maintained (GM) and locally managed (LM) Schools; in the United States, with the charter-school movement; and in New Zealand, which adapted the Canadian model as a means for developing a national system of self-managing schools called Schools of Tomorrow.

In recent years there has also been substantial change in the way in which education is structured, financed and managed in Australia. The move towards more self-managing schools, complete with school councils, school charters, school global budgets, quality assurance, school reviews, and utilising the new technologies, is now a feature of most, if not all, Australian school systems. One only has to look at the terminology used in Western Australia (Better Schools, 1987), New South Wales (School Renewal, 1989) and Victoria (Schools of the Future, 1993), and those that are emerging with Queensland's Leading Schools and Tasmania's Directions for Education initiatives to see the emphasis being placed on accountability, marketing and management, particularly as they impact on school communities.

It could be argued that this move of the world of education into the world of business has developed, in Australia at least, with the coming of age of the 'baby-boomers', that group of people born near the end of the Second World War. It also may be the case in other Western societies. Minzey (1981) once said that this group is going through society like a watermelon through a boa constrictor.

Ever since history began, each generation has been slightly better off than the one that preceded it, in educational terms, in social terms and in income terms. Those who had the power to make decisions seemed to take the view that development needed to continue. Take, for example, those involved in making decisions for the 'baby-boomer' generation in Australia. Universal secondary education was put in place after the war so that they could all get a decent education. By the time they reached university, pressure was being placed on governments to provide free tertiary education as well. By the time university or college was completed, everyone who wanted to work was able to find a job. For the first time, women entered the workforce in large numbers, and as they found inequities in the system they tried to address them. Things like equal pay for equal work, women's liberation and the assault on the 'glass ceiling' can all be attributed to the 'baby-boomer' generation.

However, somewhere along the line something seemed to go awry. We entered the age of 'me-ism'. The attention and resources devoted to this group seemed to create a monster, almost in proportion to the resources expended on them. The more education the boomers received, the better their jobs and their material wealth, the more they wanted. The selflessness of previous generations created a selfishness in the boomers that, it could be argued, largely still remains.

They dabbled in sex and drugs, and opened a Pandora's box which we still have not been able to close. Some chose not to marry or, if they did, married late and had children even later. In many cases the need to 'establish oneself' (read 'gather material resources') was given as the reason. Children were partly raised by grandparents or childcare agencies because both parents chose to stay at work. Divorce rates sky-rocketed – some would argue because the parents chose their own well-being over that of their children. The gap between the haves and the have-nots started to widen.

And where are these people now, twenty or so years later? Those who succeeded in the 1960s and 1970s are now the most powerful people in our community. They are the ones shaping decisions in government, in commerce, in society. They seem not to mind about high youth unemployment because they can look after themselves and their own families. They do not care about the demise of the public health system because they have health insurance, or the demise of public schooling because their children have gone through school and probably university, but are not yet old enough to have produced school-age grandchildren. They do not care about public transport or public housing because they do not use either.

They are at the peak of their earning capacity and they want to maximise their advantage while they can. They are the economic rationalists who demand decreased public spending so that governments can decrease taxes, thereby maximising company profits and personal gain. They are the executives seeking massive pay increases and benefits while exhorting the workers to do more for less. They wish to take money away from schools because they have finished with them. They wish to take money away from health services because they are not yet old enough to be suffering the problems of old age. [However, a sign of the future has recently emerged. A recent report (Alcorn 1997: 1, 4) describes how a drug used in the treatment of impotence has now been placed on the Federal Government's Pharmaceutical Benefits Scheme, which means that baby-boomers suffering impotence problems now pay $4 instead of $29 for an injection that enables them to perform. The taxpayer now pays 80 per cent of the cost. The medical director of the company involved said: 'The baby boomers are a big group who are going to play all sorts of havoc in the future' (*ibid.*: 4). In ten years' time we should be prepared for a massive increase in the health budget.] The unemployed have themselves to blame. Any money allocated to social service of any kind is seen as a cost to society rather than a benefit or, in the case of education, rather than an investment in the future. They have lost the sense of the common good (Galbraith 1992). Profit has come to be equated with progress, community has given way to commerce and sharing is a sign of weakness. For the first time, the generation following the baby-boomers will be poorer than their parents, in all senses of the word.

Our politicians – of all parties – have listened, and are listening to, the boomers because they are the most powerful and vocal group in society. Those arguing for downsizing public expenditure (to provide tax relief) started to hold sway over those arguing for increased public support services around the mid-1980s, which was the time when the crossroads of increasing public expenditure and increased calls for tax relief intersected. Since that time both sides of government have adopted various strategies to change the balance. They sold public assets (but only those that were profitable, since business does not want to buy those that make no money) and introduced a variety of strategies to make ends meet. They shifted money from one portfolio to another and then shifted it back a couple of years later, in an endeavour to make everyone happy at least some of the time.

They introduced 'user-pay' schemes, but it seemed that the people who most needed the service could not afford to pay and those that could afford to pay did not need the service. The user-pays mentality exacerbates this problem because it not only causes problems for individuals but actually leads to the demise of services. If the only people who require a service are those who cannot afford to use it the service itself becomes unviable and is likely to attract less government funding on the basis that no one uses the service.

'Productivity efficiencies' were introduced, which is a short way of saying that although the number of those using the service (hospitals, tertiary education) increased substantially the increase in funding lagged far behind. None of these schemes have worked well enough to satisfy the greed of the boomers. Anil Bordia (1996) argued: 'The world has enough resources for human need, but not enough for human greed.' Australia has not yet learned that lesson. The current changes to education must be seen as part of this broader social change.

The changes to education could been seen as being a destabilising force within school systems, as they place schools in competition with each other. It could be argued that, while some schools have struggled to come to grips with new requirements, new procedures and new accountability measures, others have flourished under self-management. This seems to be the classic implementation of the Chinese word 'crisis', which is made up of two characters, one meaning 'danger' and the other meaning 'opportunity'. School restructuring has been characterised by some as a danger to the public-school system, but others have seen it as an opportunity, particularly for their own schools.

This book focuses on the impact that such change has had on the primary school, the place where, for a century and a quarter, every Australian child has commenced his or her formal education journey. Only some had a pre-school education and until after the Second World War not all had a secondary education – and even fewer completed it – but all had a primary education. For about a hundred years education was stable, centralised and almost the same for everyone, but the last twenty years or so have increasingly seen management of education being returned to school communities. One of the outcomes has been a substantial variation in the type and, dare one say it, quality of education from school to school.

The introduction of self-management into Australian schools provided the opportunity for what I called 'Core Plus Education', which incorporated two components, the core plus curriculum and the core plus school:

> The core plus curriculum, which could be considered as maintaining a core of state-mandated requirements for all students, plus the curriculum determined locally (based on the needs of the children from particular communities), could be expanded to become the core plus school where the core activity, namely, the education of children, was enhanced by a range of other formal and informal programmes for the community as a whole.
>
> (Townsend 1994: 113)

However, this return of education to the control of local communities has been accompanied, almost universally, by substantial budget cuts. In the USA, Michelle Fine argued that school-based management 'has emerged at a moment of public sector retrenchment not expansion. School-based resources and decision making have been narrowed, not expanded. School-based councils feel empowered only to determine who or what will be cut' (Fine 1993: 696). In his arguments against the state of Victoria's *Schools of the Future* programme, which follows the international trends more closely than does any other Australian state and, perhaps, even pushes the boundaries internationally, John Smyth argued:

> One of the noticeable (indeed, even remarkable, or is it?) features of the move towards the self-managing school phenomenon around the world, is its occurrence in contexts of unprecedented education budget cut-backs. Whenever there is a break out of self-managing schools, the notion is used as a weapon by which to achieve the alleged 'efficiencies' and 'downsizing' of education.
>
> (Smyth 1993: 8)

This book seeks to review the impact of this change on Australian primary schools, on the people who are involved with them and the issues they face. In Chapter 1 Hedley Beare discusses the use of metaphor as a means of describing educational change. He discusses the *pre-industrial* metaphor, where the feudal system brought with it a class-based school system. Education was elitist and upper class. He then considers the *industrial* metaphor, where factory production in society spawned mass education. He discusses of some of the difficulties that we have had in moving on from this view of the world. Finally, he describes a *post-industrial* metaphor, which he calls 'Enterprise', where the rise of the market economy in society is pushing a market view of education. He argues that educators will have to learn to live with this new metaphor, but cautions that – as always – it will be the poorer children who suffer if anything goes wrong.

Part II of the book considers the people involved in the work of primary schools; principals, teachers and families. In Chapter 2 Brian Caldwell discusses the importance of the principal as a leader of educational change. He argues that past principals were heroes in the building of the nation, and that current and future principals will have to undertake a quest, as did the classical heroes of the past. He uses Jaworski's (1996) term, 'synchronicity', a meaningful coincidence of events, which originally was the coincidence of the introduction of public education and the developmental needs of the nation. He argues that in recent years this synchronicity has been lost, but that current developments in education (devolution, technological innovation) provide the opportunity for it to return. He identifies three tracks of reform currently evident, although with different time frames and stages of development in different places: the development of self-managing schools, an unrelenting focus on teaching and learning, and the move to schooling for the knowledge society. He calls on a series of allegories as a means of describing the principals' quest for synchronicity, both personally and as a profession, and identifies some of the barriers and pitfalls that might get in the way of success.

In Chapter 3 Len Cairns considers the impact of the recent changes in education on teachers. He provides a sketch of today's primary teacher, usually female, early to mid-forties and struggling to come to grips with new tasks for which she has not been trained, students who have a wider range of educational and other needs than she has previously had to cope with, and the problem of balancing a demanding job with family responsibilities. Cairns suggests that there are a number of new expectations that challenge primary teachers today, ranging from changes in our understanding of teaching and learning, through increased social expectations, to changes in curriculum. Challenges facing teachers now – and increasingly in the future – include those related to technology and the new imperatives brought by the 'information superhighway'; those that relate to the current national imperatives such as sport and LOTE (languages other than English); new social challenges such as those brought about by issues such as AIDS and drugs; and the challenges brought about by the need to make education more 'relevant' to business and industry needs. He discusses the developing themes of professionalism and professional development as critical to the future of primary teachers, using examples such as the National Professional Development Program and the National Schools Network as positive recent models for development. He argues that the most useful paradigm for primary teachers in the future is the notion of capability, which goes beyond the notion of competence by adding the characteristics of adaptability, flexibility and self-esteem.

In Chapter 4 Tony Townsend and Ian Walker consider the ways in which family life has changed since children currently completing Year 12 were in preparatory grade. They argue that families and students have changed because of demographic and economic changes, and that these changes have created new challenges for schools. Parents are generally older, more likely to be working, more likely to be single parents, more likely to come from a non-English speaking background and more likely to be struggling financially than parents of just one generation ago. At a time when more parent and community involvement is being called for, parents are finding more legitimate excuses for not being involved. At a time when more of the funding base for schools is falling to local communities, many communities are struggling to make ends meet. Yet there is no longer a doubt that parental involvement improves student performance. Townsend and Walker provide a strategy for involving parents in one of the most critical areas of learning – literacy.

Part III considers some issues critical to the ongoing development of primary schools in these changing times. In Chapter 5 Anne Kennedy discusses the early years of schooling. She considers some of the attempts to provide a national focus on the issue and addresses a range of areas, including school-entry age, school readiness, transition to school from pre-school or childcare and the need for flexible organisation structures. She argues the case for improved accountability and standards and for developmentally appropriate practice, for the importance of play and the involvement of parents as partners in the process of learning, and she argues the case for specialist teacher training for the early years of school.

In Chapter 6 John Williamson and Maurice Galton provide an overview of the role of school culture in providing a structure in which learning takes place. They discuss the current strategies for managing change, including the culture of collaboration that exists in the primary school, with the emphasis on consensus where possible. They argue that sometimes consensus as a strategy for change leads to ineffectiveness because decisions are often able to be interpreted in different ways. They also argue that current attempts at managerialism may be equally ineffective because some teachers might resist decisions in which they have no say. A third strategy, collegiality, based on a culture of collaboration, might also fail when the collegiality is either contrived or disguises a different form of managerialism. They argue the case for 'consequential collegiality' as a possible strategy for principals to use in the management of change. Consequential collegiality, which relies upon an understanding of how children think and how teachers develop their capabilities over time, is discussed as a means of promoting appropriate support for change in both the short term and the long term.

In Chapter 7 Colin Marsh considers how curriculum might be developed within the primary-school setting. He discusses the role of curriculum developers within the framework of curriculum change, innovation, diffusion and dissemination, and the notion of a curriculum continuum. The various levels of curriculum development – national, state, school and classroom – provide the focus for promoting the role of curriculum development. Marsh provides a significant section on school-based curriculum development (SBCD), which includes a discussion of the issues involved, including motivation, interest in innovation, control, responsibility and ownership, the nature of the development activity, school climate and the role of leadership. He considers the critical input requirements such as time, resources and support, and discusses the role that politics has played in SBCD. The positive impact of the national standards and outcomes-based approach to curriculum adopted by Australian states is argued, with the caution that there are still problems that need to be resolved.

In Chapter 8 John Ainley focuses on one of the elements that has been brought to centre stage by the restructuring process, that of assessment. He discusses the breadth of evidence used by modern primary teachers to establish the extent to which student learning has occurred, including observations, portfolios, projects, and paper and pen testing. He argues that for assessment to inform teachers about student learning proper interpretation of the data must occur, which includes reference to other pupils' performances, whether or not specific criteria have been achieved or how this piece of work measures up to other work that the student has done. He discusses the differences between norm-referenced, criterion-referenced and scale-referenced assessment, among other ways of assessing students. He discusses the modern techniques of profiling students, the development of curriculum frameworks and the use of assessment as part of the monitoring of students' achievement nationally, at the state level and at the school level.

In Chapter 9 Geoff Romeo discusses the impact of computer technology on both the curriculum and administration in the school. He argues there is still confusion about the exact role of the computer in the primary classroom and that computers are currently under-utilised. He suggests that there is a case for the 'Computers in Education' dream, one that has been slowed by traditional classroom practices, teachers' lack of experience in developing curriculum, lack of resources and time, and teachers' lack of computer literacy. He discusses some of the issues that primary schools must address if there is to be progress, including the selection of hardware and software, and how and where computers will be used. He considers the current use of, and trends in, computers in the library, multimedia, the Internet and Telematics, integrated learning systems and open learning. The issues of the relationship between computers and learning, the need for professional development and increased resources are considered, and the concern is expressed that access and equity issues become critical problems which must be addressed, both at the school level and by government.

In Chapter 10 Tony Townsend discusses the allocation of resources to primary schools, considering the issues at three levels. First, he discusses the national and state trends of government funding for education, which establishes how much money, in total, will be available to schools. Second, he considers how the total funding allocation might be allocated to individual schools and uses the funding allocation mechanism of the state of Victoria's Department of Education as a case study of how this might be done in a way that considers the needs of each student. Finally, he discusses how, once the school knows its total resources, it might go about planning the allocation of resources within the school so that the key programmes and priorities of the school are met. He suggests that each of these levels is linked, because if there are not sufficient total resources no means of distribution will overcome inequities in the system, and some of the school's own priorities may have to be ignored to enable all the priorities mandated by government to proceed.

In Chapter 11 Lindsay Fitzclarence, Jane Kenway, Janine Collier and Chris Bigum discuss the impact of the culture of the market economy on primary schools. They discuss the way in which the language of the market has started to infiltrate education, as students have become clients and the community has become the customer. They discuss the motivating political forces of decentralisation of management and centralisation of curriculum that have created schools as market identities. Students and parents as clients become students and parents as consumers, not only in terms of educational products, but also as consumers of products that might return a sponsorship for the school. The authors discuss their research, which includes interviews with principals, to establish their reactions to the marketisation trend. This found principals being inundated by mail containing brochures and catalogues of things that schools could buy, with a substantial number of them focusing on school fundraising. Data collected from interviews with principals variously labelled 'vigorous educational entrepreneurs' and 'cautious resisters' help to show how difficult the current times are for leaders in schools. The authors also discuss interviews with students to establish student reactions to some of the marketing techniques used by companies as a means of making contact with students as consumers of their products. The authors conclude that education should not be part of the ideology of the market, but instead must make a contribution to stemming the flow towards it.

Finally, in Chapter 12, Tony Townsend turns his thoughts to the future. He uses information gathered at three recent Australian conferences, the Successful Schools conference in Melbourne (June 1997), the Australian Council for Educational Administration conference in Canberra (July 1997) and the Australian Council for Educational Administration virtual conference (July 1997) to consider the future of primary schools. Predictions have ranged from there being almost no formal education system at all through to little real change. He discusses predictions made in 1979 about what the world would be like and what the teacher's role would be in the year 2000 to demonstrated that careful predicting can be fairly accurate. He focuses on two major differences between the 1979 predictions and the reality in 1997. He suggests that the world was predicted to be a much kinder place than it has turned out to be in reality and that the impact of technology was substantially underestimated. He argues that two alternatives face Australia as it moves into the future, the Third World option and the Third Millennium option. The former focuses on manufacturing competitiveness and the latter on information competitiveness. He argues that to adopt the latter we need to refocus our attention on what the school was designed to do and what changes are necessary in the future. He argues the case for new partnerships between primary and secondary, between school and home and, perhaps most important of all, between school and the wider community to fulfil the challenge of the future.

Tony Townsend

References

Alcorn, G. (1997) 'The generation of free love finds way to extend the fun', *The Age*, 30 July: 1, 3.

Bordia, A. (1996) 'Reviewing the results', speech made in a panel presentation at the UNESCO ACEID (Asian Centre for Educational Innovation and Development) Conference, Bangkok, December.

Drucker, P. (1993) *Post-capitalist Society*, New York: HarperBusiness.

Fine, M. (1993) 'A diary on privatization and on public possibilities', *Educational Theory* 43(1): 33–9.

Galbraith, J. K. (1992) *The Culture of Contentment*, Boston, MA: Houghton Mifflin.

Gerstner, L., Semerad, R., Doyle, D. and Johnston, W. (1994) *Reinventing Education: America's Public Schools*, New York: Dutton.

Hargreaves, A. (1994) *The Mosaic of Learning: Schools and Teachers for the New Century*, London: Demos.

Jaworski, J. (1996) *Synchronicity: The Inner Path of Leadership*: San Francisco, CA: Berrett-Koehler Publishers.

Minzey, J. D. (1981) 'Community education and community schools', address at the State College of Victoria, Frankston, Australia, May.

Smyth, J. (1993) 'Schools of the future and the politics of blame', public lecture sponsored by the Public Sector Management Institute, Melbourne, Monash University, 2 July.

Townsend, T. (1994) *Effective Schooling for the Community: Core Plus Education*, London and New York: Routledge.

ACKNOWLEDGEMENTS

I wish to express my gratitude to the editorial staff at Routledge for both their effort in producing the book and their patience when it took longer than expected, and to each of the colleagues who have contributed to its development. I have been able to bring together some of the key people working in the field in Australia and I appreciate their time and effort. Thanks also go to the staff of the Faculty of Education at Monash, particularly those who have increased their efforts in recent years to promote the development of primary teachers and primary education. Finally, I would like to recognise and thank primary-school teachers across Australia, but particularly those at Kunyung Primary School in Victoria, who guided my three adult children, Paul, Cindy and Ben, through these difficult early years of school and still have the responsibility of ensuring that Jenni turns out as well as they did.

Tony Townsend
March 1998

Part I

INTRODUCTION

1

'ENTERPRISE'

The new metaphor for schooling in a post-industrial society

Hedley Beare

relates to education
is it as a commodity
a business like
more commodity?

Introduction

Change is unlikely ever again to be gentle for schools, largely because in the newly emerging world economy a country's power to compete and the productivity of its workforce depend on education. Especially as know-how, information and brain power replace commodities as the things which are traded or which give a country its trading edge, the health of its schooling system becomes a crucial factor in managing the local economy. Furthermore, governments (and ministers) have learned not only that they must deliver, but that they must deliver fast. The processes of planned change have been researched for well over three decades, but in the 1990s much of the creed about the change process no longer works. The essential message in the new approaches is that time itself is an expense, and like all good currency it has to be invested wisely, used sparingly and not squandered. Time has to be spent as though it is money.

Thus planned change, with its neat flowcharts and lead-times, its phased introductions, its consultative frameworks, belongs with the late-industrial period and its techniques are becoming out of date, largely superseded by 'crash-through' tactics because legislators, politicians, national leaders and chief executives cannot allow as much time as we think we need. *They* do not have time on their side either. Unless they act quickly, their firm goes out of business or bankrupt, is bought out or taken over, they lose office or are replaced, or some other country, agent or agency secures an inside advantage. The change imperative waits for no one, and it is certain that there will be no reversion to pre-1983 patterns (Beare and Boyd 1993: Murphy 1991).

School leaders, most of all, must understand these contextual changes. The education departments of the 1970s no longer exist, and the administrative tactics and procedures which worked then are no longer effective. The

3

protection which principals and schools once took for granted from 'head office', from 'the Department', is no longer there; the senior positions, the assumed tracks for upward mobility, the known career paths for the promotion of insiders, the mechanisms for policy interventions have changed, and many have ceased to exist altogether. In a world context which is unsympathetic to many of the educational modes we have known in the past, prudent school managers and educators are likely to prosper, not by fighting rearguard actions aimed at preservation, but by acquiring an intelligent understanding of the emerging trends and then fashioning them in ways which will deliver to this generation of schoolchildren the best educational advantage.

Most significantly, there has been a fundamental shift in the way people discuss schooling; it represents, in fact, a change in public thinking so radical that it can be called a paradigm shift. Imaging, creating mind-pictures, and then conveying them in stories and metaphors is a process as old as human history. A picture held firmly in the mind and believed has the tendency to manifest itself and to become real. When we try to convey ideas to others we are forced to use analogies, favouring some metaphors over others. Indeed, we use them over and over again in such a way that they impose conformities on our thinking and action, coordinating thousands of unnoticed and unstudied actions and reactions. We pattern our language and behaviours on firmly held, taken-for-granted images.

Schooling has been subject to widely held pictures of what the education process is, and those images are built into the warp and weft of schools. We also know that the favoured prevailing images have always been suggested by what kind of economy the country has. So one of the reasons for the profound confusion which has accompanied the school reform movement around the world since the early 1980s is that the organising *metaphor* which explains what schooling is has changed. Furthermore, it is a roots-and-branch change, radical in the accurate sense of that word; those who have not accommodated to the new metaphors seem to be operating in a time warp, reacting to educational changes without understanding the powerful underlying logic driving them.

The pre-industrial metaphor

Before the onset of industrialisation in the Industrial Revolution a large proportion of the population lived close to the land, usually in villages. There were few large cities. The influence of the Church and the Crown was strong. It was a class-bound society in which those who owned land, often by inheritance, were considered the upper class. They were 'rich' in the sense that they owned property; their wealth was measured in terms of possessions and their power to control the work of others. It was a feudal system and the landed rich behaved as though they were born to rule.

4

In that society the lords and ladies of the realm were the patrons of the social order. They had the leisure and the money to patronise the arts and letters. Formal education was provided only for the few and the privileged; it was privately funded, the preserve of the rich, available only to those who could afford it. It dealt with intellectual pursuits like literature, languages (especially the classics – Latin and Greek 'grammar' in fact), history, the arts, philosophy and theology, and it spurned anything connected with manual occupations, the domains of the workers, the serfs and the employed. Education was about refinement; it was called 'liberal' for it freed the mind and the intellect, giving rise to the idea that 'academic subjects' are somehow superior to the technical and that 'grammar schools' are deliberately elitist and upper class.

These ideas about education have given rise to many of the images we still associate with superior schooling (though we now use terms like 'excellence'). 'Grammar schools' (the title may be implied while not used) are usually like the homes of the landed rich, set in wide green parks or estates, and their original buildings often resembled (or even were) the gracious manor houses of the affluent. Those elite schools still retain the livery of feudalism – the school shield, embossed with emblems and heraldic crests; a Latin motto; schools hymns or songs; and the regalia of the upper class reflected in the school uniform. Academic, 'intellectual' subjects are favoured over the practical; the mind is favoured above dexterity with hand, limb, or eye. Sporting contests, 'houses', class captains and prefects, and various scholastic ceremonials and assemblies still prevail in these schools.

Interestingly, the established Church and the King's army provide comparable imagery. So service to King, country, God and the Church were preached as social duties, and were made the basis for civic and personal responsibility. An ordered, godly society required moral rectitude in those born to rule it.

We need to be wary lest a cluster of images inherited from the society-before-factories – associated with the wealthy, the well-to-do, the upper-class and the newly rich and favouring pursuits of the mind above those of the hand – are preserved in the way people conceive of schools. It is a mode of thinking about education which ought to be passé, if only because it represents a society which has passed into history. The imagery, however, survives.

The industrial metaphor

Another powerful set of mind-pictures based on factory production grew up when education became universal, but they too are now obsolescent (indeed, they should be obsolete). Large-scale manufacturing was born with the Industrial Revolution. The crafts once practised in the village were broken down into their component parts and processes, systematised by experts and put on a conveyor belt, each segment of the sequence in the hands of process workers. Commodities were mass-produced, rather than individually crafted by an artisan. The production line was a huge breakthrough which transformed society, and it made dominant the large-scale organisation – the big factory, the big corporation – with a one-best-way form of management called 'bureaucracy'. Bureaucracy and industrialisation evolved together and are interconnected.

And so is the big city. The people who worked in the factories migrated from the country and had to be clustered in dormitory suburbs around the places of production. Wherever in the world we find 'newly industrialised countries' (NICs), there we also find burgeoning cities. Some are now called 'supercities' and they have become one of the greatest problems confronting the world today; they are among the world's worst polluters.

The way people thought about money also changed with the Industrial Revolution. The village or town markets were one step removed from simple bartering and exchange, but the town markets were replaced by national and international economies, still (rather oddly) called 'the international marketplace'. Money itself became one of the commodities being produced by business, and in that context the term 'wealth production' was used. A new wealthy class arose, called the *nouveaux riches*, the captains of industry – which, by and large, meant manufacturing. What was once literally 'made by hand' (*manu factum*), country crafts, was now mass-produced in a factory and on a conveyor belt.

At the same time, Europe and North America invented mass education too. From the early 1800s onwards, as rural areas lost their populations and the manufacturing cities were built up, legislation made primary (and, later, secondary) education compulsory for all, because basic literacy and numeracy, some social skills and a comprehension of what the society was were essential in every fully functioning citizen and, especially, in every worker. Production-line education arrived, in both the literal and the metaphorical sense.

To control and administer the state schools, large-scale organisations called education departments were developed. Not surprisingly, both the large schools and the large school departments were organised along the lines of the bureaucracies which characterised factory production. The same terms were used, the same ideas, the same control devices, the same framework of analogies and metaphors.

Furthermore, education itself came to be modelled on the factory metaphor. The schooling process was divided into year groups, knowledge was subdivided into subjects, teachers became specialists, and were credentialled (literally 'certificated' like tradespeople) and ordered into hierarchies, the students were placed in class groups or batches, moving in linear progression through graded curricula, from easy to more complex, from lower grades to higher grades. They were 'promoted' (as are workers in factories) up the steps until they graduated at Year 12, checked to see if they conformed to the standards and then classified with a road-worthiness

6

certificate called matriculation. So credentialled, and usually in a one-shot action which equipped them for life, they were let loose, supposedly safely, on the thoroughfares of the community. It is the factory-production metaphor applied to schooling. It is a mind-picture which ought by now to have been discarded, but the extended imagery which derives from the factory line still seems to saturate the entire fabric of schooling.

The mechanistic universe of science

The inherent problem about moving beyond this pervasive factory metaphor is that we conceive of *knowledge* and *knowledge production* (note the terminology) in exactly the same way. The scientific movement and its universal method are also outcomes of the centuries of industrialisation. The following characteristics of the scientific method of inquiry (Harman 1988: 29–33) are the canon of qualities which form the underlying creed of modern education:

- *Reductionism*: the way to understand anything is to break it down into its component bits, and to examine each part in detail. By building up a knowledge of the individual pieces we will come to an understanding of the whole. Science is therefore reductionist, and scientists become specialists, with ever increasing sophistication about particular subdisciplines. *This is how schools get their subjects, it is why we have specialist teachers, and why the curriculum is structured the way it is.*
- *Positivism*: the only defensible way to extend our knowledge about the universe is through empirical methods, by relying solely on what we can observe with our five senses. By experimentation and measurement, especially by relying upon the physical senses and the technology which extends them, we arrive at verifiable truth. Only what can be verified is trustworthy and admissible as knowledge. *This is why science and mathematics are pre-eminent in the curriculum. And this approach underlies most teaching methods.*
- *Materialism*: the empiricist works only with what appears substantial and real, insisting on evidence which can be examined. Even what we describe as consciousness or awareness are to be understood by analysing the physical and chemical processes in the body. *This is why so much of schooling is secular, and why systematic and sustained education about values has always posed problems for modern schools.*
- *Objectivity*: there is a clear distinction between the objective world (which any observer can perceive and which all observers will read in the same way) and subjectivity (which is limited to the privacy of one's own brain and consciousness). What is objective is reliable because it is replicable; what is subjective is unreliable unless the evidence is confirmed by several people in a way that can lead to an objective conclusion. *These*

7

two characteristics of materialism and objectivity provide the rationale for most curricular work in schools.

- *Rationality*: reason is the indispensable partner of empiricism and objectivity. The application of reasoning, rigorous logic, dispassionate (and therefore value-free or unemotional) rationality, especially when based upon observed phenomena, is the only safe method by means of which to advance knowledge. It is the only way of 'knowing'.

- *Quantitative analysis*: it stands to reason, then, that qualitative properties are best reduced to quantitative ones, to what can be weighed, measured, rendered objective and assessable. *These two properties of rationality and quantitative measurement explain educators' practices on examinations and assessment, on measuring progress, on promotion and certification, and our concern with outcomes and results.*

- *Anti-enchantment*: Goldberg (1983: 18) argued that 'scientism' – the unnecessary belief in the 'one best way' of science – has devoured other fields of knowledge. Flushed with success, the juggernaut of science gobbled up terrain formerly held by philosophy, metaphysics, theology and cultural tradition. We sought to apply the methods that worked so well in the material realm to answer questions about the psyche, the spirit and society. Over time, our organisations and educational institutions made scientism the *sine qua non* of knowing, the model for how to think.

As a result, the intuitive, the expressive, the unmeasurable and the intensely personal have never found a satisfactory place in the curriculum, in assessment or in the public's esteem.

In short, the problem for educators is that almost everything about twentieth-century schooling is based on the scientific method. The division of knowledge into subject areas; the way schools examine and assess student achievement, and then report it; the division of learning into age-grade levels; the way teachers specialise in subjects; the linear progression in curricula; even the way schools are organised and roles assigned among teachers – they all follow the inexorable logic of scientism. Can such schooling survive into the postmodern, post-scientific age?

As Ken Wilber (1983) and others have pointed out, a scheme for 'knowing' limited to so small a base and which dismissed as insignificant anything which was not material was bound in the end to become a nonsense. Quoting the philosopher Alfred North Whitehead, Wilber comments: 'This position on the part of the scientists was pure bluff. . . . Science was becoming scientism, known also as positivism, known also as scientific materialism, and *that* was a bluff of the part playing the whole' (Wilber *ibid.*: 23). This is the important point. The scientific method has advanced the world's knowledge enormously and its achievements are not to be devalued. It is not that science is wrong, but rather that it should not and cannot exert an exclusive claim on the generation and validation of knowledge.

One of the most profound reasons for questioning science in this way is that it has begun to recoil on itself, producing counterintuitive findings and some developments which will not fit into its own tidy, materialistic, scientific paradigm. This is the case with the purest of the pure sciences, physics. Harman says that 'the ultimate triumph of reductionist physics is to demonstrate the *necessity* of a new paradigm which goes beyond reductionist science' (Harman 1988: 106). There has been a spate of writings from scientists in recent years along these lines, questioning science's own certainties and beginning to change its metaphors.

To illustrate the extent of the change even among scientists, consider the case of Professor Gerald Edelman, winner of a Nobel Prize for his work on the nature of the human brain. He has taken to task the scientific community for using imagery about machines to describe living organisms: 'There is a tendency in every age', he said, 'to compare the brain with the toys that excite us' (Cornwell 1993: 4). The mathematician Leibniz thought of the mind as a flour-mill, a piece of machinery; earlier it had been described as a telephone; now it is typically called a computer. Edelman considers this fashionable mode of explanation to be 'profoundly mistaken' because this kind of imagery sieves out too much:

> Computer codes simply can't encompass the infinite range of human language, imagination and metaphor; our ability to hold intelligent conversation and create works of art ..., our sense of being individuals. ... It's a purely objective, determinist viewpoint that doesn't include *me*. ... Physics and computing cannot account for this sense we have of looking out on our world from within.
>
> (Cornwell 1993: 4)

Then, in an astonishing change of analogy, Edelman asserts that 'each individual's brain is more like a unique and unimaginably dense rainforest, teeming with growth and decay. It is less like a programmed machine than an ecological habitat that mimics the evolution of life itself' (Cornwell 1993: 4). Simply stated, then, the window on knowledge is being shaped by new metaphors which release us from the images or mind-pictures which now imprison us. If we are to discard the outdated metaphors which underlie most current schooling practices, has a set of metaphors emerged yet to replace those of factory production, the industrially based economy and bureaucracy? The simple answer is 'Yes'.

The post-industrial metaphor: 'enterprise'

Most Western countries are now in a *post-industrial* period. For a range of reasons, fewer people are now involved in factory production, the proportion falling from near half the population about fifty years ago to 15–10 per cent now. Manufacturing is still producing goods and profits, of course, but employment in manufacturing has been collapsing. This has resulted in mass unemployment in developed countries around the world. What new occupations and jobs there are have appeared in the services sector, in the professions and in communications. How will schooling be described in the post-industrial world, and what language or imagery will be appropriate to explain it?

The change in metaphor has already occurred. The new logic was developing throughout the 1980s as schools and school systems around the world underwent the 'restructuring movement', still described by the mechanical metaphor 're-engineering' (Hammer and Champy 1994). It was in many respects a destructive period, for the change agents often appeared not to comprehend the organising logic, and educators were crudely disregarded as being too stolid, too unionised, too unimaginative and too naive to be left in charge of education any longer. Society has paid a price for this disdain, in the form of a flight of able people away from teaching, at least in the short term. The people most needed to lead the new assault may already have fled the field or not have joined it in the first place. It was not until the late 1980s that the new metaphor which provides the rationale for the shape of post-industrial schooling solidified. In retrospect, one influential book encapsulated the new logic. It was written by the Stanford economists Chubb and Moe and entitled *Politics, Markets and America's Schools* (1990).

The metaphor of the market economy is now used around the world to justify the new policies for schooling. Most pervasively, schools are being talked of as though they are private businesses or enterprises providing a product (learning) to a set of clients (students and parents). They are also required to contribute to the economic competitiveness of the nation. Schools have to market themselves; we talk of them 'selling themselves'. They must find a niche in the market and compete for their market share. Schools are expected to be responsive to their local community, for the consumer has the power of choice. Schools are now regarded as stand-alone enterprises and as self-managing. Each school has its own single-line budget. School boards or councils not only represent the shareholders (the more usual term is now 'stakeholders') but are the means whereby the school is audited or held accountable. It is assumed that schools will compete for resources, that schools which can provide a marketable product will be worthy to survive, and that poor providers (and poor teachers) will go to the wall; that the school and its teachers will monitor their performance outcomes; and that they will be entrepreneurial (Hanushek 1994).

The big centralised bureaucracies have largely disappeared (although the rhetoric about them remains). The school system's head office has now divested itself of day-to-day control of individual schools. It puts in place accountability, regular audit and quality-control machinery, and then leaves the school alone to carry on its own business (almost literally). Departments of School Education have done away with middle management, have down-sized, outsourced any function they can give away, and now have only monitoring functions and global policy-making roles. They have shrunk to a strategic core.

This new extended metaphor is now widely accepted, and it is seductively powerful through the way it channels our thinking. Not only is it used to describe the restructuring of schools and school systems, but it has also *become the favoured way of explaining how education operates*. For more than a decade governments have been describing education like this, as a commodity to be purchased and even exported, justifying their policies by using that analogy. The education export market was estimated to be worth $16 billion worldwide in 1992. In 1996 Pauline Hanson, Independent federal member for the Oxley electorate in Queensland, ignited a racial debate with her inflammatory comments, in her maiden speech to parliament, about Aborigines and migrants (particularly Asian migrants). Her comments were condemned, among other things, because of their impact on the trade in education.

Education was also seen as a personal investment. The Australian Higher Education Contribution Scheme (HECS) was justified on the grounds that only four member countries of the Organisation for Economic Cooperation and Development (OECD) made no charge for university tuition, that most countries provide a combination of grants and interest-bearing loans to cover tertiary education costs and that since education brings higher earning capacity to degree-holders a 'user-pays' approach to funding was justified.

To explain the movement to reform the management of schools we need to understand that the same political and organisational approach has been applied across the whole range of public administration. The movement is widespread. Governments of all persuasions have begun to sell off those parts of their operations which can be run *by* private enterprise or *as* private enterprises. The sell-offs included steel mills, banks and insurance compa-nies, power plants, fertiliser factories and so on. At least twenty-five national telephone systems have been up for sale and at least ten state-owned airlines. Japan sold its tobacco manufacturing enterprise and leased its metropolitan railways back to private businesses. British Airways and British Steel were made public companies. In the United States, prisons, garbage collection, fire protection and mail services are being privatised.

The favoured mode for transforming public enterprise has been described by Osborne and Gaebler (1993) with a ten-point model; we need to translate this into schooling and the teaching service:

1   *Government should steer rather than row.* The public system, they say, should make things happen rather than carry out the functions itself.

Government should guide, not get itself into day-to-day delivery of services. Government merely facilitates, encouraging others to discharge the functions which once might have been carried out by the civil service – hence self-managing schools.

2 *Government should empower rather than serve.* The government system needs to invest others with the power to act, usually through some kind of legislation or devolution. In the case of schools this means that the public system will set only the broad parameters within which they operate but then legislate or devolve power to local schools, and hold them accountable for quality of delivery.

3 *Government should inject competition into service delivery.* The argument is that competition is the only incentive which works. Monopolies corrupt, especially among service givers. Schools in this new environment are therefore expected to be *different* from each other, success-oriented and aggressively competitive. Competition implies choice – customer choice – and choice implies variety.

4 *Government should be mission-driven.* Each school should therefore define what it intends to be and do, and be held responsible for carrying it out rather than being required to follow a rule book of government regulations.

5 *Government should be results-oriented.* Government ought to be concerned about outcomes and results, not conformities. It is assumed, therefore, that the school is driven by learning outcomes, not by resource inputs, and will be able to quote evidence that it is achieving what it is set up and paid to achieve. No one will be particularly concerned about the methods it uses to achieve its ends, provided it *does* achieve them.

6 *Government enterprises should satisfy the customer, not the bureaucracy.* Indeed, funding arrangements should put purchasing power in the hands of the customer to be served. There are now many variations on the theme of educational vouchers, including per capita funding and the Victorian (and Edmonton) idea of a Student Resource Index (SRI). In this scheme a bounty reflecting the cost of education is placed on the head of each child and the school which enrols the child receives that level of funds. The funding goes wherever the child enrols. This is the approach underlying the present federal policy on new schools. It is what Hywel Thomas has called 'the *child* as voucher' (Thomas 1993: 33).

7 *Government enterprises should earn where they can, not merely spend.* A government enterprise (in this case the individual school) should be encouraged to earn its way wherever it is able to, rather than merely to spend tax dollars ('enterprising government'). It might make money by hiring out its facilities, by selling its staff's expertise in various consultancies and professional advisory services, by inventing new uses for and services with the school's resources, and often by asking the user to pay, especially where a non-essential or discretionary service is supplied.

8   *Government enterprises should be proactive, aiming to prevent rather than to cure.* So the school should anticipate, plan ahead and take evasive action rather than try to mop up after a disaster has struck, that is, to solve problems reactively after they have arisen.

9   *Government should be decentralised.* Government should move away from hierarchy, from top-down controls – in the education profession, both within the school and in the system. So the authoritarian, controlling, militaristic principal has no place in this system, where the emphasis is on teamwork, professionalism, participation, and on sharing responsibility and power.

10 *Government should be market-oriented.* Hence economic rationalism, of course. Osborne and Gaebler (1993) mean here that schools – public schools – should use the market and its inherent competitiveness to develop leverage from which to achieve its public benefits. The school and the system need to shape their processes and services so that the incentives arise naturally from the way the enterprise is situated in its community.

Ask yourself, then, how well Osborne and Gaebler's portrait of a public enterprise suits your school:

> New kinds of public institutions (schools) are emerging. They are lean, decentralised, and innovative. They are flexible, adaptable, quick to learn new ways when conditions change. They use competition, customer choice, and other non-bureaucratic mechanisms to get things done as creatively and effectively as possible. And they are the future.
>
> (Osborne and Gaebler 1993: 2)

What emerges is a new picture of school and a new kind of school system, both of them with different orientations from those heavy-limbed, large-scale, hierarchical, control-driven schools and school systems modelled on the Industrial Revolution's factories. The old-style government-school system is obsolescent. In the past public schools tended to operate within tight controls imposed by education departments, which handled much of the day-to-day management centrally. Central management, centralised control of resources and the built-in accountabilities (such as they were) which came with bureaucracy made the centre answerable for the excellence of the system. Self-management changes all that (Caldwell and Spinks 1992).

Put simply, the new ideology is to regard schools as enterprises – not as places to confer privilege, not as factories, not as social welfare outlets, not as part of the fabric of a big civil-service bureaucracy. Like enterprises, they will survive by delivering a demonstrably high-quality service to each of their students. To come to terms with the ramifications of the new model, the new paradigm, let us list some of the logical consequences.

13

Management structures

A new management model for the delivery of education is clearly emerging across the world, almost universally derived from the way private enterprise works and based upon each unit in the system having managerial autonomy. It is best epitomised as a shift from 'educational administration' to 'efficient management'. The ideas of efficiency (in management), effectiveness (in measuring outcomes), accountability (in financial responsibility) and productivity (in meeting the market's requirements) were inherent in almost all of the reports written in the 1980s and early 1990s.

The new management structures are modelled on the modern corporation, the flexible conglomerate which keeps central control of the essential and strategic areas but allows entrepreneurial freedom to the operating units which make up the body corporate. Schools and education systems are once again borrowing both the names and the concepts of business, and building the organisational structures which appear to give the flexibility to operate in volatile market conditions and also the means of staying in control of events. Over the past two decades around Australia, in system after system, the big central bureaucracies have been pared down, divested of educator staff and their operational functions reassigned to regions, clusters and schools. If the present trend continues there will be very few staff left at the centre.

School responsibilities

Schools are thus gaining increased legal and professional responsibilities in the form of a global budget, wide discretion over funding, the responsibility to select their own staff and fill their promotion positions from the principal down, the management and upkeep of their physical plant, and so on. Put simply, the combined impact of the trends towards a denuding of the head office, towards self-managing schools, towards a shrinking of system-provided education services and back-up, and towards financial stringency will be the emergence a set of what might be called *public* private schools.

Funding and school clustering

Most of the money allocated for education will go straight from government to individual schools. Already in Great Britain over 90 per cent of the money voted from Whitehall to the local education authorities must be passed on direct to the schools. The same trend is clearly evident in Australia and New Zealand. Individual schools will therefore have to go into the marketplace and buy any specialist services which are required to supplement the work of their own teachers and general staff. School-based coalitions, like the New South Wales (NSW) 'clusters' or the South

Australian and Tasmanian 'districts', are being asked to share their expertise, pool resources or 'contract in' services by each contributing to the cost of a specialist consultancy. School support centres (in Victoria) and education resource centres (in NSW) have often served as broker for a set of schools, owned and managed by school clusters rather than controlled by head office. Most recently, even they have been disbanded through economy measures.

Privatised support services

What schools lose in the restructuring is allies at head office, support in terms of curriculum and professional services, a range of free professional advice and protection from political changes. As a result, a host of private agencies, consultants and professional firms are beginning to fill (for a contracted price) the gap left by the dissolution of the services which were once provided free and by the system itself. The new service agencies compete for custom, and the schools are in a position to require quality, school-specific and thoroughly professional services. The new agencies are tending to operate across state and national boundaries and recruit into their firms some of the best teachers out of schools. Individual schools may also develop a consultancy arm, earning additional revenue by selling the skills of their own staff and the learning materials generated from that school base. In short, new kinds of career prospects will open up for able educators.

Privatised school reviews

We may well be surprised at how many educational services can be privatised, corporatised or commercialised. In 1991, for example, the British government implemented a scheme whereby school inspections were contracted out to private enterprise and Her Majesty's Inspectorate was translated into OFSTED (Office of Standards in Education) to run the new scheme.

Professionalised management

The new format will give a better appreciation of what the local school is and of the role of its head. If one aggregates the salary bill in any normal-size school of, say, about forty staff members, the capital value of the buildings and equipment, the costs of maintenance and supplies, and its other recurrent expenditures, it immediately becomes apparent that the school is an enterprise with a multimillion-dollar annual turnover. The school is, in fact, usually the largest enterprise in town; certainly, in any country town or suburb, not only is the school the municipality's biggest company, but it also usually occupies the largest piece of real estate in the locality.

The managers of these enterprises are no longer 'middle management'; they are not subordinate parts in a big bureaucracy. Instead, school principals are among the most highly skilled and qualified executives in the community, running a firm much more complicated than any other local business, because its purposes are more complex, more public and more politically sensitive. The school directly affects a far larger proportion of the community than any other enterprise, and by its very nature it requires the delicate exercise of human relations, not merely among the enterprise's own staff, but also with a large and volatile set of customers or clients.

The teaching service

The way teachers are employed and deployed changes under the new model (Ashenden 1990). If the new metaphor takes hold, teacher career patterns will change, moving away from a salaried service and into a contract system, with teachers being paid a market-determined fee-for-service for discharging an agreed professional function. The nature of the school and its staff may not need to change, but the people serving on the staff will probably be on contracts negotiated by a professional company of which they are principals or partners. The position of Head of School will therefore become more complicated and may be transformed into a management team with a congeries of skills, some of them legal and industrial. The days of the centre as the employer of salaried teachers who are then assigned to schools could be passing.

The curriculum in market terms

The most profound change is the imagery relating to the curriculum: how the learning programme is being redefined in terms of a product to be bought and sold. For decades schooling (especially learning and the curriculum) has been depicted as climbing stairs (the word 'grade' is derived from the Latin for 'step', *gradus*). So the student is promoted (literally 'moved forward') through 'grade levels' until he or she 'graduates', even proceeding to 'higher' education, where the student will be granted a 'degree' (a word whose prime meaning, the Oxford Dictionary tells us, is 'one of a flight of steps, a rung of a ladder'). Or again, the student undertakes 'courses' (a word derived from the Latin for 'I run', *curro*). The very word 'curriculum' (literally, a small running track) is part of this cluster of metaphors. The problem is that these analogies present learning too simplistically. They depict learning as:

- *Linear*: there is one best set of graded exercises for each subject area. The student proceeds from simple to more complex ideas in one logical progression.

- *Age-related*: It suggests that certain skills belong with certain age groups. This poses artificial problems for adult learning and for deciding how studies are labelled. When graduate students undertake initial learning in a foreign language, why is it called 'tertiary study' for them when it is almost identical to what primary-school students undertake?
- *Split into discrete subjects*: those official and acceptable subjects are now called key learning areas but they still approximate to the official disciplines in tertiary education.

The market metaphor has been used so widely by politicians, business people and the public that it is no longer merely a convenient metaphor to explain the new patterns of educational funding and resource management. *It has now become the favoured way of explaining the education process itself.*

As a result, the curriculum is now being re-imaged, often by forces outside education, into something resembling the cluster or network organisation. So we speak now not of a 'a curriculum' but of 'pathways', of several alternative routes through a plurality of learning programmes. The elements are 'modularised' (like modern car parts) for multiple usage, and they can be assembled into optional packages. There are now 'generic' (general) and 'specific' (occupation-determined) skills and knowledge. It is no longer possible to advance a cohort of students in lock-step through years of instruction. They will branch out into 'learning trees'. There is much discussion of 'credit transfers', joint degrees, educational consortia which provide components for credentials across institutions. In short, we are witnessing the working out of a new metaphor of networking.

Because the new ideas about learning are built on market or business analogies it should not surprise us to see the extent to which schooling is depicted as utilitarian, as serving economic purposes. Educational discourse has changed, moving away from concerns about students and towards concerns about curriculum content. We hear less about individual differences (except when it concerns the education of the able and the gifted, who are viewed as national resources worth investing in), or about the processes of learning, or about individual fulfilment and self-actualisation. Parents and teachers may talk this way, but not policy-makers. On the other hand, a great deal is said about standards, about general levels of achievement, about certificates and credentials, and about core curricula. What is to be learned has occupied more attention than the nature of the learner. Education is about tradeable skills and workplace components; not much is said these days about personal formation. In fact 'progressive education' is maligned, labelled as passé, and regarded as something aberrant and wrong. To be blunt, and in spite of the political rhetoric, schooling is no longer talked of as being about individual fulfilment but, rather, as being about standard learning, about conformities, about being useful. In a sense, the

curriculum itself has been invaded by economic rationalism and commodi-
fied.

The juggernaut of funding

Underlying all of the above is *cost*. Modern education has become so expensive that it is beyond the capacity of governments to finance everything they
would like to in education. Ironically, at a time when higher levels of education are needed to support the kind of economy the country requires if it is
to remain internationally competitive, governments appear to have exhausted
their options for funding education along traditional lines. Some new devices
and policies are emerging.

Several levels of government and some powerful actors outside education
(the business community, for example) have an intense interest in what
happens in education. But it is only a partial interest, and they are prepared
to finance only that part of the educational operation which affects their
interests. Education is no longer thought of as an automatic public good, to
be funded without question from the public purse. Some elements of it are,
but not all of it. What is likely to develop, therefore, is split-level funding,
and possibly also split-level provision. For example, *national government* is
deeply concerned about those aspects of education which affect the
country's economy, the productivity of its workforce, its relationships with
its neighbouring countries, its health (to name four areas in which it exercises legal authority). We have already seen national governments adopt
interventionist strategies regarding the skills of the workforce and migrant
education (migration is a national responsibility), and in language learning.
State or provincial governments are directly concerned with community well-
being and are prepared to pay for those parts of schooling which make for
social harmony, for the development of the skills of the workforce, for the
understanding of political systems and the processes of government, and so
on. They are likely to support, in other words, the provision of education in
key learning areas, in the domains which will make for good citizenship,
social responsibility and a sense of community. In these areas, largely utilitarian and instrumental, state and territory governments are providing
funding, including subsidies for independent schools. In this respect, the
state schools are largely 'provisions of last resort'. Provincial government is
happy for some schools to be provided at parent expense, but will continue
to ensure that every child has access to an education in those areas it deems
important to society. Where no one else will provide education the state will.
This is the logic of the market metaphor.

It is now evident that governments are not particularly interested in
funding those educational provisions which are obviously personal or which
are inessential from their perspective. So an education to ensure that every
child meets his or her full potential is a *personal or parental* concern rather

than a governmental one, and the recipient (or his or her parents) might be asked to pay for or subsidise those aspects of schooling. The old certainties of progressive education – education for individual differences, a full education for all, 'education for life' and the other catch phrases of the 1960s and 1970s – are past. Those areas of personal development or personal formation may have to be funded by someone other than government, probably parents. Clearly, some children will miss out.

In short, post-industrial schools – once the new metaphor of markets and consumer choice takes hold – are likely to receive split-level funding from a plurality of financing bodies. It is also probable that there will be split-level provision, some of what we once associated with schooling now provided by bodies which until now we have not regarded as 'schools'.

Conclusion

Educators may or may not like the new metaphor, but they seem to have no choice. They did not particularly like the factory metaphor either, but learned to live with it and make educational sense of it. At least the new image positions schools at the centre of education, frees educational providers from an overabundance of centralised controls on their daily operations, reconfigures schooling in a way which places it close to and makes it amenable to its recipients, and creates a climate in which teachers can become completely professionalised, and their work differentiated and appropriately rewarded (if market forces operate properly).

The fact is that there are very few bad schools, and if application of the market metaphor causes some to go broke, usually by their overstretching themselves, it is almost always the poor children who suffer – the ones who are unable to move. So the theory about competition and choice may sound good to middle-class parents, but the metaphor may not do much for those at the bottom of the heap. In the end, it will be discovered that society must pay for the essential education of all its members, literally as well as figuratively. The new metaphor will be found useful for a time, but eventually limited, just as were the ones it has now displaced.

References

Ashenden, D. (1990) 'Award restructuring and productivity in the future of schooling', *VIER Bulletin* (Victorian Institute of Educational Research) No. 64, June.

Beare, H. and Boyd, W. L. (eds) (1993) *Restructuring Schools: An International Perspective*, London: Falmer Press.

Caldwell, B. J. and Spinks, J. M. (1992) *Leading the Self-managing School*, Lewes, Sussex: Falmer Press.

Chubb, J. E. and Moe, T. M. (1990) *Politics, Markets and America's Schools*, Washington, DC: Brookings Institution.

Cornwell, J. (1993) 'Just what do we think' (a profile on G. Edelman), *The Weekend Review (The Australian)*, Sydney, NSW, 21 August.

Goldberg, P. (1983) *The Intuitive Edge*, Los Angeles, CA: J. P. Tarcher.

Hammer, M. and Champy, J. (1994) *Reengineering the Corporation*, St Leonards, NSW: Allen & Unwin.

Hanushek, E. (1994) *Making Schools Work: Improving Performance and Controlling Costs*, Washington, DC: Brookings Institution.

Harman, G. S., Beare, H. and Berkeley, G. (1991) *Restructuring School Management: Recent Administrative Reorganization of Public School Governance in Australia*, Deakin, ACT: Australian College of Education.

Harman, W. (1988) *Global Mind Change*, Indianapolis, IN: Knowledge Systems, Inc.

Murphy, J. (1991) *Restructuring Schools: Capturing and Assessing the Phenomena*, New York: Teachers' College Press.

Osborne, D. and Gaebler, T. (1993) *Reinventing Government*, New York: Plume.

Thomas, H. (1993) 'The education-reform movement in England and Wales', in H. Beare and W. L. Boyd (eds) *Restructuring Schools: An International Perspective*, London: Falmer Press.

Wilber, K. (1983) *Eye to Eye: The Quest for the New Paradigm*, Garden City, New York: Anchor Books.

Part II

PEOPLE IN THE PRIMARY SCHOOL

2

SYNCHRONICITY AND THE HEROIC QUEST

The primary principal in an era of dramatic change

Brian J. Caldwell

Introduction

Primary schools have made a major contribution to the well-being of society. This is especially the case in Australia, where thousands of small and remote schools have provided an education for much of the nation, including leaders in every field of endeavour. Searing heat and devastating drought interspersed with untimely floods have characterised these settings to the degree that they furnish the national stereotype. Yet many primary schools are located in urban areas as complex and challenging as those that may be found in cities such as Los Angeles, London and New York. If primary schools have made such contributions under these exacting conditions, then their principals are surely among the heroes in the building of the nation.

The starting point for this chapter is a celebration of these achievements and acknowledgement that the role of the primary school and its principal will be no less important in the future. However, the fulfilment of this mission will require the successful negotiation of the same major transformation in the concept of school that is reshaping virtually every element of society. This transformation is the most far-reaching since the Industrial Revolution, which created the conditions that gave rise to systems of public education in the first place, an accomplishment that ought to be included among the great success stories of social organisation. Celebrations are under way at the time of writing, for 1997 marked the 125th anniversary in Victoria of free, compulsory and secular government schooling.

Given this history and anticipating this mission, it is hard to accept that primary schooling will not continue as it has in the past. Surely, one might argue, the primary school ought to be the one haven that is secure in a sea of change. Teachers and principals in primary schools will likely reject the view that their workplace in recent years could possibly be described as a haven. Yet some may harbour a hope that it will all go away and that the waters will be stilled once again. As soon as we write the words, we know that this will not occur, such is the extent of change and the evidence of its continuation.

The purpose of this chapter is to describe and analyse current and emerging trends in primary education, giving particular attention to the role of the primary principal. While the domain is primarily Australia, attention will also be given to developments in Britain, New Zealand and, to a lesser extent, the United States. This is intended to be a positive account because the role calls for unprecedented levels of professionalism, which, paradoxically, restores the primacy of the principal as leader in learning.

Synchronicity

The core concept in this chapter is synchronicity, a term adopted by Jaworski (1996) to describe an aspect of leadership that is especially important at this time. He borrowed it from the psychologist Carl Jung, who defined synchronicity as 'a meaningful coincidence of two or more events, where something other than the probability of chance is involved' (cited in *ibid.*: ix). While the phenomenon is intended to apply to deeply personal experiences, Jaworski explores the possibilities for collectivities, and so they are applied in this chapter to the primary principalship – personally, on an individual level, and collectively, on a professional level.

There seems to have been a measure of synchronicity in the creation of the public primary school and the developmental needs of the Australian nation over the last 125 years, but there has been a disjunction in recent times. The challenge now is to restore that synchronicity, not only for the collectivity, but also personally, as the search for synchronicity is also an heroic quest on an individual level – not in an exclusive or hierarchical sense, but in the manner of a personal journey that all can make.

School reform and the primary principal

There are common characteristics to school reform in Australia, and their impact on the role of the primary principal is now becoming clear. Self-managing schools have been created in systems of public education, a state of affairs in which there has been significant and consistent decentralisation to the school level of authority to make decisions on the allocation of resources, defined broadly, within a centrally determined framework of goals, policies, priorities, standards and accountabilities.

The shift to self-management has been under way for more than two decades but has moved ahead rather dramatically in some states. It has gone further in Victoria, with the implementation of the Schools of the Future initiative after 1992. New South Wales moved in the same direction in 1989 but did not go as far as Victoria. More recently, Tasmania, a pioneer of the self-managing school in the 1970s, took a further step forward with its Directions for Education initiative. Queensland has been the most cautious of all states but it now has a modest programme under the banner of Leading Schools.

Among these initiatives in Australia, particular attention is paid to Victoria, given the scope of the change. Comparisons are made with experience in New Zealand, where similar changes were set in train with Tomorrow's Schools in 1989, and also with Britain, with its schemes of self-managing and self-governing schools.

Schools of the Future

There are four main elements to Schools of the Future in Victoria. A Curriculum and Standards Framework was established for all years from preparatory to Year 10, designed by the Board of Studies. About 90 per cent of the state's school education budget was decentralised so that each school had a 'school global budget' to manage virtually all areas of recurrent expenditure, including teaching and non-teaching staff, the only exceptions of note being capital expenditure and certain categories of expense for system and school support. Regional and central offices were downsized, with the number of employees at these levels being reduced from more than 2,300 to less than 600. Local selection of teachers was introduced, although permanent teachers continued to be employed by the education department. The capacity to select teachers at the school level and to develop a school workforce plan was curtailed in the early years by the fact that the total number of teachers in the system was still considered to be in excess of requirements, so many schools carried a number of 'over-entitlement' teachers. A Professional Recognition Programme was introduced to provide a new career structure for teachers. A performance management framework was established for principal-class personnel. The accountability system provides for annual reports to the education department and school community, and a process of triennial review was trialled for implementation in 1997. A Learning Assessment Project was established at the primary level, with all students being tested at Years 3 and 5 in English, Mathematics and one of the other six key learning areas. Results were used for school-level planning and to report to parents. These features were all implemented within the framework of a school charter, a short document that sets out the priorities, programmes and special characteristics of each school. This constitutes an agreement between the school, its community and the education department that will shape its operations for a period of three years.

Schools of the Future is similar in almost all respects to Tomorrow's Schools in New Zealand and to the local management of schools in Britain. For the latter, under the reforms of successive Conservative governments since 1988, there is a national curriculum, decentralisation to the school level of about 85 per cent of funds in local education authority budgets, testing of students at key stages at primary and secondary schools, with publication of school rankings in 'league tables', and the local selection of staff. These arrangements apply to about 24,000 of around 25,000 primary and secondary schools. For about 1,300 schools, the arrangements are different because these schools opted, on a majority vote of parents, to leave their local education authorities and become 'grant maintained', receiving a larger budget than if they had remained locally managed, since the costs of services provided by the local education authorities are now included in the budget. The future of locally managed and grant-maintained schools under the Labour government is considered in another section of the chapter.

Impact on the role of the primary principal

The impact of these reforms on the role of the principal has been well documented in three reports in Britain, culminating in that by Bullock and Thomas (1994), a range of studies and reports of surveys in Victoria, the most recent being that of the Cooperative Research Project (1997), and a range of studies in New Zealand, including one by Wylie (1997) focusing exclusively on the primary principal.

Wylie's study of the primary principalship in New Zealand is of particular interest, not only for its focus, but also because it covers a longer period of time. The centre piece of her study was a series of twenty-five interviews with a cross-section of principals. Her major findings were these:

- Educational leadership is the most important part of the principal's role. It involves less direct teaching or work with teachers than it used to, and more planning, facilitation, motivation and resource provision. Educational leadership now includes guidance, advice and motivation for the parents on the school's board of trustees as well as the school's teachers.
- Some aspects of administration are now commonly seen as part of educational leadership; particularly work related to resourcing the school or supporting teachers. However, administration is still competing with educational leadership for priority, and takes more of a principal's time.
- Although the pastoral aspects of the principal's role are largely ignored in official descriptions, it has become more important for many principals, particularly those whose schools serve low-income and rural communities.
- Management of the school's roll, its reputation and its buildings and grounds is more central to the principal's work and concerns now than they were before decentralization.

- Administrative work has increased substantially with decentralization. Many schools are not adequately funded to allow the principal to delegate this work. Others depend heavily on the voluntary work of their boards of trustees.
- Principal workloads have increased since 1989 by an average of 10 hours a week. The average workload is now 59 hours a week.
- Teaching principals are particularly hard-pressed to balance the different aspects of their role. Their average workload is 5 hours a week more than non-teaching principals.
- Although many principals have enjoyed the challenge and stimulus of decentralization, only half describe their morale as good or high. There are clear signs that the continued high and intensive workload is taking its toll on principals' energy, and may be making the principalship less attractive to teachers.
- Principals are able to give less time now to their own professional development. Yet one important aspect of their current role is to provide each other with mutual support and advice in the absence of external support. There is increasing interest in some external support system for principals and schools.

(Wylie 1997: iii)

The most comprehensive information about the impact of Schools of the Future on the role of principals in Victoria comes from the Cooperative Research Project, established at the outset of the reform in 1993 to monitor its processes and outcomes. It is a cooperative effort of the Department of Education, University of Melbourne, Victorian Association of State Secondary Principals and Victorian Primary Principals' Association. Surveys of principals have been conducted with each intake of schools into the programme (four), with two surveys being conducted after all schools had entered and all elements of the reform had been implemented (see Cooperative Research Project 1994, 1995a, 1995b, 1996, 1997). There have also been fifteen focused investigations conducted by postgraduate students at the University of Melbourne.

Master's research by Patricia Ford (1995) provides a comprehensive and detailed picture of the new role of the primary principal. Her starting point was a set of eight Key Result Areas for principals developed by the Directorate of School Education following consultation with principals in Schools of the Future:

- school ethos and learning environment;
- vision and future directions;
- implemented school charter, particularly goals and priorities;
- curriculum overview and monitoring of student outcomes;

- resources utilisation and pursuit;
- personnel selection, performance and development;
- interdependent organisational structure and key teams performance;
- policy development and support for school council.

Ford developed a set of ten tasks in each of these eight Key Result Areas and surveyed a representative sample of primary principals in one metropolitan region in Melbourne. She found that there was high agreement among respondents on the importance of all eighty items, indicating the extraordinarily rich and complex role of the primary principal under the new arrangements. The tasks of highest importance were concerned with educational issues, financial management, establishing priorities, establishing an ethos of shared aspirations, communicating with school council and implementing council policies (Ford 1995: 123).

Most striking among Ford's findings were those related to gender. For 73 of the 80 items, women gave higher ratings of importance than did men, with differences being statistically significant in 27 instances. Among the latter, those of greater importance to women:

> concerned the valuing of participation to achieve consensus in school ethos, a common vision, team development for leadership density, planning and review of school operations, and school budgeting. As well, the female respondents were more future oriented and valued analysing social and educational trends. Educationally, they valued, significantly more than their male colleagues, catering for individual differences, independence in learning, improving the teaching learning processes and refining assessment and reporting procedures.
>
> (Ford 1995: 125)

In the matter of gender, Ford suggested that 'females perceive their role through a richer tapestry of dimensions than do their male colleagues' (*ibid.*: 125).

No evidence is available about the different capabilities of men and women in performing these new tasks. The findings suggest, however, that women principals tend to be attitudinally more disposed than men to the emerging role of principal in the self-managing school, at least in the Victorian setting. In general terms, this new role is consistent with that of primary principals in New Zealand, as described by Wylie.

On matters related to satisfaction and workload, findings from surveys in the Cooperative Research Project are of interest. There were few important differences between the responses of primary and secondary principals, and key findings in respect of the role of the principal are cited here (Cooperative Research Project 1997: 12–13).

The mean rating of job satisfaction was 4.3 on a 7-point scale, compared to 5.3 in the baseline survey of intake-one principals in 1993; 5.1 in the 'one year later' survey of intake-one principals in 1994; 4.9 in the survey of intake-two principals; 4.6 in the survey of intake-three principals; and 4.6 in the 1995 survey of all intakes. Overall, it is apparent that the trend in the levels of job satisfaction is downwards.

Principals were invited to indicate if their satisfaction was higher, the same or lower than twelve months ago. Higher levels of job satisfaction were reported by 18.2 per cent of principals, the same levels of job satisfaction were reported by 38.1 per cent of principals, and lower levels of job satisfaction were reported by 43.8 per cent of principals.

The mean number of hours worked by principals in this survey was 59 hours, identical to that reported in the previous survey and the same as that reported by Wylie (1997) for primary principals in New Zealand. The modal range was 60–9 hours, with over 82 per cent of principals indicating that they work between 50 and 69 hours. As in earlier surveys, principals also stated whether the time they devoted to Schools of the Future was less than expected, the same as expected or more than expected; 69 per cent reported that the workload was higher than expected, a level comparable to the high of 70 per cent recorded in 1995 and up from the 34.2 per cent for principals of intake-one schools in the baseline survey of 1993. Only 30 per cent reported that the workload was the same as expected, down from the 63.1 per cent in the baseline survey.

Preferences for new arrangements

An important issue is the extent to which principals prefer the new arrangements for self-managing schools, particularly in view of the dramatic change in role and the much heavier workloads. This issue has been addressed in all settings under consideration here, with the most recent and comprehensive being in Schools of the Future in Victoria, where principals were asked 'Taking all things into account, would you wish your school to return to previous arrangements, prior to implementation of Schools of the Future, in each of the four frameworks of Schools of the Future?' (Cooperative Research Project 1997: 75). The four frameworks were curriculum, resources, people and accountability. In addition, they were asked to make an overall judgement for their school. Responses were limited to a choice between returning or not returning to pre-Schools of the Future arrangements. The results are summarised in Table 2.1. Across all questions, more than 75 per cent of principals prefer the current arrangements to those that existed before Schools of the Future. The resources area produced the strongest response, with 88.5 per cent of principals preferring the current arrangements. Overall, 86.4 per cent of principals preferred the new arrangements.

Table 2.1 Preference for arrangements under Schools of the Future

Area	Principals who wish to revert to previous arrangements (%)	Principals who wish to stay in current arrangements (%)
The Curriculum Framework	18.1	81.9
The Resources Framework	11.5	88.5
The People Framework	23.0	77.0
The Accountability Framework	23.4	76.6
Overall for your school	13.6	86.4
For you as principal (for those with principal experience under both systems)	30.4	69.6

Source: Cooperative Research Project (1997: 75)

The second section related to the principal, but was restricted to principals who had served during Schools of the Future and prior to implementation. Principals were asked, 'Taking all things into account, if you have served under both systems as a principal, which would you prefer: being a principal of a school since implementation of *Schools of the Future*, or being a principal of a school prior to implementation of *Schools of the Future?*' (Cooperative Research Project 1997: 76). Of the total number of respondents, 84 per cent provided a response, of whom nearly 70 per cent indicated that they prefer being a principal 'now' (late 1996) rather than prior to Schools of the Future. Given the dramatic change that has occurred in the work of principals this is a remarkable finding.

In Britain, Bullock and Thomas (1994) reported an increasing preference for new arrangements among primary principals, with 70 per cent in 1991, 76 per cent in 1992 and 81 per cent in 1993; and among secondary principals, with 85 per cent in 1991 and 1992, and 93 per cent in 1993. This suggests the same broad acceptance of self-managing schools under Schools of the Future in 1996 as developed by mid-decade in Britain for the local management of schools.

There are, however, some interesting differences when the Schools of the Future findings are broken down on a primary and secondary basis. In Victoria, overall, 87 per cent of primary principals in 1996 would not wish their schools to return to pre-Schools of the Future arrangements, a higher figure than the 81 per cent preferring local management in Britain; whereas 82 per cent of secondary principals in 1996 would not wish a return, compared to 93 per cent in Britain. In both instances, the surveys were taken about three years after most schools had entered the reform programme. It appears that primary principals in Victoria are more accepting of the new arrangements than their counterparts in secondary schools and in Britain.

Noteworthy is the fact that principals have a preference for the new arrangements despite concerns evident in the ratings of principals, especially in respect of workload, job satisfaction and principal performance management. A similar point was made by Tony Misich, who, while serving as President of the Western Australia Primary Principals' Association, received the Australian Primary Principals' Association 1995–6 Telstra Research Award to study developments in Australia and New Zealand. He observed that:

> one common variable is that all Principals, having gone down the path of devolved decision making, do not wish to return to a more centralized system, regardless of the extra work and responsibility. There is far greater satisfaction in schools being 'in charge' at the local level.
>
> (Misich 1996: 3)

> Principals everywhere have hailed the devolved budget as the most concrete tool to affect any real decision for school improvement.
>
> (Misich 1996: 7)

Tracking change in school education

While an international comparative perspective has been adopted thus far, it is helpful to place these reforms in an even bigger frame, taking an historical and future perspective. Caldwell and Spinks (1998) see reform proceeding on three tracks. Action on each track is analysed here to discern the current and likely impact on the role of the primary principal.

• Track 1: building systems of self-managing schools;
• Track 2: unrelenting focus on learning outcomes;
• Track 3: creating schools for the knowledge society.

These are tracks rather than discrete or sequential stages. Evidence of each may be found in different settings: schools, school systems and nations vary in the distance they have moved down each track.

Track 1: building systems of self-managing schools

The shifting of significant responsibility, authority and accountability to the school level within a Curriculum and Standards Framework, with new alignments of personnel and other resource functions, will probably become the norm for the management of schools in the public sector. On the evidence before us, no system that has moved in this direction is likely to return to arrangements which provided good service over much of the last century but are now obsolete.

The experience of Britain best supports this expectation, given that each of the major political parties went to the 1997 election intending to retain the key elements of reform that centre on the concept of self-management, notably the local management of schools within a centrally determined Curriculum and Standards Framework. It seemed that each party was raising the stakes in terms of the percentage of the available budget that would be devolved to schools. Despite the contentious nature of their intro- duction and the fact that many issues remain to be resolved, it seems that the national curriculum and, especially, the local management of schools have been among the success stories of the 1988 Education Reform Act. In respect of the latter, the secretary of state for education in the new Labour government, David Blunkett, made clear that 'We're committed to devolving a greater part of the budget' and set in train a review to determine how this could be accomplished (cited in St John-Brooks 1997: 1).

The possibility of going beyond the self-managing school towards the self-governing school was raised by the minister for education in Victoria, Phil Gude, in mid-1997. He established a task force to look at more autonomous schools, taking account of developments in other countries, including grant-maintained schools in Britain and charter schools in the public sector in the United States. Under Labour, grant-maintained schools will be renamed foundation schools and come under local control again, but maintaining a higher level of autonomy. Tony Blair sends his son to a grant-maintained school in London. The counterpart in the United States is the relatively small number of publicly funded charter schools. Several states have legislation that allows schools to leave the administrative umbrella of their school district and be fully funded from the public purse. There is bipartisan support for this initiative, with President Clinton's 1997 budget doubling the amount of federal support to more than $130 million.

Taking all of these developments into account, it seems that a settle- ment on the new structural framework for public schools has been reached or is emerging, at least as it concerns the concept of the self-managing school.

Track 2: unrelenting focus on learning outcomes

With settlement on the major dimensions of school reform as far as organi- sational arrangements are concerned, it is likely that momentum will build for reform on Track 2 of change in school education. This calls for an unre- lenting focus on restructuring learning and teaching.

In effect, movement on Track 2 recognises that reform on one track alone will not, by itself, have an enduring impact on the quality of schooling. New responsibilities, authorities and accountabilities must be used to improve learning and teaching. Evidence of how this has been accomplished is now emerging. Really significant change now depends on schools taking up and applying knowledge about school and classroom effectiveness and improvement, and this body of knowledge is richer and deeper than ever. There are some imperatives around which consensus is building, including early literacy, adoption of approaches which smooth the transition from primary to secondary, and managing increasingly complex arrangements in programmes at senior secondary. 'Unrelenting' is an appropriate word to describe the commitment that will be required to ensure that all students learn well, with new learning and relearning through teacher education and professional development.

Much has been written about the extent to which Track 1 reforms have had an impact on outcomes for students. It seems obvious that if explicit links are not made with the processes of curriculum, teaching and learning there will be no impact, and this is precisely what the research has shown. This is most evident in recent meta-analyses on the impact of school-based management (SBM). One of the best is by Summers and Johnson (1996).

Summers and Johnson located seventy studies that purported to be evaluations of school-based management, but only twenty of these employed a systematic approach and just seven included a measure of student outcomes. They conclude, with justification, that 'there is little evidence to support the notion that SBM is effective in increasing student performance. There are very few quantitative studies, the studies are not statistically rigorous, and the evidence of positive results is either weak or non-existent' (Summers and Johnson 1996: 80). Apart from the 'overwhelming obstacles' in the way of assessing the impact of SBM, Summers and Johnson draw attention to that fact that few initiatives 'identify student achievement as a major objective. The focus is on organizational processes, with virtually no attention to how process changes may affect student performance' (*ibid.*: 92–3).

It is interesting that Marshall Smith, under-secretary of the US Department of Education, in commenting on the reform agenda of the Clinton administration (Smith *et al.* 1996), draws attention to the importance of linkage by referring to the findings of a study by the Organisation for Economic Cooperation and Development (OECD) which parallel those of Summers and Johnson (OECD 1994):

> to the degree that a reorganization effort is conducted with a clarity of purpose to improve classroom teaching and learning, positive outcomes may accrue. In other words, to improve student learning, the content and instruction delivered to students must change as

well as the organizational structure of the school. They complement each other.

This is not rocket science.

(Smith *et al.* 1996: 21)

It is timely to ask if these linkages have been made in recent reforms such as those in Victoria. Schools of the Future affords an opportunity to explore the impact of school-based management because linkages of the kind described were intended in the design of four elements: a curriculum and standards framework, a people framework, a resources framework and an accountability framework.

A noteworthy finding in the Cooperative Research Project (1997) relates to outcomes for students, since it was the view of the majority of principals that there have been gains in the areas of curriculum, teaching and learning, either in improved outcomes or in improved capacities to carry out the work of the school. For example, 85 per cent of principals gave a rating of 3 or more on a 5-point scale of 'low' to 'high' on the extent to which the expected benefit of 'improved learning outcomes' had been realised in their schools. These are, of course, opinions or perceptions; no baseline data on student achievement were available.

It is possible to undertake analysis of responses in the survey to determine the direct and indirect effects of selected factors on learning. Such analysis will help us gain an understanding of how schools are moving beyond self-management to high performance and to discern the role of the principal.

The approach known as structural equation modelling was employed on the data from the Cooperative Research Project study, using LISREL 8 (see Jöreskog and Sörbom 1993). This approach allows the analysis of ordinal-scaled variables such as those utilised in the items of the Cooperative Research Project study. This analysis was undertaken on the 1995 data (reported in Caldwell 1996) and on the 1996 data, with the findings for the latter reported here.

The first step was to take clusters of related items in the survey and to treat these as constructs. Seven constructs were formed: Curriculum and Learning Benefits (three items), Personnel and Professional Benefits (seven items), Planning and Resource Allocation Benefits (nine items), School and Community Benefits (six items), Curriculum Improvement due to the Curriculum and Standards Framework (CSF) (seven items), CSF Curriculum Support (four items) and Confidence in Attainment of Schools of the Future Objectives (nine items). A one-factor congeneric measurement model was used to examine the relative weight that each item contributes to a particular construct. All but eight of the forty-five items contributed to the various constructs, with those contributing the most being consistent with an intuitive explanation of which capacities in Schools of the Future ought to have an impact on curriculum and learning. These included greater financial and administrative flexibility, enhanced capacity to attract staff, higher community profile, planning the provision of curriculum, course advice in support of the curriculum and standards framework, and confidence in an objective of Schools of the Future to encourage continuing improvement to enhance learning outcomes. Reliability ranged from 0.79 to 0.94, indicating in the case of the latter a 94 per cent probability that another sample of the principal population would have produced a similar pattern.

Further analysis was conducted to determine the 'goodness of fit' between the data and a model formed by the constructs described above. Figure 2.1 contains the explanatory regression model, which shows the interdependent effects among variables (in this instance, latent variables that represent the constructs) on the variable Curriculum and Learning Benefits. Standardised path coefficients are shown, representing the direct effects (all paths are statistically significant beyond the $p < 0.05$ level by univariate two-tailed test). The fit between data and model is very good indeed, with an adjusted goodness of fit index of 0.947, indicating that about 95 per cent of the variances and co-variances in the data are accounted for by the model.

The path coefficients may be interpreted as follows. The direct effect of School and Community Benefits on Personnel and Professional Benefits is indicated by a path coefficient of 0.479. This indicates that an increase in the measure of School and Community Benefits of 1 standard deviation produces an increase in the measure of Curriculum and Learning Benefits of 0.479 of a standard deviation.

The explanatory model derived from findings in the 1996 survey is similar to that derived one year earlier (see Caldwell 1996), indicating a high degree of stability in the explanatory model. A noteworthy difference is the stronger effects of the three constructs that have a direct impact on Curriculum and Learning Benefits: Personnel and Professional Benefits (0.464 in 1996 compared to 0.217 in 1995), Curriculum Improvement due to the CSF (0.332 in 1996 compared to 0.271 in 1995) and confidence in the Attainment of School of the Future Objectives (0.227 in 1996 compared to 0.195 in 1995). Also noteworthy is the low correlation between individual and school characteristics of respondents and the various dimensions of the model. In other words, the explanatory model stands independent of the nature of respondents and their schools.

While these findings are based on the perceptions of principals, the direct, indirect and total effects are consistent with expectations for the successful implementation of a scheme of school-based management. The structural features of reforms such as the shift of authority, responsibility and accountability to the school level are unlikely, by themselves, to have either a direct or an indirect effect on curriculum and learning unless the capacities that may be nurtured within such arrangements are developed. Clearly, the principals who report curriculum and learning benefits tend to

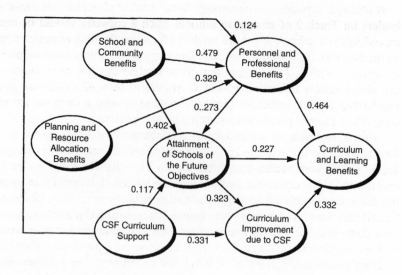

Figure 2.1 Explanatory regression model showing interdependent effects among factors influencing perceived Curriculum and Learning Benefits showing standardised path coefficients

Source: Cooperative Research Project (1997: 80)

Note: CSF = Curriculum and Standards Framework

be those who have reported benefits in other domains of the Schools of the Future programme, including the capacity to select staff, increased flexibility in the use of resources, and the involvement of the community.

The model in Figure 2.1 suggests pathways for the exercise of leadership in self-managing schools where there is a commitment to high performance. While further research is under way to determine the manner in which these pathways are travelled in schools that have evidence of improved outcomes for students, they appear trustworthy and are consistent with a 'theory of action' for the self-managing school. Referring to items on which constructs were derived, such action in respect of direct effects concerns, for example, better personnel management, increased staff satisfaction, enhanced professional development, shared decision-making, enhanced capacity to attract staff (these being in the Personnel and Professional domain); and planning the provision of a curriculum program, establishing levels and standards in key learning areas, focusing attention on key learning areas, basing curriculum around intended learning outcomes, responding to the range of students needs and reporting outcomes to parents (these being in the Curriculum domain). In respect of indirect effects, for example, these concern a higher level of self-management, increased financial and administrative flexibility, and better resource management (these being in the Planning and Resource Allocation domain).

36

Building a capacity to accomplish these tasks is clearly a role for school leaders on Track 2 of change in schools. Such a capacity should be deeply embedded in a school, for there ought to be many leaders engaged in such work, not just the school principal. Contrary to concerns – or perhaps in response to research evidence – that work to date has not been so focused, the direct effects of action in the Curriculum domain should be noted. Leadership and management should be balanced, with a focus on learning, curriculum and the people resources of the school.

While these findings are helpful in describing a preferred role for school leaders, they do not capture the scope and sense of urgency for change on Track 2. The word 'unrelenting' was used to describe the focus on learning and teaching. Robert Slavin uses the word 'relentless' to describe an imperative for action in schools which seek to succeed in early literacy. His Success for All and Roots and Wings programmes are among the nine designs in the New American Schools programme that raise the stakes in terms of work to be done in the USA.

The Labour government in Britain and governments in other countries are making clear that standards-driven reform must lie centre stage. Indeed, in Britain one of the first two education bills presented in the House of Commons after the election in May 1997 was concerned with standards and how to deal with 'failing schools'. Perhaps the most significant appointment in education by the Labour government was the selection of Professor Michael Barber of the University of London to head a new School Standards and Effectiveness Unit. In political terms, in other countries as well as in Britain, there seems to be bipartisan agreement on this issue.

This means that school leaders on Track 2 must, first and foremost, be educational strategists, for they will need to know much about what works and why in an era when the levels of knowledge on these matters is higher than it has ever been. Working with teams of teachers to gather data on student achievement, on entry and in relation to standards for different levels of schooling is central to this task. The concept of 'value added' in respect to the contribution of the school will preferably replace the raw score-based 'league tables' in some countries, notably Britain, despite their growing acceptance by the community and increasing skill on the part of teachers in utilising the results.

These are demanding and highly skilled roles for school leaders, with capacities dispersed in the school rather than focused in the person of the principal. The implications for the preparation and ongoing professional development of teachers and their leaders are profound. It is noteworthy that the Labour government in Britain now requires a formal qualification in leadership and management for school principals.

Track 3: creating schools for the knowledge society

Developments in recent years suggests a third track for change in school education. Track 3 cannot be described in detail but may be presented as a vision, illustrated in Figure 2.2 in a *Gestalt* – 'a perceived organized whole that is more than the sum of its parts' (Concise English Dictionary). This is schooling for the knowledge society because we have entered a new age where those who manage information to solve problems, provide service or create new products form the largest group in the workforce. They have displaced industrial workers, who formed the largest group following the Industrial Revolution and who, in turn, displaced the agricultural and domestic workers who had dominated in pre-industrial times.

Dramatic change to approaches to learning and teaching is in store as electronic networking enables 'cutting across and so challenging the very idea of subject boundaries' and 'changing the emphasis from impersonal curriculum to excited live exploration' (to use the words of Papert in *The Children's Machine* (1993)). At risk is the balkanised curriculum that has done much to alienate children from schooling, especially in the middle years of the transition from primary to secondary (G1, Connectedness in curriculum).

Schools as workplaces are transformed in every dimension, including the

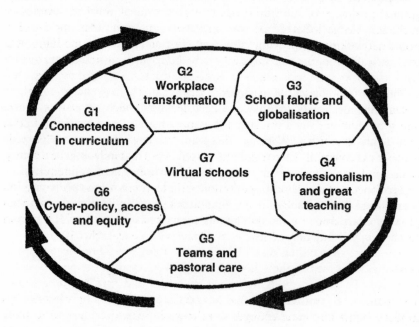

Figure 2.2 A vision for schooling in the knowledge society illustrated in a *Gestalt*
Source: Caldwell and Spinks (1998)

scheduling of time for learning and approaches to human resource management, rendering obsolete most approaches that derive from an industrial age, including the concept of 'industrial relations' (G2, Workplace transformation).

The fabric of schooling is similarly rendered obsolete by electronic networking. Everything from building design to the size, shape, alignment and furnishing of space for the 'knowledge worker' in the school is transformed. In one sense, of course, the school has no walls, for there are global learning networks, and much of the learning that calls for the student to be located at school occurs in many places, at home and, at the upper years of secondary schooling and for life-long learning, in the workplace. (G3, School fabric and globalisation).

A wide range of professionals and para-professionals support learning in an education parallel to the diversity of support that may be found in modern healthcare. The role of teacher is elevated, for it demands wisdom, judgement and a facility to manage learning in modes more complex and varied than ever. While the matter of intellectual capital must be resolved, the teacher is freed from the impossible task of designing from their own resources learning experiences to challenge every student: the resources of the world's great teachers will be at hand (G4, Professionalism and great teaching).

A capacity to work in teams is more evident in approaches to learning, given the primacy of the work team in every formulation of the workplace in the knowledge society. This, of course, will confound those who see electronic networking in the form of an outdated stereotype of the loner with the laptop. The concept of 'pastoral care' of students is as important as ever for learning in this mode, and in schools which, quite literally, have no boundaries (G5, Teams and pastoral care).

Dale Spender's challenge in *Nattering on the Net* (1996) to formulate 'cyber-policy of the future' is a priority. The issues of access and equity will drive public debate until such time as prices fall low enough to make electronic networks as common as the telephone or radio, and that may soon be a reality, given trends in networked computers (G6, Cyber-policy, access and equity).

The concept of the virtual organisation or the learning-network organisation is a reality in the knowledge society. Schools take on many of the characteristics of such organisations, given that learning occurs in so many modes and from so many sources, all networked electronically (G7, Virtual schools).

Tracking changes in the role of the primary principal

The work of the primary principal has certainly changed in profound ways in recent years and more changes seem to be in store. It is helpful to track this change as a way of summarising the main themes and imperatives in this chapter.

In Australia and comparable countries, the role was relatively stable and straightforward until the last quarter of this century. For the principal, it was largely a matter of administering a standard curriculum that did little to accommodate a range of student aptitudes and interests. Few students reached the end of secondary school and most secured employment in their local communities. There was little involvement of parents, except for minor fundraising and social activities, and no substantive role in decision-making. Resources were allocated to schools by formula and no funds as such were devolved to the school level. The principal was expected to 'run a tight ship' as far as staff were concerned, be a model teacher and regularly visit the classrooms of the school.

The role began to change in the 1970s and early 1980s as policies to redress disadvantage and empower communities were enacted. Funds were allocated for particular purposes and in some cases these were devolved to schools, with a more powerful role for teachers and parents in decision-making. For the most part, however, these funds were retained centrally in an increasing array of organisational units in an expanding bureaucracy. It was around this time, in 1983, that the author began research on effective schools, paying particular attention to those which allocated their resources effectively. A model derived from this research helped define a new role for school leaders in goal-setting, policy-making, priority-setting, planning, budgeting, implementing and evaluating, with these activities based around programmes of learning and teaching, and the support of learning and teaching (Caldwell and Spinks 1988).

This role became important as governments around the world restruc-tured their systems of public education, with local management within a centrally determined framework becoming the norm (Track 1). Cultural leadership, strategic leadership, educational leadership and responsive lead-ership were important dimensions of the work of school leaders in a period of rapid change (Caldwell and Spinks 1992).

It is now clear that the concept of the self-managing school is beginning to settle, as evidenced in Britain and New Zealand, and now in Australia. The most important aspect of the emerging role of the principal is concerned with improving the quality of learning for all students, with stan-dards-driven reform now gaining bipartisan support in most places (Track 2). School leaders must be educational strategists, working with others to develop a capacity for state-of-the-art learning. Work in this area is best illustrated at present by the priority given in most places to improving stan-dards of literacy for all students in primary schools.

At the same time as these matters have settled (Track 1) or have gathered momentum (Track 2) there is evidence that school education is being rein-vented, largely driven by advances in technology. It is not possible to be certain about the detail of reform, but the domain for the exercise of leader-ship in the achievement of high performance on Track 3 will be dramatically expanded in the years ahead.

Taken together, this sounds like a rich and rewarding role for school leaders at the dawn of the third millennium.

The search for synchronicity

Much of the chapter has focused on the profound changes affecting the primary school and implications for the principal. These are now placed in a still broader frame with the assistance of some seminal writing on the personal or inner dimensions of leadership.

Much is being written to help us gain an understanding of what is happening in society at the dawn of the third millennium – and why – and this understanding can empower the principal leader. Peter Drucker's (1995) *Managing in a Time of Great Change*, Bill Gates's (1995) *The Road Ahead*, Kenichi Ohmae's (1995) *The End of the Nation State* and John Naisbitt's (1995) *Megatrends: Asia* are examples of such writing (see Caldwell 1997 for application of their work to an understanding of the nature of schooling in the new millennium).

These books deal with the bigger picture in an external sense. They are concerned with major societal change and implications for the tasks of leadership. The new writers considered here also deal with the bigger picture, but they dwell on the inner life of the leader. The starting point is the notion of the psychic prison, choosing the allegory of shadows on the wall in Plato's cave. Attention is then given to the paradox that the more successful we are, the more we place ourselves in jeopardy. This is the Icarus paradox. Gareth Morgan's classic writing on *Images of Organization* (1997) deals with the allegory and the paradox. The core concept of the chapter is then considered in more detail, with reference to Joseph Jaworski's eloquent account of a personal journey in *Synchronicity: The Inner Path of Leadership* (1996). The same themes are given focus in David Loader's remarkable account of *The Inner Principal* (1997), which places the emphasis four-square on the principalship in an era of change.

PLATO'S CAVE

Gareth Morgan (1997) uses the image of Plato's cave to describe the challenge we face in understanding the new realities. He is referring here to Socrates' allegory, in Plato's *The Republic*, in which we are encouraged to imagine people chained to the wall of an underground cave. Outside the cave is a fire, behind which people go about their various activities, making sounds and moving objects. The cave dwellers can only see the shadows of these movements on the wall in front of them, and they try to make sense of their causes and their relationship with the sounds.

Morgan uses this allegory to suggest that our organisations become 'psychic prisons', in which 'organizations and their members become trapped by constructions of reality that, at best, give an imperfect grasp of the world' (Morgan 1997: 216). In school education – and perhaps especially in primary education – it is relatively easy to become trapped in this manner, with little opportunity to be directly involved in or gain a deep under-standing of the wider workplace locally, let alone globally. The forces shaping the transformation of society have led to the most dramatic changes in the nature of work since the Industrial Revolution, developments which can, quite understandably, appear like the shadows on the wall of Plato's cave.

Another part of Socrates' allegory concerns what might occur if one of the prisoners in the cave manages to escape and leave the cave, to see and understand exactly what is happening out there. Should that person return to the cave, he or she could never live the same way again and, should he or she share what had been discovered with fellow prisoners, it is likely that that person would be ridiculed, if not rejected, for his or her efforts. Is this not the way we have changed, and been received on return, when we have had the opportunity to experience at first hand what is occurring outside the world of school education, or when we have had the opportunity to travel widely and frequently, or when we have had the good fortune to engage in an extended and challenging professional development programme?

The implication for the primary principal is to seek out ways to escape the 'psychic prison' and provide every opportunity for colleagues to do the same. Globalisation, the knowledge society, the information revolution, the re-engineering of the public service, standards-driven reform and the new world of work will not be seen as shadows on the wall, opposite which we sit chained and powerless. We shall be unchained and empowered to engage with the realities of the remarkable events around us.

THE ICARUS PARADOX

Morgan (1997: 217) draws on *The Icarus Paradox* (Miller 1990) to remind us that, over time, the strengths of organisations may become weaknesses, leading eventually to their downfall. Icarus was the figure in Greek mythology whose artificial wax wings enabled him to fly so high that he came close to the sun. The wax melted and he plunged to his death.

We are challenged here to reflect on the extraordinary success of primary schools, which served so well over more than a century. They enabled the nation to make its way in the world, even after advantages through the era of gold strikes and the ride on the sheep's back had run their course. We are now exposed to the competition of a global economy and the need to restructure the world of work to keep pace with those now starting to pass us by. International comparisons of educational achievement and approaches to learning and teaching are becoming increasingly intense, as evidenced in the Third International Mathematics and Science Study, the largest international comparative study ever undertaken in school education. With the Icarus paradox, what served us so well in schools in the past may not stand the heat of the demands of the knowledge society and a global economy. The image provides no answers but, like Plato's cave, we are challenged to gain an understanding of the forces transforming society and their impact on schools.

Synchronicity

Joseph Jaworski borrowed the concept of synchronicity from the psychologist Carl Jung to describe a phenomenon of central importance to leadership. Synchronicity is 'a meaningful coincidence of two or more events, where something other than the probability of chance is involved' (Jung; cited in Jaworski 1996: ix).

It was suggested at the start of the chapter that there was a happy conjunction between the creation of a system of public primary schools and the developmental needs of the nation. In a sense, this is synchronicity on a grand scale, the successful coincidence of organisational form and national need. Jaworski explored such possibilities for organisations and other collectivities but was concerned mainly with a personal journey for leaders. He sees this as an heroic quest, not in an exclusive or hierarchical sense, but more along the lines portrayed so well in Joseph Campbell's landmark book *The Hero With a Thousand Faces* (1988) and subsequent television series.

Campbell (1988: 245–6) presented an archetype or template of the hero's journey to which Jaworski gives personal testimony in his own work in establishing the American Leadership Forum, and which can be a guide to all. In simple terms, this journey is characterised by a call to adventure, with perhaps an initial refusal of that call; the availability of a guide; crossing the threshold of adventure; the tests and trials that occur along the way; those who give support to the effort; perhaps a supreme ordeal leading to a sense of exultation or personal apotheosis; a return from that adventure; and, finally, success and satisfaction, for oneself and others, being the gift of elixir (Jaworski 1996: 89).

Dimmock and O'Donoghue (1997) provide accounts of life histories of successful school principals. Each has characteristics of the heroic quest, with success built around work that pervades the new role of the principal (values, vision, goal-setting, goal achievement).

Synchronicity occurs when in the course of the heroic quest one is presented with and accepts opportunities that seem to appear with greater probability than chance alone. Every reader will readily identify instances where such events have occurred in his or her own journey. They are evident in the life histories recounted by Dimmock and O'Donoghue.

Peter Senge has done more than anyone else to develop the notion of 'the learning organisation' (Senge 1990). He wrote an introduction to Jaworski's

(1996) book and included these thoughts about leadership, which appear to have direct application to the primary principalship:

> Leadership exists when people are no longer victims of circumstances but participate in creating new circumstances. ... It's not about positional power; it's not about accomplishments; it's ultimately not even about what we do. Leadership is about creating a domain in which human beings continually deepen their understanding of reality and become more capable of participating in the unfolding of the world. Leadership is about creating new realities.
>
> (Senge 1996: 3)

Senge believes we are all 'wrestling with the profound changes required in public and institutional leadership in the twenty-first century ... [in which] Our lifelong experiences with hierarchy cast a long shadow, making it difficult for us to think outside the framework of hierarchical leadership' (Senge 1996: 4). For principals of primary schools in the public sector, this is the challenge of leadership in the self-managing school and beyond the self-managing school, for those who set out on an adventure in greater autonomy, outside the frameworks that have served so well in the past but may melt away in the heat of change ('the Icarus paradox'). This is the challenge of leadership that seeks to escape the 'psychic prison'. For principals of all schools, public and private, this is the challenge of leadership that seeks to create the new realities of schooling that will emerge in the new millennium.

The inner principal

The inner path of leadership is described in engaging fashion by David Loader in *The Inner Principal* (1997). David Loader is the principal of Australia's largest private school, Wesley College in Melbourne, but is best known internationally as Principal of Methodist Ladies' College (MLC), also in Melbourne, from 1978 to 1996. It is likely that MLC has accepted the challenge of information technology to a greater degree than any other school, nationally or internationally, with more than 2,000 of the 2,300 students having their own laptop computers. Virtually every aspect of schooling, for students and teachers, has been transformed at MLC. For his role in this transformation, David Loader is widely recognised as an outstanding strategic thinker in school education.

These are the external accomplishments in the leadership of David Loader. He has helped create the 'the new realities' of schooling for MLC, in the style of leadership set out by Senge (1996: 3; cited above). In *The Inner Principal* he has written about his personal journey. His chapter on 'The stumble principal' harmonises with Jaworski's concept of synchronicity, for

Loader recounts the way he literally stumbled on opportunities which then became the new realities.

In what, in the author's view, is the most insightful chapter in the book, Loader draws on Coelho's modern fable to describe 'The alchemist principal' (based on Coelho 1993). This fable concerns a boy named Santiago who travels the world seeking the treasure of his dreams. It is an adventure remarkably like the heroic quest described by Joseph Campbell. There is the call to adventure, the guides along the way, the tests and trials, even a supreme ordeal where death seems imminent, and a return, quite literally, to his home, where he finds the treasure beneath his feet. Santiago reflects on his heroic quest: 'It's true; life is generous to those who pursue their destiny' (Coelho 1993: 176). The power of synchronicity prevailed, for 'Where you stumble, there your treasure lies' (Joseph Campbell; cited by Jaworski 1996: 119).

Barricades, traps and the elixir of learning

There are, of course, some barricades that are making things difficult for the primary principal. In the matter of workload and job satisfaction, those in the public sector may look with envy on many of their colleagues in the private sector who have a large staff to support them in administration. It is not simply a matter of delegation. Resource issues are dealt with in another chapter. The author addresses them in more detail elsewhere, drawing lessons from recent efforts in the reform of public education (Caldwell and Hayward 1998).

Jaworski identifies three traps which seem especially relevant to the work of the primary principal, namely the trap of responsibility, the trap of dependency and the trap of overactivity (Jaworski 1996: 118–30). The trap of responsibility is encountered when one feels that one has responsibility for everything, and the workload expands and the number of sleepless nights increases. ('I would wake up in the middle of the night thinking of all the people whose jobs depended on me' (ibid.: 120).) Once recognised, according to Jaworski, the trap loses its potency, but seeing oneself as one of many who are all involved in or committed to the enterprise will assist ('operating in the flow of the universe' (ibid.: 125)). The trap of dependency is the flip side, relying excessively on the contribution of others, compromising on achievement rather than energising the commitment of all to the dream. ('The traps of responsibility and dependency generate a lot of energy from the fear of no alternative' (ibid.: 128).) The trap of overactivity is experienced when one gets bogged down in the detail. It seems that this is a pathological aspect of recent reforms in education, given the increase in workload of teachers and principals, as is evident in New Zealand and Victoria (see Hargreaves and Goodson (1996) for an account of intensification in the professional lives of teachers). For Jaworski, 'the key to overcoming the trap of overactivity is in doing the inner, reflective work, individually and collectively necessary to regain our balance' (Jaworski 1996: 129).

Traps and barricades are no reason for refusing the call to adventure. The treasure for the principal is the elixir of learning. The heroic quest will inevitably lead us back to where we began, and the synchronicity that marked the last century of primary education will be achieved in the next.

References

Bullock, A. and Thomas, H. (1994) *The Impact of Local Management in Schools: Final Report*, Birmingham: University of Birmingham and National Association of Head Teachers.

Caldwell, B. J. (1996) 'Factors associated with improved learning outcomes in the local management of schools: early findings from Victoria's *Schools of the Future*', paper presented in a symposium on the Processes and Outcomes of Schools of the Future at the Annual Conference of the British Educational Management and Administration Society, Coventry, 20 September.

—— (1997) 'Thinking in time: a gestalt for schools of the new millennium', in B. Davies and L. Ellison (eds) *School Leadership for the 21st Century: A Competency and Knowledge Approach*, London: Routledge.

Caldwell, B. J. and Hayward, D. (1998) *The Future of Schools: Lessons from the Reform of Public Education*, London: Falmer Press.

Caldwell, B. J. and Spinks, J. M. (1988) *The Self-managing School*, London: Falmer Press.

—— (1992) *Leading the Self-managing School*, London: Falmer Press.

—— (1998) *Beyond the Self-managing School*, London: Falmer Press.

Campbell, J. (1988) *The Hero With a Thousand Faces*, London: Paladin Grafton.

Coelho, P. (1993) *The Alchemist*, San Francisco, CA: Harper San Francisco.

Cooperative Research Project (1994) *Base-Line Survey*, report of the Cooperative Research Project on Leading Victoria's Schools of the Future', Directorate of School Education, Victorian Association of State Secondary Principals, Victorian Primary Principals' Association, University of Melbourne (Fay Thomas, Chair) [available from Department of Education].

—— (1995a) *One Year Later*, report of the Cooperative Research Project on Leading Victoria's Schools of the Future, Directorate of School Education, Victorian Association of State Secondary Principals, Victorian Primary Principals' Association, University of Melbourne (Fay Thomas, Chair) [available from Department of Education].

—— (1995b) *Taking Stock*, report of the Cooperative Research Project on Leading Victoria's Schools of the Future, Directorate of School Education, Victorian Association of State Secondary Principals, Victorian Primary Principals' Association, University of Melbourne (Fay Thomas, Chair) [available from Directorate of School Education].

—— (1996) *Three Year Report Card*, report of the Cooperative Research Project on Leading Victoria's Schools of the Future, Directorate of School Education, Victorian Association of State Secondary Principals, Victorian Primary Principals' Association, University of Melbourne (Fay Thomas, Chair) [available from Department of Education].

—— (1997) *Still More Work to Be Done But ... No Turning Back*, report of the Cooperative Research Project on Leading Victoria's Schools of the Future, Department of School Education, Victorian Association of State Secondary Principals, Victorian Primary Principals' Association, University of Melbourne (Fay Thomas, Chair) [available from Department of Education].

Dimmock, C. and O'Donoghue, T. A. (1997) *Innovative School Principals and Restructuring: Life History Portraits of Successful Managers of Change*, London: Routledge.

Drucker, P. F. (1995) *Managing in a Time of Great Change*, Oxford: Butterworth-Heinemann.

Ford, P. M. (1995) 'Role perceptions and professional development needs of primary principals in Schools of the Future', unpublished master's thesis, Department of Education Policy and Management, University of Melbourne.

Gates, B. (1995) *The Road Ahead*, New York: Penguin.

Hargreaves, A. and Goodson, I. (1996) 'Teachers' professional lives: aspirations and actualities', in I. Goodson and A. Hargreaves (eds) *Teachers' Professional Lives*, London: Falmer Press.

Jaworski, J. (1996) *Synchronicity: The Inner Path of Leadership*, San Francisco, CA: Berrett-Koehler Publishers.

Jöreskog, K. G. and Sörbom, D. (1993) *LISREL 8: User's Reference Guide*, Chicago, IL: Scientific Software, Inc.

Loader, D. (1997) *The Inner Principal*, London: Falmer Press.

Miller, D. (1990) *The Icarus Paradox*, New York: HarperBusiness.

Morgan, G. (1997) *Images of Organization*, Thousand Oaks, CA: Sage.

Naisbitt, J. (1995) *Megatrends: Asia*, London: Nicholas Brealey.

OECD (1994) *Effectiveness of Schooling and of Educational Resource Management: Synthesis of Country Studies*, Points 22 and 23, Paris: OECD, Directorate of Education, Employment, Labour and Social Affairs, Education Committee.

Ohmae, K. (1995) *The End of the Nation State: The Rise of Regional Economies*, London: HarperCollins.

Papert, S. (1993) *The Children's Machine: Rethinking School in the Age of the Computer*, New York: Basic Books.

St John-Brooks, C. (1997) 'Blunkett pledges to clear the funding fog', *Times Educational Supplement*, 16 May: 1.

Senge, P. (1990) *The Fifth Discipline*, New York: Doubleday.

—— (1996) 'Introduction', in J. Jaworski *Synchronicity: The Inner Path of Leadership*, San Francisco, CA: Berrett-Koehler Publishers.

Smith, M. S., Scoll, B. W. and Link, J. (1996) 'Research-based school reform: the Clinton administration's agenda', in E. A. Hanushek and D. W. Jorgenson (eds) *Improving America's Schools: The Role of Incentives*, Washington, DC: National Academy Press.

Spender, D. (1996) *Nattering on the Net: Women, Power and Cyberspace*, North Melbourne: Spinifex.

Summers, A. A. and Johnson, A. W. (1996) 'The effects of school-based management plans', in E. A. Hanushek and D. W. Jorgenson (eds) *Improving America's Schools: The Role of Incentives*, Washington, DC: National Academy Press.

Wylie, C. (1997) *At the Centre of the Web: The Role of the New Zealand Primary Principal Within a Decentralized Education System*, Wellington: New Zealand Council for Educational Research.

3

TEACHERS, TRAINING AND DEVELOPMENT

Len Cairns

Introduction

Primary teachers have been struggling with a period of immense pressure and change in the past decade. The pressures, largely associated with a time of substantial school restructuring, have been international and pervasive (Lieberman *et al.* 1991; Beare and Boyd 1993; Stringfield *et al.* 1996, Goodson and Hargreaves 1996). As a consequence of these pressures, changes have occurred in the nature of who the primary teachers are and the school contexts in which they work. In addition, there have been considerable changes in the range of responsibilities today's primary teachers are required to fulfil, in the curriculum they have been asked to teach, and in the additional pressures and challenges they have been expected to endure and meet (Keeves 1987; Hughes *et al.* 1987; Woods 1995; Busher and Saran 1995). At the same time, their training and professional development have been less dramatically changed and in only a few areas have they been able to assist teachers in their need both to 'keep up' and to try to 'stay on top'. It has become evident that there is a need to develop and enhance professional development, and to reconsider the defining characteristics of the profession, professionalism and professional development approaches (Hughes 1991; Goodson and Hargreaves 1996).

This chapter begins with a brief picture of primary teachers today and then traces some of the issues associated with the changing role of primary teachers, the new demands made upon them and the need for the professional development of a dynamic teaching force for the new century.

Being a primary-school teacher is seen by many members of society as akin to being a highly paid babysitter, yet this aspect of schooling is charged with the most important aspects of our children's development. The frequent lack of a clear understanding of the significance and the professional contribution made by teachers at this level cannot be sheeted home to the usual scapegoats such as the media or the fact that everyone is familiar with primary schooling so they are all armchair critics. The profession itself must take responsibility for any poor perception within society and any less-ening of the status of primary teachers. We (and I include myself in the primary-teacher category) need to stand a little taller and speak very care-fully about the role of the primary teacher in schooling and society, how we act and profess what we do. Some recent writing by Peter Woods (1995), where he describes what he calls *Creative Teachers in Primary Schools*, is a good start to this, as is the volume by Patrick Whitaker on *Primary Schools and the Future* (1997), which he admirably dedicates 'to all lovers of primary schools and those who work in them'.

It is suggested that the changing roles of the primary teacher, and the pressures and challenges facing each one of them necessitate a paradigm shift in thinking about what type of teacher we need for the twenty-first-century primary school (Kuhn 1962). It is the thesis of this chapter that the notion of the capable primary teacher is what we should be actively pursuing. A capable teacher is one who is able to move beyond basic compe-tence (knowledge and skills) towards a flexibility (coping with present twists and turns) and an adaptability (coping with uncertain futures) in a manner that demonstrates potential and professionalism. The capable teacher – with that blend of high skills and knowledge, wedded to strong self-efficacy beliefs and intertwined with central values of and for learning and the devel-opment of learners who manage their own learning for life – is the essence of future teaching and development for the next century. Capable teachers place learning, by pupils, self and community, at the heart of their teaching work (Cairns and Hase 1996).

Change might be all around us in terms of restructuring our schools as organisations, but any decent study of the change process in organisational theory will point to the 'people' aspect as a key factor (Hesselbein *et al.* 1997). The roles developed and played by the primary teacher are therefore central to the whole enterprise.

Who are today's primary teachers?

If we were to describe a composite Australian primary teacher based on much of the available evidence we might emerge with someone like Janice.

Janice is a teacher of third grade at Beaumont Primary School in the metropolitan suburbs of a capital city. She is 43 years old, married (for the second time) and she has two children of her own (one of each sex, aged 14 and 11 years). She has been teaching for fourteen years, with a break of 'family leave' for eight years in the middle (it was to have been five years but she successfully extended it). She has been back teaching in the state system for the past six years. Janice was originally a three-year trained primary teacher at a college of advanced education and during her first eight-year teaching stint she managed to undertake a fourth-year upgrade to a Bachelor of Education by distance education. During that eight-year period she taught at four different schools, including two years in the country. She married in her fifth year of teaching and divorced when her second child (her daughter) was 3 years old. She spent a year as a single parent sorting out her life before remarrying and returning to teaching after an eight-year break.

Janice's school is in a fast-growing suburb with a mixed population, including a number of non-English speaking families. It has a male principal and a female deputy. Within the school Janice is heavily involved in curriculum implementation committees for literacy and maths. She chairs the maths group.

Janice works hard. She also has an active role in the community (she lives locally), where she runs the local cubs group, and takes after-school parent-education classes in literacy and trains the Maths Mothers helper group once a week.

Her third-grade class has two boys who have been diagnosed as attention-deficit disorder (ADD) and she has one 'integration' child, who is hearing-impaired and intellectually retarded, and she is assisted by an integration aide for part of each day (mornings). Janice has thirty-one children in her class. One child in the class is also about to be assessed (at the parents' request) for giftedness. He is described as an unusual child and tends to be a behaviourally difficult pupil in the classroom.

The School has Italian, taught as a language other than English (LOTE) by a specialist teacher (part time), and has a reading recovery teacher.

Under the new system, the school has a local (approved) charter which specifies that its major emphases are on technology and literacy.

The school motto is 'Educating for the Future'.

The point of painting Janice as we have in this chapter is not to emphasise any particular aspects but to 'colour in' some of the current reality of our profession as we attempt to sketch aspects of the typical primary teacher working in our schools. Janice is not 'every teacher', but she represents a good number of the statistics extant in the profession. There are many more women than men. The proportion of males in promotion positions, while slowly falling, is still high compared with the overall proportion in the teaching force. The average age of the teaching force has been climbing. There are more teachers with four-year qualifications than there were, say, five years ago. Most of our teachers completed their basic training some ten years or more ago. There are few, if any, incentives to upgrade qualifications other than professional pride and dedication. Many of the women involved have 'broken' careers. A number have children and have experienced marital disruption. The tasks and the children they are now facing in their class-rooms are described in different terms from those which were the pattern when they initially trained as teachers. The types of roles they are now asked to fulfil and the organisation of the schools in which they work are very different from what they were at the outset of their careers. Some of the new expectations are in areas where the teacher has little or no experience or expertise (such as technology). Both the time and the set of new roles are laden with potential tension and anxiety for many teachers.

There are other characteristics of today's primary teachers worth noting in this descriptive overview and not mentioned in the case of Janice. There are community pressures on teachers and there is some difficulty in projecting the role as a true profession (Robertson 1996). One such aspect has surrounded publicity about the educational ability of teacher entrants. The quality of pre-service teacher education students has been a topic of considerable debate over the past decade. The concern is that there has been a decline in the level of academic achievement (as indicated by end-of-high-school results) of entrants into pre-service teacher education courses, particularly those preparing teachers for the primary level. At the same time as this has been a noticeable feature, there has been considerable restructuring within state school systems in many Australian states, which has led to considerable downsizing of the teaching service (most notably in Victoria) and few entry-level appointments of young, recently trained teachers. The profession has thus been targeted for a good deal of public scrutiny and, for many, it has been found wanting.

The end result of these efforts has been that in the late 1990s the primary teachers of Australia are a smaller, gradually ageing teaching force attempting to come to grips with massive changes in structure and curriculum. At the same time, they have to deal with poor press and public perceptions. Today's primary teachers are also faced with a set of new and ever-changing challenges which present them with issues which they need to address and to which they must respond. As we shall discuss in a later section of this chapter, the need for professional development and support at this time and in this context is heightened in significance by these changes, pressures and challenges, and becomes a central element in the development of the future-oriented capable teachers we need.

The changing role of primary teachers

The primary teacher of the 1990s is a far cry from what most adults currently over 40 would have experienced as pupils themselves. There are a number of significant changes to the role of the primary teacher that have occurred in relation to classroom teaching, shifts in theoretical understanding of learners, the curriculum involved, the breadth of individual differences in classrooms, and the specialist knowledge and support areas they are expected to respond to or manage.

Changes in teaching and social expectations

The modern primary teacher has a vast array of research and theoretical views impinging upon his or her professional practice, each crying out for consideration and many being adopted as 'bandwagons', with slogan-like support in staffrooms, in-service courses and the media. The past decade has been the age of 'process writing', 'whole language', 'genre writing', 'technology' (in all its various meanings), 'multiple intelligences', 'cooperative learning', 'peer tutoring', 'reading recovery', 'authentic assessment', 'portfolios', 'profiles', 'reflective teaching', 'mentoring', 'teaching on (or with) the Internet', and so on. One could put together a large and detailed table of such aspects, to which most primary teachers would nod in agreement. Australian primary teachers have what has been, for some, an unenviable reputation as among the most inclined to join a 'bandwagon' of all international teachers. For example, we were the leading purchasers – per capita – of the famous Science Research Associates (SRA) Reading Laboratories in the 1960s and 1970s. We embraced 'process, or conference, writing' like no other nation in the 1980s and we have grasped Reading Recovery in some states as the panacea for reading problems in the late 1980s and 1990s, to name just a few. I do not mean to say that each of these aspects has little or no value, or that they might not be useful and helpful elements of the primary teacher's array of ideas and techniques. The point is that Australian primary teachers seem to have a penchant for the adoption of schemes and approaches. While such a predisposition – if that is what it appears to be – might be criticised as educationally unfortunate, it could also be seen as a very useful and advantageous flexibility, if the adoptions were based on thoughtful evaluation of the available evidence and the theoretical stance of the innovation purveyors.

Among the more prevalent trends in relation to planning and performance of classroom teaching in the past few years has been the influence of the theories, research and practical implications associated with what is now most frequently referred to as the social-constructivist view of teaching and learning. Developing out of the implications of the work of theorists such as Piaget and Vygotsky, this view has placed greater emphasis on the child/learner as a social constructor of meaning and less emphasis on the teacher as imparter of knowledge. An overview has been succinctly put by C. T. Fosnot in the 'Preface' to the volume she edited on this topic:

> Although constructivism is not a theory of teaching, it suggests taking a radically different approach to instruction from that used in most schools. Teachers who base their practice on constructivism reject the notions that meaning can be passed on to learners via symbols or transmission, that learners can incorporate exact copies of teachers' understanding for their own use, that whole concepts can be broken into discrete subskills, and that concepts can be taught out of context. In contrast, a constructivist view of learning suggests an approach to teaching that gives learners the opportunity for concrete, contextually meaningful experience through which they can search for patterns, raise their own questions, and construct their own models, concepts, and strategies. The classroom in this model is seen as a minisociety, a community of learners engaged in activity, discourse, and reflection. The traditional hierarchy of teacher as the autocratic knower and learner as the unknowing, controlled subject studying to learn what the teacher knows begins to dissipate as teachers assume more of a facilitator's role and learners take on more ownership of the ideas. Indeed, autonomy, mutual reciprocity of social relations, and empowerment become the goals.
>
> (Fosnot 1996: ix)

Many of these principles, beliefs and associated attitudes are also at the heart of much of the whole-language movement (Goodman 1986), which, like constructivism, is not a set of teaching techniques *per se*, but rather a set of beliefs and attitudes about learning and the important roles played by the active learner as a constructor of meaning. Australian (and, even more so, New Zealand) primary teachers are regarded as being at the forefront of this work on the conceptualisation of language teaching.

An additional change in the classroom teaching expectations of today's primary teacher has been the movement, as a policy of many governments and educational bureaucracies, for children designated as having 'special needs' (the physically, intellectually and behaviourally impaired) to be included or 'integrated' into the mainstream classroom. The movement away from exclusion into special schools and classes has led to local primary schools having a wider range of individual differences within the school. A teacher may now be responsible for the day-to-day education and developmental supervision of children who are hearing- or sight-impaired, intellectually retarded or autistic, for example. Some systems provide a range of teacher-aide support and some have specialist teachers attached to schools or groups of schools. Today's primary teacher, however, is the 'frontline' educator with the key responsibility. Many of the teachers faced with this range of children are anxious because they have had little, if any, specialist training, and they are fearful of the extra demands and that their skills may be inadequate. In addition, they now have to supervise the work of their teacher aide closely.

Alongside many of these ideas and collections of ideological positions (such as, say, whole language), teachers at the primary level have also faced pressures associated with the prevailing trends in educational practice and approach at the macro-level. For example, during the 1970s and most of the 1980s the move towards a social justice and critical pedagogy model of thinking about schools and schooling (Carr and Kemmis 1986) heavily influenced much classroom practice through government policies, teacher unions and various aspects of teacher symposia, publications and in-service programmes. Some teachers readily embraced such notions; others felt either uncomfortable or overly challenged in their roles by many of the emerging ideas. The end result was further anxiety and confusion for many. This aspect of teacher professional practice, reflection and critique is still very much alive as an issue (Smyth 1996),

Jones and Maloy (1996) have very neatly summed up some of these competing pressures as a feature of the present and recent past in most (post)modern Western societies as a matter of operating within what they term 'contested terrain' between 'industrial-era and information-age ways of making sense of schools and society' (*ibid.*: xvi). They present the 'contested terrain' in a diagram as follows:

an industrial economy <-> a post-industrial economy
hierarchical prospects for jobs <->aspirations for a meaningful life
supervision in hierarchical structures <-> cooperative decision-making
behaviorism in an objective world<-> social construction of meanings
schooling to reproduce categories <-> exploring new roles and values
learning in academic frameworks <-> transdisciplinary approaches
authoritative adult knowledge <-> jointly constructed understandings
replicating class, race and gender <-> crossing cultural boundaries
corporate domination of democracy <-> democratic discourse and
social justice

Jones and Maloy suggest that, within this field:

School structures still embody the assumptions and beliefs of the left column while students and emerging information-age organizations are attracted to those in the right column. Teachers find themselves uncomfortably in between, trying to mediate or reconcile approaches that are contradictory.

(Jones and Maloy 1996: xvi)

Suffice it to say at this stage that a primary teacher like Janice currently faces decisions about the extent to which she adopts and/or adapts ideologies such as whole language, social-constructivist approaches or direct instruction in basic skills. Fundamental aspects of the teacher's role as facilitator or didactic instructor, once resolved, lead her on to examine aspects of her roles as curriculum implementer or curriculum devisor, cooperative team member or lone ranger, reflective practitioner, partner with the parents, and part community social worker. Each of the complex facets of the modern primary teacher's role needs to be examined and acted upon at some stage of his or her development and practice. This remains, for many, a daunting task. It is also clearly no matter for the ill-informed or naive, but rather one for well-educated professionals. In order for Janice to emerge as a sophisticated primary teacher in the future she will need to be assisted to develop attitudes, values and approaches which will help her to build upon her skills base and to be confident, flexible, adaptable and ready to take charge of uncertainty as a 'paradigm shifter' (Kuhn 1962; Whitaker 1997; S. P. Marshall 1997). These aspects constitute attributes which take her beyond simply the development of pedagogical expertise and into the realms of what the author would argue is the emergence of the capable teacher.

Changes in curriculum

At the same time as the primary teacher faces such fundamental and personal style choices, there has been a set of changes associated with the way schools are now structured and what the basic curriculum standards ought to be. The many elements of primary-school restructuring are the focus of the whole volume of this book and will not be separated out in this chapter; nor will the details of curriculum change and development (see Chapter 7). However, the moves, within most Australian states, towards a more central specification of overall curriculum structures with appropriate goals/outcomes and standards for age/grade (or 'bands' of) achievements will be briefly mentioned.

The main movement over the past five years within the Australian curriculum context has been towards the establishment of greater correlation of state-based curricula (though the attempts to introduce something akin to a national curriculum or an agreed 'core' model were only partially successful), with a focus on 'key' statements of 'levels', 'bands' and 'profiles', and a preoccupation with the terms *outcomes* and *standards* evident in many state documents. In Victoria, for example, the centrally developed and issued Curriculum Standards Framework (CSF) offers a much more structured set of expectations (standards) in levels and bands than did curriculum documents in that state in the previous decade. A good deal of teacher input and development is still needed at the local-district and even school level with the CSF approach, but there is much less of an emphasis on what was termed School-based Curriculum Development (SBCD) in the past.

Primary teachers are now expected both to be aware of the standards and the documentation set by the state education authorities and to be able to account to parents and the system within the terms and standards set by the state. There has been some movement, as well, towards the development and administration of state-wide tests of basic skills and achievement. This movement, while not of the same ilk as that in countries such as the USA, has gained a degree of political and community support, but has angered many teachers and other educators, who see it as the thin end of a wedge to move to wider and more insidious test-dominated modes of instruction, with all the obvious attendant ills associated with this idea and practice.

Much of the participation by classroom teachers in the curriculum debate seems, in 1997, to have quietened down and the major contested terrain is currently in the areas of assessment and reporting. Primary teachers appear to have less effective ability directly to influence the wider community with educational argumentation on many of these issues than their secondary and tertiary colleagues. This is most likely a further reflection of perceived status and expertise.

Current and future challenges to primary teachers

In addition to the changes and influences which have positioned the modern primary teacher at the centre of a wide range of choices and professional pressures, there are many challenges which have emerged through societal and educational developments in the past few years, and others which are harbingers of the future. These challenges reflect broader-based community and social developments which education, and primary schooling in particular, is expected to respond to, if not be actively engaged in.

In order to provide a structure and focus for this consideration of the various current and possible future challenges for the primary teacher, the topics to be examined have been grouped under four broad headings: technology and the 'information superhighway' challenges, national imperative challenges, social responsibility challenges and, finally, business and industry relevance challenges.

Technology and the 'information superhighway' challenges

There is no question that the coming of the Internet and the World Wide Web (WWW) in this computer age has heralded a set of monumental challenges for primary teachers. First, the level of equipment and associated resources to engage in this element of education has been a major delaying influence for many schools and individual teachers. Second, the level of personal expertise in this area of operation, for most primary teachers, has been one of severe under-skilling. Third, the speed with which the technology has advanced and the in-built obsolescence – so much a deliberate marketing feature of the computer industry – have meant that the educational significance, curriculum intent, learning possibilities, development of appropriate pedagogical models and the general theorising of what the whole field of activity actually means or offers for schooling, children learning and the broader society have been severely underdone.

This area of society – and, in particular, its impact upon and relevance to education – is seen by many as a key to the twenty-first century. In the USA, in both his 1996 and 1997 'State of the Union' Presidential Addresses, Bill Clinton has pledged that US schools and all libraries will be connected to the Internet by the year 2000. In the detail of the president's *Call to Action for American Education* the key 'four pillars of his technology literacy agenda' are described as follows:

1   Connect every school and classroom in America to the information superhighway.
2   Provide access to modern computers for all teachers and students.
3   Develop effective and engaging software and on-line learning resources as an integral part of the school curriculum.
4   Provide all teachers the training and support they need to help students learn through computers and the information superhighway.

(US Department of Education 1997: 41)

President Clinton and his vice-president, Al Gore, have been vanguard advocates of the significance of the Internet for education and society, and have been responsible for the US government appearing on-line in much more accessible ways than in past administrations. The interested reader may wish to examine, for example, the details of the US President's Technology programme by logging on to the White House Web site and accessing the information there (http://www.whitehouse.gov/edtech.html).

While these elements are situated in the US context, they are similar to the emerging sentiments in Australian schools and society. Australians are world renowned as great adopters of technology, and joining the 'information superhighway' has been no exception. Naisbitt (1994: 52) listed Norway as the nation with most 'Internet host' machines, with 5 per 1,000 people. Next came the USA, with 3.8, and Australia, with 3.7. Our fascination and involvement has increased in the three years since that data was published. Most of our government departments also have Web sites where details are available. Most of our daily newspapers also offer electronic versions, and the international news conglomerate headquartered in Australia, News Ltd, has a large and burgeoning classified advertising location on the Internet. An excellent site (known an SoFweb) has been set up by the Victorian Government's Department of Education and can be accessed at http://www.dse.vic.gov.au.

At one extreme in the 'hype' (pardon the pun) about the power and significance of the impact of the Internet is the argument, best exemplified by Perelman (1992: 23) that, in the near future, schools as we know them will be replaced (and should be) by vast computer networks and technological advances in what Perelman refers to as Hyperlearning. There is no doubt that the educational future will depend upon and heavily involve whatever networks and advances we are yet to see as major driving and structural components. There is a need to ensure, as educators, that there are clear and sensible pedagogical theories, models and informed practices which best utilise this amazing new resource. We are only just beginning to examine the educationally necessary theoretical considerations in this field (Jones and Maloy 1996; Jonassen 1996), and various practitioners are beginning to offer more flexible classroom ideas and advice beyond the skill, drill and game formats which first emerged (Lasarenko 1997).

The educational significance of the technological revolution, as some wish to characterise the era, has popular appeal (Ravitch 1993; Gates 1996) as well as critics (Postman 1995; C. Stoll 1995), and there are those who have pioneered applications and ideas in particular computer languages and settings such as LOGO and the use of LEGO. (Papert 1980, 1993; Resnick 1996). In addition, courses are now emerging on the Internet offered by commercial and university enterprises, and targeting teachers who wish to start and develop this area with their pupils (Royal Melbourne Institute of Technology University (RMIT), Edith Cowan and Monash, for example). Many schools and even individual pupils have World Wide Web home sites where anyone with the address or able to seek out the topics can log on and read about the place, the pupil or whatever has been loaded (Goldberg and Richards 1995, 1996) (see, for example, the Co-NECT schools site, http://co-nect.bbn.com/, or the excellent US National School Network site at http://nsn.bbn.com/). A number of universities in Australia are also cooperating with schools in Web projects (e.g. Monash, http://www.education.monash.edu.au/, and Griffith University, http://www.edn.gu.edu.au/). As soon as the matter of secure and sensible ways of charging is better resolved than has been the case to date, there will be much more trade on the Internet.

These aspects are rapidly (in an exponential manner) changing the way many children think about knowledge and their interaction with it, all without any teacher intervention being necessary. It is growing and emerging all around them, in the media, in their daily interaction and in the street (new Internet booths in shopping centres and on street vans are beginning to emerge across the world, and cyber-cafés are a reality). We need to imagine and develop ways to demonstrate how and why teacher intervention in this area, probably in ways we are just beginning to see, should lead to better utilisation and understanding of the whole technological world enterprise. There is also a need to examine what teachers' attitudes are to this burgeoning area and whether there are relationships between teachers' views of learners, learning and their potential to adopt and utilise computers and the new associated technologies effectively. Some early steps have been taken in this direction (Hannafin and Freeman 1995: 55) which seem to indicate that in the USA, at least, older, more experienced teachers have more 'objectivist' than 'constructivist' views of learners and the learning process, and may therefore be less likely to adopt computer-based materials and models based on constructivist philosophies. In addition, Hannafin and Freeman have suggested that 'experienced teachers are more likely than their less experienced colleagues to believe that students are not qualified to manage their own instruction' (*ibid.*: 55). Such views as these, if they are also held by Australian teachers, may be a major stumbling block to progress in educational patterns such as the Learning-centred Classrooms and Schools of McCombs and Whisler (1997), or the Learning School of Nixon *et al.* (1996). To say that this area is a huge challenge to today's primary teachers is an understatement.

Current national imperative challenges

Among the extended list of challenges to primary teachers mentioned above were two aspects which focus on particular areas of the curriculum content. Both of these aspects can be characterised as *current national imperatives*, not to inflate their significance as issues, but more to reflect the nature of their roots and their role in challenging teachers and schools today. In today's societies, with increased trade and travel internationally, and with the advent of sport and recreation as major industries with huge international audiences and large income-generating prospects, the fields of physical education and sport, and the learning of a range of useful languages other than English have become challenges placed firmly in front of the primary teacher.

Today's teacher is being pressed to introduce to children, and to develop their interest and expertise in both these areas as national imperatives. Primary teachers are expected to assist in the maximal development of future adults who are fit and athletic, and, in some cases, heavily competitive and able to take their place in sports and activities which will enhance them. The potential for some pupils to go further at levels such as the Olympics and the world of competitive national and/or international professional sport is also an underlying factor of many efforts in this area. There is huge money to be earned in this latter arena, and many parents and communities now expect more of schools and teachers in the identification, fostering and support of young potential athletes, gymnasts and sports people. Some of the expected support may involve differential treatment at school and 'understanding' as to the preferred options of the pupil and the parents. This can create extreme stress and difficulty for some teachers in some settings. Pressure is emerging for more than the 'games' lessons of the past and for more informed physical education, diet supervision, and credible coaching and skill development. World champions in various sports (for example in ice skating and tennis) are frequently aged around 14 and have been identified and supported from early primary-school age. The morality, the ethics, the pressure of such aspects constitute one set of challenges for the teacher; another set is the expertise and professional judgement needed to assist, if that is desired. Many primary teachers are turning to specialists in this field and some systems are encouraging this development, while others are apparently ambivalent.

It is possible in this regard that Australia might see, in the not too distant future, a situation similar to the USA, where sports coaches draw the largest salaries and are viewed by much of society as the most significant educators in the secondary- and tertiary-education setting. Whatever actually develops, there is no doubt that these aspects are a set of challenges to the modern primary teacher and that they represent another aspect of change and development. It is important, however, that a balanced approach is maintained in this area. Few children will be aiming for elite athleticism. Few parents actually see this route as one for their child. However, there is a heightened awareness that there is now a greater role for the primary school in good exercise, informed training and fitness regimens, and sensible skill development than there was in the past.

This area of physical education, possibly more than many others in the primary curriculum set, appears to have raised the issues of the 'generalist' teacher versus the 'specialist'. This is an extension of this area of challenge and also an aspect related to some of the pressures, mentioned above, that various changes have placed upon the primary teacher. As Berliner (1991) has argued, teacher expertise has a great deal of contextual significance, with regard to both subject matter (social studies, art or physical education) and grade level. He even argued that 'subjects such as physical education, social studies and mathematics are associated with different epistemologies' (*ibid.*: 147). Whether the case is fully made for subject specialists or for better context and content awareness in primary teachers is yet to be decided, it is, however, a live issue worthy of more research and debate. It is particularly relevant to discussion and design of pre-service teacher education courses.

Australia went through a period in the early 1990s when it recognised, politically and socially, that its geographic location and its trading partnerships make its connections to Asia more significant than was previously realised. This became a somewhat contentious aspect of government and social policy in late 1996 and early 1997, but the debates and assertions do not alter the realities of location, trade and interaction. This development comes on top of the work over the past two decades to raise Australia's internal social consciousness of the reality of its multicultural nature as a nation and, with that, to create a greater awareness of languages and other cultures.

Amidst this realisation and the subsequent planning for development a greater imperative has emerged for Australians to study languages other than English and, in particular, to focus on Asian languages such as Indonesian, Japanese and Mandarin. Most state school systems have identified a set of 'priority' languages, and are pursuing increased teacher education and curriculum development in this area. One of the key curriculum areas in the national set and within the relevant state versions of this curriculum concept has been LOTE.

This national imperative challenge has not only challenged many of today's primary teachers but also threatened them. The challenge lies in the 'how?' How does today's primary teacher start a language in her class if she has no background or training at all in such an area? How does she ensure that any support she seeks from, say, parents and community members in a language is adequate, professional, skilled, etc.? How does she access appropriate training and in-service support (assuming there is appropriate goodwill and intent, which is not universal in this regard)? A number of state education authorities have joined together to provide satellite-linked broadcast lessons in various languages, with tutorial support for classroom teachers. Others have attempted to utilise district experts and consultants via Telematics and other similar types of technological support to assist grouping and remote provision. The area has been made a priority for many pre-service teacher education courses, and universities are attempting to develop the language-teaching areas. The time-line for most of these initiatives, however, means that there will be little positive impact for a decade.

The threat, for many of the primary teachers in the LOTE area, also lies in the lack of perceived expertise and preparation to teach such an aspect of the curriculum. Many teachers know that one cannot acquire a new language to fluency in a few in-service sessions, or even over a one-year programme. Many see a long and very difficult road ahead if they even wish to enter this area. Others simply argue that it is a role for specialists. This latter aspect, then, further breaks up the fairly integrated and 'holistic' generalist primary curriculum and, potentially, further subdivides the primary school in ways similar to the secondary system.

Both of these challenges, characterised here as national imperative challenges, demonstrate further that today's primary teacher is facing additional pressures beyond those associated with role and restructuring changes.

Social responsibility challenges

The third area of challenges which today's primary teacher must face, meet and respond to is described here as the *social responsibility* set of challenges. This term is used to cover those aspects of the schooling curriculum and the operation of schools which are regarded by society as areas where community and interpersonal responsibility need to be both highlighted and monitored, and the school (or, more broadly, usually 'education') is seen as the site and answer to these aspects of social responsibility or these problems. The Organisation for Economic Cooperation and Development (OECD) report on *The Teacher Today* describes this situation thus: 'And new moral and social questions are being added to their brief: to enhance awareness of the environment and pollution, to educate about drug abuse and AIDS, to be watchful for signs of child abuse in the home' (OECD 1990: 114). Each of the elements mentioned by the OECD in 1990 has emerged in Australian education as a major issue. These aspects are prominent also in political and media admonitions as areas where 'more education' is needed to assist society to deal with, and possibly resolve, aspects of the social torment to which they are related.

Most state systems have specific projects, awards and campaigns associated with environmental issues and pollution. Many industrial groups have found it advantageous to be associated with campaigns to 'clean up' or 'green' the nation in various ways. National and state bodies have embarked upon numerous projects to publicise and support awareness of the dangers of AIDS and other sexually transmitted diseases. Surprisingly, the discussion of what a decade ago would have been taboo for primary-aged children is now seen as a social imperative. Many primary schools are now engaging in special courses for parents about AIDS and in more detailed sex education than would have been either normal or permitted by parents, lobby groups and community standards only a short time ago. There is still some degree of greater sensitivity about certain aspects of drug education with younger children, as the assumption still appears to be prevalent that this is predominantly a youth problem and that the 'education' function therefore resides more in the secondary sector. Nevertheless, drug and 'substance abuse' are discussed and figure in the lexicon of primary-aged pupils in our schools.

Finally, the issue of mandatory reporting by teachers of suspicions about child abuse has now become a legal issue within most states and territories. Teachers may have had some difficulty understanding and implementing this area as one of absolute compliance and legal responsibility, with little if any degree of discretionary element, as it is required in most of the laws enacted. This remains a difficult and, in some small communities, at times a potentially explosive aspect of the educational work of a primary teacher.

Business and industry relevance challenges

The final area of challenges which today's primary teacher must be aware of and face is described here as the set of *business and industry relevance* challenges. In examining this aspect the word 'relevance' becomes a key concept, as it is part of the rhetoric of business leaders (the so called 'captains of industry') that schools are not producing students who 'fit' the world of work. This phenomenon is also international and pervasive (Finn, Carmichael and Mayer reports in Australia, National Vocational Qualifications (NVQs) in the United Kingdom and the rise of industry partnerships in US schools), with very similar rhetoric in a multitude of nations. Robertson, in a forceful critique, argues that these trends have amounted in Australia to a 'loss of ideological control' by teachers over 'the goals, objectives, and policy directions of their work' (Robertson 1996: 44). As she argues the position:

> The fact is, the goals, objectives and policy directions for schools are not for teachers to determine. Rather, the organization of schooling and teachers' work must take its cue from the needs of industry. An array of committees and forums, such as the Finn Committee under the chairmanship of Brian Finn (IBM general manager) reviewing post-compulsory schooling, the Mayer Committee to implement the competency-based curriculum under the chairmanship of Eric Mayer (National Mutual Life Insurance), the Industry Education Forum, with representatives from all the large transnational corporations, and the federal Economic Planning and Advisory Council (a coalition of state, corporate capital and peak unions), have all laid out the ideal worker for the new regime: multiskilled, efficient, self-reliant, team-oriented, adaptable and flexible. The task for teachers is to develop new approaches to teaching which efficiently produce the ideal worker.
>
> (Robertson 1996: 44)

The Australian scene is not the only site for such shifts. The movement towards the notion of students in the school system as developing 'human capital' has been a feature of this development in the USA for some time (Reich 1983; Becker 1993; Sweetland 1996). Much of this rhetoric came to the political and social fore following the release of the government report *A Nation at Risk* during the Reagan administration (National Commission on Excellence in Education 1983). This document, with such a provocative title and intent (somewhat facetiously dubbed 'the mother of all critiques' by Berliner and Biddle (1995)), spurred many a 'business leader' in the USA to criticise schools as out of touch and not delivering what business needed for America to be internationally competitive. This catch phrase became almost a 1990s mantra.

The debate is still raging in the USA, in particular. One book, *Thinking for a Living* (Marshall and Tucker 1992), is reported to have been set by Bill Clinton for all his campaign staff to read. The latest in a long line of such advocacies, written by an economist and an educator, recommends that a set of 'new basic skills' needs to be built into the school system. Of course, these skills come from a business framework. We have not heard the last of these challenges.

In the United Kingdom, similar trends have been identified and criticised, as exemplified by this section of a recent paper by Hyland:

> stemming from these radical shifts within the public sector, professional studies and education and training generally have been forced to change in order to accommodate what Elliot (1993) calls the 'social market' model according to which the 'outcomes of professional learning are construed as quantifiable products which can be pre-specified in tangible and concrete form' (pp. 16–17). A major vehicle for such change has been the competence-based education and training strategy popularised through the work of the National Council for Vocational Awards (NCVQ) and now officially endorsed by and enshrined in Employment Department (ED) and Department for Education (DFE) policy through national targets and funding regulations (Burke, 1995).
>
> (Hyland 1996: 169)

In an even-handed and useful contribution to this issue, Jamieson (1996) argued that the education and business agenda was leading in the UK to a form of 'confluence' in which schools were being moved towards a form of 'marketization'. Jamieson's point is that if schools do take on more market-like behaviours and the links between business and schooling become clearer and better focused, then some of the possible partnerships may have a positive impact on aspects of social and community regeneration.

In Australia, while the major impact of this challenge (usually referred to as 'industry-led', but that is open to some debate in Australia) has been in the area of secondary schooling, and the TAFE and training areas, there has been movement in the primary sector as well. The trickle-down effect of much of the rhetoric and some of the agenda has occurred through a greater emphasis on the needs of the primary school to develop strong, measurable standards in the 'basic skills' areas of literacy and numeracy, in particular. The Key Competencies identified by the national Mayer Committee were intended to be applicable across the whole range of schooling and even to have an impact upon higher education (as was the Finn plan). The core theoretical concept in this range of reports and series of recommendations for schooling reform was the notion of competency-based education (note that in the UK this is usually referred to as 'competence-based', but the design, the rationale and the rhetoric are the same). That competency-based thinking has influenced the current curriculum and developments, and testing as well, is evident in the outcomes-based documents and tests being touted as the new 'necessary' wave of development for our society and its future. It is evident that the approach is still somewhat minimalist in its conceptualisation and that it does not embrace aspects of modern thinking on learning and educational critique, and this has been documented (Cairns 1992, 1996b; Stephenson 1994).

This challenge to today's teachers, while apparently less direct in curriculum and day-to-day impact for the primary teacher, is nevertheless probably the major trend which today's teacher needs to investigate and reflect upon. This is no passing 'fad' which, if ignored, will go away.

Professionalism and professional development

There has long been debate about whether teaching is or is not 'a profession' (Goodson and Hargreaves 1996) and this brief chapter is not the place for further deliberation of this significant issue. What is to be discussed in this penultimate section is the matter of professionalism and professional development in teaching. Teachers, as important social and educational role players in society, have much to be concerned about in the professionalisation pressures and in the matter of their personal and group professional development.

As Hargreaves and Goodson have argued, there are at least six differing 'and often overlapping discourses' about teachers as professionals (Hargreaves and Goodson 1996: 4). They describe these 'forms' as:

classical professionalism: traditional status-conscious professional claims);
flexible professionalism: treating professionalism as more of a local matter for smaller 'communities of practice';
practical professionalism: according dignity and status according to the teachers' practical knowledge and skills;
extended professionalism: arguing that teachers' professionalism is extended rather than restricted and that this new professionalism deals with aspects beyond just the classroom;
complex professionalism: teaching professionalism should be judged on the basis of the very complex nature of the task;
postmodern professionalism: a 'new' grouping proposed by Hargeaves and Goodson which draws on postmodern thinking – this 'form' of professionalism discourse is, Hargreaves and Goodson state, almost the same as what was termed 'interactive professionalism' by Fullan and Hargreaves (1996).

The key aspect of this parade of 'forms' is not merely to emphasise that times change or that this is a complex area, but rather to point out that there is a wide range of perspectives which have an impact upon the discussion and conceptualisation of teacher professionalism. Each perspective offers a view of the nature of the job, the role or the profession. Each perspective, we argue, also offers a view of the nature and the purpose of any professional development which teachers plan, engage in or expect. It is important, therefore, that today's primary teachers stop and consider the view from which they see the complex role they are engaged in and examine what this implies for their current and further professional development. Professional development is not just a matter, for primary teachers, of updating their pedagogical techniques or examining new demands by way of mandated curricula. It involves a broader set of issues and awarenesses. It has political, social, emotional and personal dimensions as well as pedagogical aspects. As Hargreaves has so sensibly put it in another of his many publications on this topic:

> The practice and research of teacher development, I have argued, should address the technical competence of teaching, the place of moral purpose in teaching, political awareness, acuity, and adeptness among teachers, and teachers' emotional attachments to and engagement with their work. None of these dimensions alone captures all that is important or all there is to know about teacher development. What really matters is the interactions among and integration between them.
>
> (Hargreaves 1994: 26)

One of the key subjects which has emerged from the debates both about the business and industry relevance challenge to schools and teachers and about aspects of teacher professionalism has been what has been characterised as the issue of 'intensification' versus 'professionalisation' (Hargreaves 1994). Put simply, this notion, which owes its roots to the work of Larson (1977) on the 'proletarianisation' of 'educated workers' suggests that as the economy becomes more and more advanced many of the tasks associated with the educated worker become more routinised and there is less time to complete tasks, reskill or indulge in other activities. Apple (1986) and Apple and Jungck (1992) have also offered some interesting analyses based on this idea. For some writers and commentators, technology – particularly such aspects as the Internet – is directly or at least partly complicit in this intensification process (Robertson 1996). While Hargreaves (1994), after a detailed study of teacher preparation time and its relationship to the intensification thesis, concluded that some aspects of intensification appeared to be at work, he had some 'qualifications' about the notion which arose from his data. He argued that his findings, while not 'disconfirming' the intensification thesis, did 'raise doubts about its scope and singularity as an explanation of changes in teachers' work' (*ibid.*: 137).

A strong case is, nevertheless, mounted by a number of the authors cited above to suggest that teachers, as technology and further restructuring impact upon them, become less able to practise in a professional manner, and that many are 'deskilled' by the changes in curriculum, school structures and expectations, and modern 'accountability' exercises. If this case is accepted as approaching accuracy, then the teaching profession, as such, is under great threat and pressure.

Professional development, in such a set of context aspects, is, then, a difficult and yet no less significant area of concern. Both pre-service teacher education and in-service professional development have undergone significant change, pressures and shifts in the basis of finance and support in Australia in the past decade. In the pre-service teacher education programmes for primary teachers there has been a gradual decline in the cut-off mark levels of commencing students as they emerge from the various state high-school programmes. This appears to reflect a decline in the appeal of the profession. Innovations in courses such as school-based teacher education, more 'reflective' programmes and a wide range of new double degrees have been moderately successful. There has also been an overall reduction in numbers undertaking primary-teacher education in this period.

In the in-service professional development area, the popular 'one-shot' visiting speaker, consultant or 'guru' day event is seen to be of limited value by many teachers and their schools, though these events still take place quite frequently. The popularity of more extended and well-developed 'in-service' strategy courses, such as ELIC (Early Literacy In-service Course) and the even more ambitious and ritualised reading recovery (both from the stable of Marie Clay in New Zealand), has assisted in some major rethinking by many primary teachers about just what 'good in-service education' might be.

One of the more pervasive aspects of research on teachers' work and professional development amongst university academics over the past decade in Australia has been the movement which can best be described as the Reflective Teaching/Reflective Practitioner genre. While much of the terminology has penetrated everyday 'teacher speak', it is as yet unclear to what extent the concept and the effects have actually penetrated to classroom practice. Centring mainly on the writings of Donald Schon of the Massachusetts Institute of Technology (MIT) (Schon 1983, 1987), and the interpretations and extensions of his work by Zeichner (most recently summarised in Zeichner and Liston 1996), the adoption of this idea and advocacy of elements of the process as a major teacher-development approach appear to have been more highly visible in teacher education in Australia than in some other nations (Boud *et al.* 1985; Smyth 1996). While the basic notion of thinking about actual practice during and after the event (Reflection-in-action and Reflection-on-action) is patently a sensible one for teachers, the concept and some of its excesses in various applications have not gone by without some thoughtful critique (Shulman 1988; Fenstermacher 1988; Court 1988; Hargreaves and Goodson 1996). The notion has been linked to the critical-theory element, as mentioned before, as a basic ideological bedfellow (Smyth 1996). This aspect requires (and it is starting to receive) considerable careful consideration in the literature and in practice in Australian primary schools.

Most systems at the state department of education level and in the Catholic schools system have adopted various people-network and team-group approaches, and are attempting to utilise computer networking as a new and additional feature to ensure adequate follow-up and interaction over more extended time and locations.

A significant element in the professional development of teachers in Australia over the past few years has been the National Professional Development Programme (NPDP), funded by the federal government through what was then the Commonwealth Department of Employment, Education and Training (DEET). The significant element of this programme was that funds (and substantial amounts have been distributed) were allocated to applicants who addressed the National Priorities (as published each year) and applications were expected to have tripartite support documented (higher education, employers and professional associations). Many groups did benefit substantially from grants under this programme, while some unions and some university advocates were less impressed by the range of restrictions and attempts by some state government education departments to hijack the process. However, the basis, the funds and the approach have been the subject of review and replacement by the incoming federal government.

In Victoria the state education system has emphasised professional development within its restructuring approaches, and requires teachers to develop a professional development plan and schools regularly to review and report on progress through the Schools of the Future programme. Promotion and progress for teachers also have a significant element of professional development expectation built into the processes.

Among the many innovations and attempts to highlight the significance of professional development in this time of educational change and reform has been what has become known as the professional development school notion (Darling-Hammond 1994). This approach, which has a long history and many variations, has re-emerged in the USA in particular as a joint venture between universities and schools whereby a large proportion of the pre-service teacher-education programme takes place in a school designated as a professional development school. The school, together with the university programme, offers, via the teachers, sections of the course and, in close cooperation with the university, deals with a range of aspects of the course and teacher professional development which enhance the programme at both ends of the partnership. This has been tried in various ways in Australia as well, with combinations of school-based and Professional Development Schools, all of which have a strong intention to enhance partnerships among the university, the schools and the community (Cairns 1995a, 1996a; Cairns *et al.* 1995).

In the United Kingdom the advent of more formally required school-based teacher education (under legislation) has led to close attention to 'mentoring', whereby classroom teachers are taking greater responsibility for the teacher education of pre-service students and the university is in more of a peripheral than central role. This has led many university academics and teachers into greater partnership models and to more research attention being focused on the mentoring role (McIntyre 1993; Tomlinson 1995).

Another significant innovation in the professional development of Australia's teachers has been the Australian Teaching Council (ATC) and National Schools Network (NSN) joint National Professional Development Schools held over vacation periods (either three days or one week residential) and funded by the DEET. These 'schools' (the title was deliberate) were well funded (to the tune of around A$1 million per year), with the intention of making a major impact upon teachers in developing the ideas and an understanding of the National Agenda for Education and School Reform (including National Curricula and Competency-based Education). The schools were overseen by a large and representative advisory committee, with the programme being developed and carried out by the NSN, and the administration by the ATC. Unfortunately, the ATC has contracted after federal funds were discontinued (partly due to a change of government); however, the NSN continues and now also administers the Professional Development Schools. A key feature of these schools has been an intensity of involvement and a collegiality of involvement (leaders have been very carefully selected, trained and quality-controlled) by both the workshop leaders and the participant teachers. The focus on learning for all involved in these workshops has been a deliberate and well-fostered approach. Details of the NSN and the Professional Development Schools can be obtained from their web site at http://www.schnet.edu.au/nsn/.

The NSN, in its own right, has been a strong and interesting development as an approach to school reform and teacher professional development in Australia. The original basis of the project was largely set up with teacher union and federal government agreement (the federal government at the time was a Labor government) to assist schools to adjust and redevelop or restructure. Robertson describes the aims in more politicised terms as: 'to embed a new set of work practices within schools which works toward realizing the industry-endorsed worker competencies, while at the same time aligning the organization of schooling with the organization of the workplace' (Robertson 1996: 47–8). Robertson additionally cites other aspects of the project, such as the tight specification of the framework and the commitment to an outcomes and competencies approach as 'further evidence of ideological proletarianization' (*ibid.*: 48). These criticisms, however, refer to the early days of the initiative and there has been a wider set of objectives within a multifaceted approach over the past four years.

School who wish to 'join' the NSN (there are reportedly over 300 member schools across the nation) are expected to sign on with agreement to the basic set of the NSN Principles of Participation (see NSN Web site, 1997). These are:

> an acceptance of the school's responsibility for improving learning outcomes for all students;
>
> a commitment to greater student participation in the learning process;
>
> agreement that reforms in the Network will be based on a commitment to establish equality of access, opportunity and outcomes for all students;
>
> a willingness to examine current work organisation in order to identify good practice and impediments to effective teaching and learning;
>
> a willingness to develop a model of participative workplace procedures and appropriate decision-making that includes the whole staff;
>
> an understanding and acceptance of the industrial rights and responsibilities of all parties;
>
> an acceptance that the whole community will be involved in the decision-making about the reform process.

It is apparent from a perusal of these seven principles that some of the points Robertson criticised are embedded. The 'industrial rights and responsibilities' principle appears to be one influenced by the teacher-union element, and represents an apparently necessary assertion at a time of some threat and potential change in this area in some states.

The multifaceted approach referred to above is a key and innovative concept in the NSN approach. The NSN has set up two aspects directly aimed at improved and well-informed professional development for teachers but, significantly, also developed *by* and *with* teachers. These two aspects are the Innovative Links Project and the University Roundtables. Both of these aspects involve cooperation between classroom teachers and university academics in projects, professional development activities, workshops and other cooperative ventures (critical friends for innovative approaches, for example), and there have been interesting and favourable results (Yeatman and Sachs 1995). A further aspect of this multifaceted approach has been to set up a register of educational researchers, who in joining the NSN Register are signalling that they are willing to be involved in projects with member schools.

The NSN, along with the now struggling ATC, has also participated in aspects of what was a major national project, the National Project on the Quality of Teaching and Learning (NPQTL). This project, over a three-year period, examined and extensively developed (together with the Australian

Council of Deans of Education, the Australian Teacher Education Association and other groups within the industry) a set of proposed National Competencies for Beginning Teaching (1994). While this work focused both on the pre-service sector and on attempting to ensure that the competency-based approach penetrated one of the largest professions in the nation, it nevertheless has relevance for the discussion of teacher professional development. It is also an area where there is clear concern internationally about the potential dangers of taking a narrow, competency-based approach (Lester 1995).

Currently, a new national committee, chaired by the chairperson of the Australian Deans of Education Council, is re-examining (under the new government's auspices) the issues around National Standards and Guidelines for initial teacher education. It is possible that such aspects may lead to some understandings about national teacher registration and improved portability, as well as opening up and continuing the debate on continuous professional development and quality.

With the prospect of a return to university fees in Australia (particularly possible for upgrading and higher degrees by coursework, where teachers have been the mainstay), there is a likelihood of further reductions in the numbers of teachers studying for higher qualifications. There has never been a tradition of much financial support by employers of teachers for such university work, nor has there been much overt salary or promotion-element support related to increased qualification at this level. This aspect of the importance of credentials as one marker of professionalism (Ingersoll 1997) should not be ignored in the debate.

Tomorrow's teachers and developments

The final section of this chapter briefly addresses the question of where primary teachers might advance to in the future. Such quests are inevitably doomed to failure since accurate predictions are rare indeed, but the whole essence of structural, pedagogical, curricula and professional reform at this time of anxiety about the close of one millennium and the commencement of another begs the question and some projections.

Lest there be some concern among educators and the community, it should be stressed that, despite much of the international pressures for school reform and restructuring, and assertions that schools have somehow faltered (or even failed) in their educational mission, it should be unequivocally stated that primary schools are a vital and necessary element of future educational development for the twenty-first century. Few of the most vociferous critics or the 'hyped' technology advocates have argued for the demise of schools. Many have argued for change and rethinking, and that is what this volume also discusses.

It is apparent, from any reading of the international education literature of the past five years that there is wide-ranging and international concern about the state of schooling in most advanced societies. Change is a major factor. Most systems of public education have restructured or redesigned their schooling enterprises, or are in the process of doing so.

In the United Kingdom (curiously 'un-united' in education, since Scotland has always done its own thing) there has been the national curriculum, the emergence of grant-maintained schools and the infamous 'opting-out option'. Vouchers have also been an agenda item in many discussions and political meetings. Education has been railed about, standards and tests have been set and administered, and there has been huge restructuring and change.

As detailed above and elsewhere in this volume, in Australia aspects of the current period have been similar. Systems have 'downsized', we have set up projects such as the Victorian Schools of the Future (within the state system). Standards have been a much-debated topic, as has a more unified approach to national curriculum. At the same time as much of this preoccupation with structures, standards and status has been dominating discussion and much of the public rhetoric, a useful and educationally based set of concepts and ideas has been emerging.

These arguments arose most visibly during the early 1990s, and quite pervasively across education (at the levels of schooling and adult learning in higher education) and within the business organisation area (particularly the human resources area in companies). The basic underlying idea has been the advocacy of the centrality of the learning process and the relative autonomy of the learner. These trends can be seen in the emergence of such ideas and ideals covered by the closely ideologically related terms the Learning Society (Maxted 1996; RSA 1996; Antikainen *et al.* 1996), the Learning Organisation (Senge 1992; Argyris 1992; Chawla and Renesch 1995), Learning Companies (Pearn *et al.* 1995; Starkey 1996), the Learning School (Nixon *et al.* 1996) and the Learner-centred School (McCombs and Whisler 1997).

These aspects are yet to 'gel' into anything like a unified view or school of thought, yet there are emerging similarities and a converging lexicon within this corpus of work internationally. Peter Vaill, a leading American business educator and writer on management, has described the trend in the title of his most recent and influential book *Learning as a Way of Being* (1996). Learning and its significance for the future are the central feature of all these approaches.

The converging ideas and terms are beginning to gain some common ground in the concept of *capability* and its application to learning and learners in business and education (Stephenson and Weil 1992; Cunningham 1994; Cairns and Hase 1996; DiBella *et al.* 1996; Ulrich 1997). Labelling theory tells us of the usefulness of having terms to describe organising notions or ideas. The term capability is offered as one such useful term – a rubric under which to organise the ideas and elements for educational development in the twenty-first century. What this term is used to mean in most of these varying contexts is best summed up as follows:

> Capability can be defined as the set of characteristics (skills, knowledge and attributes) that when combined with values and self-esteem enables people to manage themselves in both familiar and unfamiliar circumstances.
>
> - A Capable person is adaptable and flexible and is a self-managing learner in life.
> - A Capable company or business is adaptable and flexible – with a conscious involvement in supporting learning as a company and its employees as self-managing learners.
> - A Capable education system supports and develops the expertise and skills for students to be self-managing learners and to become capable citizens and workers.
>
> (Cairns and Hase 1996: 1)

Capability as a concept offers education and training more than does the concept competency (Barnett 1994; Stephenson 1994; Cairns 1996b). It is clear that the future is about coping with the unknown, the unfamiliar and the unpredictable. This is an aspect clearly within the ambit of the capability notion. As Barnett so clearly says, 'the idea of a competence that allows for unpredictability is ultimately incoherent' (Barnett 1994: 81).

The notions of capability, capable organisations and even the significance of capable schooling are beginning to enter much of the current discussion. In some cases the uses of the terms are deliberate, are conscious of the emerging theory and extend that work. Others are merely fortuitous usage which adds to the familiarity and extends the frequency of the public airing of the terminology. However, most of these comments are identifiably in line with the general principles of the notion and contextually very similar. As Stephanie Pace Marshall (a former president of the Association for Supervision and Curriculum Development, USA) outlines in her recent essay on 'Creating sustainable learning communities for the twenty-first century', 'If we are truly going to create learning communities for the twenty-first century, we must view our schools as dynamic, adaptive, self-organizing systems, not only capable but inherently designed to renew themselves and to grow and change' (S. P. Marshall 1997: 184). In the business world, a leading organisational theorist has offered some useful advice that is clearly also relevant to this discussion. Ulrich has argued that 'my intent is to shift the focus in organizational thinking away from structure, forms, rules, roles, and accountabilities and into a debate on capability' (Ulrich 1997: 195).

The implications for tomorrow's primary teacher are clearly that the concepts of capability and the capable teacher need exploration, and the classroom implications need to be drawn out of the rather broad conceptualisation as mentioned in the definition. Both pre-service teacher education and in-service professional development need to consider the elements of capability, as it implies change and development of courses and approaches. This type of consideration is under way, as exemplified by the work of Whitaker (1997) in his chapter on 'Meeting the future', in which he sees capability as the educational-system outcome, through the work of the Higher Education for Capability Centre in Leeds, in the UK (http://www.lmu.ac.uk/hec/) and the recently formed Australian Capability Network (http://www.nor.com.au/community/ACN/). These groups are currently engaged in research and publication which clarifies and develops the ideas and the notion for practical application in schools, training and universities.

What we need as tomorrow's primary teachers are those who are capable, teachers who 'have adaptability and flexibility to cope with ever-changing sets of circumstances' (Woods 1995). As Beare and Boyd put it, 'Only the resilient, adaptable, quick and creative will thrive. This is the challenge of Tomorrow' (Beare and Boyd 1993: 11).

As a final word, the 'Introduction' to Hugh Busher and Rene Saran's *Managing Teachers as Professionals in Schools* (1995), entitled 'Schools for the Future', offers a summary:

> A vision of schools moving into the twenty-first century is that they are rapidly becoming centres of learning, not just for students but for all involved with the institution, including staff (both teaching and support staff), parents and members of the local community. This new role is not easily assumed by some teachers as they see learners primarily as students who are the recipients of knowledge which they transmit. It will be in addition to the other specified roles of staff, such as teacher, senior manager or site supervisor. This visionary view of schools points to an entirely new setting for the work of teachers, support staff and school governors. It has implications both for the management of teachers in schools and for understanding teacher professionality and staff development.
>
> This vision is not far fetched. A review of school effectiveness research shows one of the 11 characteristics for such an institution to be 'a learning organisation' with 'school-based staff development'.
>
> (Sammons *et al.* 1994; cited in Mortimore 1995: 11; all quoted in Busher and Saran 1995)

References

Annenberg Institute for School Reform (1996) *Walter H. Annenberg's Challenge to the Nation: A Progress Report*, Providence, RI: Annenberg Institute.

Antkainen, A., Houtsonen, J., Kauppila, J. and Houtelin, H. (1996) *Living in a Learning Society*, London: Falmer Press.

Apple, M. W. (1986) *Teachers and Texts*, New York: Routledge & Kegan Paul.

Apple, M. and Jungck, S. (1992) 'You don't have to be a teacher to teach this unit: teaching, technology and control in the classroom', in A. Hargreaves and M. G. Fullan (eds) *Understanding Teacher Development*, London: Cassell.

Argyris, C. (1992) *On Organizational Learning*, Oxford: Blackwell.

Australian Education Council Review Committee (1991) *Young People's Participation in Post-compulsory Education and Training* (chairman: Brian Finn), Canberra: Australian Government Publishing Service.

Barnett, R. (1994) *The Limits of Competence*, The Society for Research into Higher Education and Open University Press, Buckingham.

Beare, H., and Boyd, W. L. (1993) *Restructuring Schools. An International Perspective on the Movement to Transform the Control and Performance of Schools*, London: Falmer Press.

Becker, G. S. (1993) *Human Capital: A Theoretical and Empirical Analysis With Special Reference to Education*, 3rd edn, Chicago, IL: University of Chicago Press.

Berliner, D. C. (1991) 'Educational psychology and pedagogical expertise: new findings and new opportunities for thinking about training', *Educational Psychologist* 26(2): 145–55.

Berliner, D. C. and Biddle, B. J. (1995) *The Manufactured Crisis: Myths, Fraud, and the Attack on America's Public Schools*, Reading, MA: Addison-Wesley.

Boud, D., Keogh, R. and Walker, D. (eds) (1985) *Reflection: Turning Experience into Learning*, London: Kogan Page.

Brooks, J. G. and Brooks, M. G. (1993) *In Search of Understanding: The Case for Constructivist Classrooms*, Alexandria, VA: Association for Supervision and Curriculum Development (ASCD).

Busher, H. and Saran, R. (eds) (1995) *Managing Teachers as Professionals in Schools*, London: Kogan Page.

Cairns, L. G. (1992) 'Competency-based education: Nostradamus's nostrum?', *Journal of Teaching Practice* 12(1): 1–31.

—— (1993) 'Learner managed learning: a metaphor for educational revolution', in N. Graves (ed.) *Learner Managed Learning: Practice, Theory and Policy*, Leeds: World Education Fellowship (WEF)/Higher Education for Capability (HEC).

—— (1995a) 'Professional Development Schools', *Partnerships in Teacher Education*, Melbourne: Standards Council of the Teaching Profession.

—— (1995b) *Capable Education and Training Reform: The Australian Capability Network*, Lismore, NSW: Australian Capability Network.

—— (1996a) 'Making connections: revising and rebuilding teacher education in a rural region', paper presented at the Twenty-sixth Annual Conference of the Australian Teacher Education Association, Launceston, Tasmania, July.

—— (1996b) 'Capability: going beyond competency', *Capability* 2(2): 79–80.

Cairns, L. G., and Hase, S. (1996) 'Capability and re-engineering in educational change', paper presented at the Second ACEID-UNESCO International Conference, Re-engineering Education for Change: Educational Innovation for Development, Bangkok, Thailand, December.

Cairns, L. G., Southcott, J., Osborn, M. and Clingan, R. (1995) 'An exercise in partnership: the Monash Gippsland school-based primary teacher education programme', paper presented at the Twenty-fifth Annual Conference of the Australian Teacher Education Association, Sydney, July.

Carr, W. and Kemmis, S. (1986) *Becoming Critical*, London: Falmer Press.

Chawla, R. and Renesch, J. (eds) (1995) *Learning Organizations: Developing Cultures for Tomorrow's Workplace*, Portland, OR: Productivity Press.

Committee to Advise the Australian Education Council (AEC) and Ministers of Vocational Education, Employment and Training (MOVEET) on Employment-related Key Competencies for Postcompulsory Education and Training (1992) *Putting General Education to Work* (chairman: Eric Mayer), AEC and MOVEET.

Court, D. (1988) '"Reflection-in-action": some definitional problems', in P.R. Grimmett and G. Erickson (eds) *Reflection in Teacher Education*, New York: Teachers' College Press.

Cunningham, I. (1994) *The Wisdom of Strategic Learning*, London: McGraw-Hill.

Dainty, P. H. and Anderson, M. (1996) *The Capable Executive: Effective Performance in Senior Management*, London: Macmillan Business.

Darling-Hammond, L. (ed.) (1994) *Professional Development Schools: Schools for Developing a Profession*, New York: Teachers' College Press.

Department of Education (1997) *A Call to Action for American Education in the 21st Century*, Washington, DC: US Government Printing Office.

DiBella, A. J., Nevis, E. C., and Gould, J. M. (1996) 'Organizational learning style as a core capability', in B. Moingeon and A. Edmondson (eds) *Organizational Learning and Competitive Advantage*, London: Sage.

Employment Skills Formation Council (1992) *The Australian Vocational Certificate Training System* (chairman: Laurie Carmichael), Canberra: National Board of Employment, Education and Training.

Fenstermacher, G. (1988) 'The place of science and epistemology in Schon's conception of reflective practice?', in P. R. Grimmett and G. Erickson (eds) *Reflection in Teacher Education*, New York: Teachers' College Press.

Fosnot, C. T. (1996) *Constructivism: Theory, Perspectives, and Practice*, New York: Teachers' College Press.

Fullan, M. and Hargreaves, A. (1996) *What's Worth Fighting For? Working Together for Your School*, Milton Keynes: Open University Press.

Gates, B. (1996) *The Road Ahead*, revised edn, London: Penguin (with N. Myhrvold and P. Rinearson).

Gerstner, L. V., Jr (1994) *Reinventing Education: Entrepreneurship in America's Public Schools*, New York: Penguin (with R. D. Semerad, D. P. Doyle and W. B. Johnston).

Goldberg, B. and Richards, J. (1995) 'Leveraging technology for reform: changing schools and communities into learning organizations', *Educational Technology*, September–October: 5–16.

—— (1996) 'The Co-NECT design for school change', in S. Stringfield, S. Ross and L. Smith (eds) *Bold Plans for School Restructuring: The New American Schools Design*, Mahwah, NJ: Lawrence Erlbaum Associates.

Goodman, K. S. (1986) *What's Whole in Whole Language?*, Toronto: Scholastic.

Goodson, I. F. and Hargreaves, A. (eds) (1996) *Teachers' Professional Lives*, London: Falmer Press.

Guskey, T. R. and Huberman, M. (eds) (1995) *Professional Development in Education: New Paradigms and Practices*, New York: Teachers' College Press.

Hannafin, R. D. and Freeman, D. J. (1995) 'An exploratory study of teachers' views of knowledge acquisition', *Educational Technology*, January–February: 49–56.

Hargreaves, A. (1994) *Changing Teachers, Changing Schools: Teachers' Work and Culture in the Postmodern Age*, New York: Teachers' College Press.

Hargreaves, A., Earl, L. and Ryan, J. (1996) *Schooling for Change: Reinventing Education for Early Adolescents*, London: Falmer Press.

Hargreaves, A. and Goodson, I. (1996) 'Teachers' professional lives: aspirations and actualities', in I. Goodson and A. Hargreaves (eds) *Teachers' Professional Lives*, London: Falmer Press.

Hesselbein, F., Goldsmith, M. and Beckhard, R. (eds) (1997) *The Organization of the Future*, San Francisco, CA: Drucker Foundation Press/Jossey-Bass.

Hughes, P. (ed.) (1987) *Better Teachers for Better Schools*, Carlton, Victoria: Australian College of Education (with C. E. Deer and D. Neal).

Hughes, P. (ed.) (1991) *Teachers' Professional Development*, Hawthorn, Victoria: Australian Council for Educational Research (ACER).

Hyland, T. (1996) 'Professionalism, ethics and work-based learning', *British Journal of Educational Studies* 44 (2): 168–80.

Ingersoll, R. M. (1997) *The Status of Teaching as a Profession: 1990–91*, National Center for Educational Statistics, Statistical Analysis Report, Washington, DC: US Department of Education (with P. Quinn and S. Bobbitt).

Jamieson, I. (1996) 'Education and business: converging models', in C. Pole and R. Chawla-Duggan (eds) *Reshaping Education in the 1990s: Perspectives on Secondary Education*, London: Falmer Press.

Jonassen, D. H. (1996) *Computers in the Classroom: Mindtools for Critical Thinking*, Englewood Cliffs, NJ: Prentice-Hall.

Jones, B. L. and Maloy, R. W. (1996) *Schools for an Information Age: Reconstructing Foundations for Learning and Teaching*, Westport, CT: Praeger.

Keeves, J. (ed.) (1987) *Australian Education: Review of Recent Research*, Sydney: Allen & Unwin.

Kuhn, T. (1962) *The Structure of Scientific Revolutions*, Chicago, IL: University of Chicago Press.

Larson, M. S. (1977) *The Rise of Professionalism: A Sociological Analysis*, Berkeley, CA: University of California Press.

Lasarenko, J. (1997) *Wired for Learning*, Indianapolis, IN: QUE.

Lester, S. (1995) 'Beyond knowledge and competence', *Capability* 1(3): 44–55.

Lieberman, A., Darling-Hammond, L. and Zuckerman, D. (1991) *Early Lessons in Restructuring Schools*, New York: National Center for Restructuring Education, Schools and Teaching (NCREST).

McCombs, B. and Whisler, J. S. (1997) *The Learner-Centered Classroom and School: Strategies for Increasing Student Motivation and Achievement*, San Francisco, CA: Jossey-Bass.

McIntyre, D. (1993) *Mentoring*, London: Kogan Page.

Marshall, R. and Tucker, M. (1992) *Thinking for a Living*, New York: Basic Books.

Marshall, S. P. (1997) 'Creating sustainable learning communities for the twenty-first century', in F. Hesselbein, M. Goldsmith and R. Beckhard (eds) *The Organization of the Future*, San Francisco, CA: Drucker Foundation Press/Jossey-Bass.

Marton, F. and Booth, S. (1997) *Learning and Awareness*, Mahwah, NJ: Lawrence Erlbaum Associates.

Maxted, P. (ed.) (1996) *From the Ivory Tower ... to the Street: Putting Learning Theory into Practice*, London: RSA.

Murphy, J. (1991) *Restructuring Schools: Capturing and Assessing the Phenomena*, New York: Teachers' College Press.

Naisbitt, J. (1994) *Global Paradox*, New York: Avon Books.

National Center for Educational Statistics (1996) *Preparation For Work*, Washington, DC: US Department of Education.

National Commission on Excellence in Education (1983) *A Nation at Risk: The Imperatives for Educational Reform*, Washington DC: US Department of Education.

Nixon, J., Martin, J., Mckeown, P. and Ranson, S. (1996) *Encouraging Learning: Towards a Theory of the Learning School*, Buckingham: Open University Press.

OECD (1990) *The Teacher Today*, Paris: OECD.

Papert, S. (1980) *Mindstorms: Children, Computers and Powerful Ideas*, New York: Basic Books.

—— (1993) *The Children's Machine*, New York: Basic Books.

Paris, D. C. (1995) *Ideology and Educational Reform: Themes and Theories in Public Education*, Boulder, CO: Westview Press.

Pearn, M., Mulrooney, C. and Roderick, K. (1995) *Learning Companies in Practice*, London: McGraw-Hill.

Perelman, L. J. (1992) *School's Out*, New York: Avon Books.

Postman, N. (1995) *The End of Education*, New York: Vintage Books.

Ravitch, D. (1993) 'When School comes to you', *Economist* (*150 Economist Years Supplement: The Future Surveyed*) 328(7828): 43–9.

Reich, R. (1983) *The Next American Frontier*, New York: Penguin.

Resnick, M. (1996) 'Toward a practice of "constructional design"', in L. Schauble and R. Glaser (eds) *Innovations in Learning: New Environments for Education*, Mahwah, NJ: Lawrence Erlbaum Associates.

Robertson, S. L. (1996) 'Teachers' work, restructuring and postfordism: constructing the new "professionalism"', in I. F. Goodson and A. Hargreaves (eds) *Teachers' Professional Lives*, London: Falmer Press.

RSA (1996) *Campaign for Learning*, London: Royal Society of the Arts.

Schauble, L., and Glaser, R. (eds) (1996) *Innovations in Learning: New Environments for Education*, Mahwah, NJ: Lawrence Erlbaum Associates.

Schon, D. (1983) *The Reflective Practitioner*, New York: Basic Books.

—— (1987) *Educating the Reflective Practitioner*, San Francisco, CA: Jossey-Bass.

Senge, P. M. (1992) *The Fifth Discipline: The Art and Practice of the Learning Organization*, Sydney: Random House.

Shulman, L. S. (1988) 'The dangers of dichotomous thinking in education', in P. R. Grimmett and G. Erickson (eds) *Reflection in Teacher Education*, New York: Teachers' College Press.

Sizer, T. R. (1992) *Horace's School*, New York: Houghton Mifflin.

Smyth, J. (1996) 'Developing socially critical educators', in D. Boud and N. Miller (eds) *Working with Experience: Animating Learning*, London: Routledge.

Starkey, K. (ed.) (1996) *How Organizations Learn*, London: International Thomson Business Press.

Stephenson, J. (1994) 'Capability opinion: capability and competence, are they the same and does it matter?', *Capability* 1(1): 3–4.

Stephenson, J. and Weil, S. (1992) *Quality in Learning: A Capability Approach in Higher Education*, London: Kogan Page.

Stoll, C. (1995) *Silicone Snake Oil*, New York: Doubleday.

Stoll, L. and Fink, D. (1996) *Changing Our Schools*, Buckingham: Open University Press.

Stringfield, S., Ross, S. and Smith, L. (eds) (1996) *Bold Plans for School Restructuring: The New American Schools Designs*, Mahwah, NJ: Lawrence Erlbaum Associates.

Sweetland, S. R. (1996) 'Human capital theory: foundations of a field of inquiry', *Review of Educational Research* 66: 341–59.

Tomlinson, P. (1995) *Understanding Mentoring*, Buckingham: Open University Press.

Ulrich, D. (1997) 'Organizing Around Capabilities', in F. Hesselbein, M. Goldsmith and R. Beckhard (eds) *The Organization of the Future*, San Francisco, CA: Drucker Foundation Press/Jossey-Bass.

US Department of Education (1996) *Preparation for Work*, Washington, DC: Office of Educational Research and Improvement.

—— (1997) *A Call to Action for American Education*, Washington DC: US Government Printing Office.

Vaill, P. B. (1996) *Learning as a Way of Being*, San Francisco, CA: Jossey-Bass.

Whitaker, P. (1997) *Primary Schools and the Future*, Buckingham: Open University Press.

Woods, P. (1995) *Creative Teachers in Primary Schools*, Buckingham: Open University Press.

Yeatman, A. and Sachs, J. (1995) 'Making the links: a formative evaluation of the first year of the Innovative Links project between universities and schools for teacher professional development', Ryde, NSW: National Schools Network.

Zeichner, K. M. and Liston, D. P. (1996) *Reflective Teaching: An Introduction*, Mahwah, NJ: Lawrence Erlbaum Associates.

4

DIFFERENT FAMILIES

New issues for schools

Tony Townsend and Ian Walker

Introduction

Schools exist within a context of parents, community, school
districts, other educational organizations and institutions, and
levels of government. Each of these groups or institutions has
an agenda, each has 'turf' or self-interest to protect, and each
wants to have an impact on schools and, through schools,
pupils. Schools can, as many do, isolate themselves to maintain
control and avoid criticism. In doing so, they not only build
barriers against potential partners, they contribute to the inco-
herence of pupils' lives.

(Stoll and Fink 1996: 133)

There have been many changes to primary schools over the last twenty years,
some of which have been described in other chapters of this book, but
perhaps no change has been as dramatic as that related to the changes to the
community that the primary school serves, the students and their families in
various community settings. A review of Australian and Victorian
Yearbooks from 1988 to 1997 provided data that reflected the changing
Australian community. These data are used here to look at the impact that
demographic change – and, in particular, three elements of that change –
has had on the operations of the primary school and the ways in which the
administrative changes to schools in the past decade have, in turn, impacted
on families. The three elements are:

- changes in attitudes towards having children;
- changes in migration policy;
- changes in employment.

The chapter will then look at how schools and teachers might best
encourage families to play an active role in their child's education, with a

particular case study of parent involvement in one of the curriculum areas considered to be most important in primary schools: literacy development.

The changing Australian community

Changes in attitude towards having children

A quarter of a century ago, at a time when many current primary-school parents were just starting their own primary-school careers, the Australian community was a very different place. For a start, primary-aged children made up a higher percentage of the population. In 1971 28.7 per cent of the population was under the age of 14, and many of these were primary-school children. By the mid-1990s this figure had dropped to around 21 per cent. This resulted from a combination of many factors, including:

- men and women marrying later (between 1971 and 1975 the average age of a bride was 21.4 years and a bridegroom was 23.9 years; by 1995 it was 25.3 years for a bride and 27.3 years for a bridegroom);
- children being born later (in 1964 peak fertility was among 24-year-old women, with 23 per cent having babies; by 1994 peak fertility was among 29-year-old women, but only 13 per cent had babies);
- families having fewer children (the fertility rate for women in 1970 was 2.86; by 1995 it was less than 2);
- parents divorcing far more frequently (40 per cent of first marriages now end in divorce; in 1979 there were 3 divorces per 1,000 people, by 1995 this had reached 12.3 per 1,000).

Many of these factors are a response to broader issues in our community. People stay on at school (and higher education) longer than they did previously, and the economic situation and the need for security have led couples to hold off on having children while they establish themselves at both work and home.

This has led to a situation where there are fewer primary-aged children now than there were one generation ago, with a large percentage of the parents of these children being older, better educated and having more life experiences than their counterparts. In some respects, this should make the home–school relationship easier than it has been for a number of years. However, having both parents working has created difficulties in communication between home and school, and has lessened the opportunity for parents to play active roles in their child's education.

It has also meant that Australia's population is ageing and the priority accorded to families with dependent children is less than it was. These families are now in the minority. Whereas 54.7 per cent of Australian families in 1984 had one or more dependent children, now only 49.5 per cent have. These two factors lead to the possibility that healthcare for the aged may well replace education for the young as the major concern for society, with a shift of resources from education to healthcare a probable result.

Changes in migration policy

In 1971 79.8 per cent of the Australian population had been born in Australia and a further 17.2 per cent had been born in Europe, with the majority of these people born in the UK or Ireland. Only 1.3 per cent of the Australian community came from Asia. By 1995 77.2 per cent had been born in Australia, 13.1 per cent in Europe and around 5 per cent in Asia. This had come about largely because of the changing patterns of migration. In 1982 54.5 per cent of arrivals were of European background and only 3.3 per cent from Asia, but by 1994 57 per cent of arrivals were from Asia and only 29.5 per cent from Europe.

This development has created other changes as well. In 1991 13.6 per cent of the Australian community spoke a language other than English at home. Of this group, 19.4 per cent of those who were born overseas did not speak English at all, or did not speak it well (Australian Yearbook 1997). Even 5.1 per cent of those born in Australia fell into these categories. The cultural changes extend to religion as well. Whereas in 1971 86 per cent of the Australian community stated that they were Christian and only 0.8 per cent non-Christian, by 1991 only 74 per cent of the Australian community said they were Christian and 2.6 per cent were non-Christian. The figures also indicate the diminishing value placed on religion, as those who classified themselves as non-religious or having no religious preference increased from 13 per cent to 24.4 per cent over that same period. It could be argued that this changing status of religion has brought with it a substantial change in the values held by the community. Adults of just one generation ago are horrified by some of the language, violence and depictions of male–female relationships that are readily available in the media and, increasingly, through the new technologies.

Primary schools, as does the community in general, now have to cope with the different situations that a multicultural community with widely differing value-systems can bring. They must respond to new languages, new cultures, new values and new patterns of relationships between adults and children. There has been increased need for language-support teachers, for recognition of different religious holidays and for vigilance where potential racial problems might arise. Australia has prided itself on being a tolerant nation, but recent events suggest that economic circumstances can have an impact on the level of tolerance that people have for each other.

Changes in employment

The third area of the changing demography of Australia has been brought about by the comparatively recent restructuring of the Australian economy. In the hope that Australia would become more competitive internationally, and with the advent of new technologies, there have been changes in employment patterns which affect families and, hence, students and schools.

Total employment in Australia grew by around 17 per cent between 1987 and 1996, from just over 7 million to 8.3 million people. However, a more detailed analysis shows that the growth patterns have not been uniform. Table 4.1 indicates that the unemployment rates in 1996 are approximately the same as those of 1984; however, in 1984 unemployment was on the rise, whereas in 1996 there was a downward trend. The figures discount those who were undertaking either part-time or full-time employment while studying at school or university.

However, simply to report the overall growth rate disguises a rapidly changing set of employment options. These figures can be further analysed on the basis of three factors critical to our communities. The first is the difficult situation of youth unemployment, the second is the move from full-time to part-time employment, and the third is the difference between male and female employment growth. Table 4.1 shows that it was more difficult in 1996 for young school leavers to become employed than it was in 1987.

There is also a rapidly changing proportion of people that are employed part time rather than being fully employed. Table 4.2 indicates that, although overall growth was 17 per cent, the growth in full-time jobs was just 11 per cent. Most of the new jobs were part time, where there was a 43 per cent growth between 1987 and 1996. Also, male employment grew by just 11 per cent (full time 6 per cent, part time 65 per cent), while female employment grew by 27 per cent (full time 20 per cent, part time 38 per cent).

What these tables indicate is that much of the responsibility for growth in employment has been thrust upon people, particularly women, who are prepared to work part time. There has been very little growth in employment for males, particularly younger males, who are more likely to leave school early and be looking for full-time work. Young males, who perceive themselves

Table 4.1 Changes in employment

Employment	Australia 1987	Australia 1996
Full time	5,656,200	6,260,500
Part time	1,416,900	2,029,200
Male unemployment	8.7%	8.7%
Female unemployment	8.3%	9.3%
15-19 unemployment	20.6%	34.7%

Table 4.2 Employment growth

Growth in Employment in Australia 1987–96	Full time (%)	Part time (%)	All employment (%)
Total	11	43	17
Male employment	6	65	11
Female employment	20	38	27

as having few prospects in the future, have responded to this with violence to others and themselves through suicide and massive increases in drug and alcohol abuse.

These statistics have an impact on education too, because the shift from full-time to part-time employment has had the effect of lowering the overall income levels of families, making it necessary for both parents to work. With both parents working, the levels of family support and guidance, particularly for those who have language, cultural or learning difficulties, have diminished. The changing patterns of work (or non-work) may be the root cause of many of society's current ills.

The changing nature of work has also had an impact on the comparative wealth of families. Table 4.3 shows the comparative rates of pay for 1984 and 1996. It indicates that average adult weekly pay, before overtime, has increased substantially. But if we add the information from Table 4.2 we find that, more and more, those in full-time work are becoming much better off than those in part-time work or those who are unemployed. As most of the new work is part time this gap is getting wider.

Table 4.4 compares the purchasing power of the 1984 family with that of 1997. It indicates that, whereas average weekly household income has increased by 59 per cent over the period 1984–97, the increase of 66 per cent in mean weekly expenditure per household perhaps more accurately reflects the impact of inflation over that time. Tables 4.3 and 4.4, together, show us that whereas less than 60 per cent of families had household incomes less than average adult weekly earnings in 1984, by 1997 this figure had risen to around 70 per cent of households.

The increases in income and expenditure have not been uniform across the income groupings. The lowest 20 per cent of families increased their weekly household income by only 31 per cent, but increased their household

Table 4.3 Changes in pay rates

Employment	Australia 1984 (A$)	Australia 1996 (A$)
Average adult weekly pay	375	715

Table 4.4 Mean household weekly income and expenditure

Mean household weekly income and expenditure	Income 1984 (A$)	Expenditure 1984 (A$)	Income 1997 (A$)	Expenditure 1997 (A$)
Lowest 20% of households	116	164	152	303
2nd lowest 20%	238	262	354	426
3rd lowest 20%	389	347	592	573
4th lowest 20%	569	428	909	714
Top 20%	957	607	1,609	994
Average across Australia	454	362	723	602

expenditure by 85 per cent. At the other end of the social ladder the top 20 per cent increased their household income by 68 per cent and increased their expenditure by 64 per cent. The figures indicate that, on average, families in the lowest 20 per cent of household income spend about A$150 per week more than they bring in (utilising credit or other lending facilities) and that families in the top 20 per cent of household income are able to save about A$600 every week. Given the pattern indicated by the figures, it would be plausible to suggest that the top 5 per cent of households were substantially ahead of where they were in 1984 in terms of wealth, the next 15 per cent are about the same as they were in 1984 and everybody else is worse off. Any reasonable reading of the figures would suggest that there has been a shift of wealth from the poorest to the richest in our communities since 1984.

The household income and expenditure figures confirm the anecdotal evidence provided by research, such as that done by the Smith Family and the Brotherhood of St Laurence (Brotherhood of St Laurence 1996), that families at the lower end of income generation are having to deal with an unacceptable proportion of the economic change that has taken place. Table 4.5 indicates that the proportion of families with dependent children struggling against all the economic odds is also growing each year. A recent report by Monash University researcher Bob Birrell, reported in *The Age* (Milburn 1997: 1), suggests that up to one in three adults and 41 per cent of children rely on government welfare payments to survive. In real terms, the number of children in chronically poor homes (1995 incomes less than A$24,000) has risen from 93,000 in 1987 to 688,000 in 1995.

Table 4.5 Dependent-child families in low-income homes

	Australia 1984	Australia 1997
% of families with dependent children in the lowest 40% of income categories	7	17

Impact on students

Recently the federal minister of education, Dr Kemp, expressed concern that the literacy levels of about 30 per cent of Year 8 students was not as high as it should be. Certain groups within our community, such as Aborigines and those with non-English-speaking backgrounds fared even worse. However, if one takes this list of issues currently affecting our community and adds to it issues such as the drug and alcohol problem, single-parent families, family violence and child abuse, and the disturbing trend towards lower levels of physical well-being brought about by poor health, poor diet and the increasing cost of health services, which have not been discussed, could we seriously expect students to perform to the best of their ability?

Given all of the changes that have been wrought upon our communities, it is remarkable that schools have been able to maintain, let alone increase, the capabilities of students in areas such as literacy, numeracy and the like. Other countries do not fare nearly as well. The American *Goals Report* document, reporting on America's progress in education towards its Goals 2000, suggests that, nationally, 93 per cent of black children and 89 per cent of Hispanic children do not meet the grade 4 proficiency standards in reading, and 97 per cent of black children and 94 per cent of Hispanic children do not meet the grade 4 proficiency standards in mathematics.

Thus schools may have students coming to school hungry, or abused, or dispirited because of family breakdown or parent unemployment. When a school camp is mentioned some children know they will not be able to go; when some are reminded about their parents not paying their school fees the child is paying for the parents' financial situation. All of these things provide barriers to student learning that the teacher perhaps does not even know about.

Impact on families

For many parents, education is very low on the list of concerns. Many had poor educational experiences themselves; some may be illiterate or not speak English well. Others may be more concerned about where their next meal comes from than going to a parent–teacher meeting. When requests come home for excursion money, some will see this as another meal they cannot have. They are unable to help with homework because they cannot read well, and changes to the way in which mathematics operates mean that if they try to help they may in fact be hindering their child's understanding. Some will become abusive whenever the child asks for assistance; some are abusive for much of the time.

Given these circumstances, some parents will never feel comfortable about even going to the school, let alone making a positive contribution, yet all the evidence suggests that we must reach out to parents if we are to do the best for their children. Edwards and Jones Young argue:

It is necessary to sort out the group called 'parents', noting the range in their experiences, in their relationships with their children, in their feelings about school. Some have high regard for education; for others, their children's schooling is a relived struggle amid more pressing concerns. The goals and values of individual families will vary and may differ from those of the teacher and the school. It is this individuality that parents bring to parent involvement efforts.

(Edwards and Jones Young 1992: 74)

Restructuring and home–school relations

The rationale for the introduction of the Schools of the Future programme in Victoria was that 'quality outcomes of schooling can only be assured when decision-making takes place at the local level' (Directorate of School Education 1993: 1). Schools of the Future, it was claimed (Hayward 1993), would (among other things):

- encourage parents to participate directly in decisions that affect their child's education;
- enable communities, through the school charter, to determine the destiny of the school, its character and ethos;
- be accountable to the community for the progress of the school and the achievements of its students.

This combination of responsiveness to the market (through accountability to the community) has merged with the notion of school effectiveness (or improving student outcomes) to provide the argument for a self-managing school.

The school effectiveness and school improvement movement has now in excess of a twenty-year history. It has established clear guidelines as to what specific elements of school operations assist in promoting improved student outcomes. One of the factors that is now universally accepted as doing this is the development of strong home–school relations and, more particularly, the active involvement of parents in their child's learning. The literature on home–school relations supports the idea that the more interested a parent is and the more active in his or her child's education, the better the child will do. It suggests that those interested in school effectiveness should be cultivating home influences rather than trying to negate them.

Researchers have been involved in the study of parental involvement in school improvement and student achievement for many years. As early as 1967, the background research for the Plowden Report (1967) in Great Britain examined the relationship between environmental variables and school achievement. It concluded that home circumstances were more than three times as influential as school circumstances when it came to a child's achievement levels. In fact, it also seems that the bulk of the early US school effectiveness research (Weber 1971; Lezotte, Edmonds and Ratner 1974; Edmonds and Frederiksen 1978; Edmonds 1979; Austin 1979), in responding to the Coleman *et al.* (1966) study, was purposefully attempting to show that the influences of home on a student's achievement could be overcome. It was therefore unlikely that the issue of home–school relationships would be placed on the agenda of that early research. But that concern did not prevent Edmonds from at least identifying the strength of the parent position: 'Some schools are effective because they have a highly politicized Parent Teacher Organization that holds the schools to close instructional account' (Edmonds 1979: 22). Edmonds seems to be suggesting that some effective schools are that way because parents demand that they are. If they hold the school to account it is likely that they will also have an influence on their child's attitude to school.

However, research has now accepted that the home–school partnership is of critical importance to the level of effectiveness experienced by the school. It shows that the effective school is one that communicates with parents and community members, encourages parents to communicate with the school (Brookover *et al.* 1982; Eager 1988), encourages parents to accept some responsibility for their children's learning (*ibid.*) and establishes broad parameters for parent participation in their children's education. Such participation can be achieved through such things as formal organisations (*ibid.*; Rauhauser 1989), through parents assisting with learning activities either at home or in school (Stallings 1981; Brookover *et al.* 1982), or through volunteer service to the school in school canteens, libraries or helping with school sport (Gray 1984).

Parental attitudes towards education (Builder 1986) and the family's overall cultural style (Clark 1983; Dornbusch 1986) were considered stronger influences on child performance than characteristics previously considered, such as marital status, educational level of the parents, income or social surroundings. The Clark (1983) study is particularly interesting because of its analogy with an effective school. He found that certain patterns emerged in the homes of high achievers; these included frequent dialogues between parents and children, strong parental encouragement for academic pursuits, clear and consistent limits for the children, warm and nurturing interactions and consistent monitoring of how time is used. The effective home and the effective school both display a caring and safe climate, high expectations, clear rules and goals, adequate communications and consistent monitoring. One would suspect that these homes are under a system of leadership that enables the rest of the characteristics to emerge, in which case all of the major features of an effective school can be duplicated in the home environment. This would indicate that the students involved would have common forms of purpose at both home and school, which would make the learning process at school that much easier to conduct.

Other studies began to substantiate the claim that it was not simply family background that made the difference, but the level of parental involvement in their child's education that counted. Children who achieved had parents with high expectations for them (Becher 1984) or parents who were actively involved in the life of the school (Michael 1971; Armor et al. 1976; Trotter School 1977). The more parents participated in school activities, the more positive were the attitudes of the parents towards the school, the attitude of the teacher to the students and school attendance rates. Study habits and discipline within the school also improved (Schiff 1963; Rosenthal and Jacobson 1968). Declining rates of parent involvement coincided with declining rates of student motivation, performance and ability levels, even after the student's original ability level and family socio-economic status were taken into account (Coleman et al. 1966; Mayonbanks and Epstein 1987). Where parents and teachers collaborated on how to reinforce appropriate behaviour at school, the children showed improvement in academic performance, and both behaviour (Barth 1979) and 'self-concept' (Brookover et al. 1979). These results provided a clear indication that the more the school actively involved parents in their children's education, the better the child's results would be.

However, not all parents are able to attend and become actively involved in school- or classroom-based programmes. Tizard et al. (1982) demonstrated that this level of involvement was not necessary for children's attitude and performance to improve. In their study, parents of children in disadvantaged working-class areas were trained to listen to their child read at home. Not only did the children improve their reading performance, but there were also significant increases in the children's motivation for learning and in their behaviour at school. Austin (1979), Keith (1982) and Walberg et al. (1986) suggested that the amount of time spent on homework had a measurable effect on the child's achievement levels for all levels of ability within the school, and also that attitudes improved as a result of homework.

These findings suggest that there is sufficient evidence to embark on a programme of parental involvement that encourages parents to play an active part in their child's learning experiences. This could be done in the home, through the parent being interested in what the child is doing at school, reading to the child at home and actively encouraging better performance – which is the traditional view of the role of the parent – or it could be done via involvement at school, by being a 'reading mum' or helping in the classroom in other ways. Over the past two decades there has been far more encouragement for parents to undertake the role of tutor for the children both in school and at home. The case of the influence parents can have on the success of their child in the area of literacy provides an example of how schools might work with the home.

Parent involvement in literacy

In modern Western societies the value for individuals and whole communities of developing literacy skills in young children is firmly entrenched and widely acknowledged. In many of these same societies an added value is also given to parents participating in this development. This view is reflected, for example, in media comments such as this: 'Parents who are actively involved in their children's school not only aid the teacher but help their children and themselves, a leading child psychologist and educationist believes' (*Sydney Morning Herald*, 16 April 1994). What frequently is not made visible in comments such as this – or in many statements made about the benefits of parental involvement in children's learning by schools and, at times, by academics – is the meanings and assumptions which underlie them. If Australian primary schools are to respond to change and the challenge of adequately preparing children for the next century it is important to recognise that the all-too familiar terms 'literacy' and 'parental involvement' are problematic, and that their multiple meanings need to be exposed and examined.

The meaning of literacy

In an early historical examination of literacy's meaning, Graff (1986) abandoned any search for a unified, fixed and decontextualised notion and, along with other literacy commentators, opted instead for literacy's meaning to be determined by time and place and within political, social and cultural contexts (see, for example, Luke 1992–3; Baldauf and Luke 1990; Street and Wickert 1990; Apple 1988; Hunter 1987; Heath 1983). Once a socially construed notion of literacy, for example, is accepted, exploration of the meanings people make of literacy and their involvement in it becomes critical. The ethnographic work of Barton (1989), Taylor and Dorsey-Gaines (1988) and Heath (1983), amongst others, is especially useful here in that these researchers highlight the multiplicity of literacy's meanings and bring into sharper focus the fact that, at any one time and in any one location, different 'literacies' may be operating in both continuous and discontinuous ways. The significance of these sorts of studies lies in their recognition of the differential contribution made by children's home and community experiences to their literacy learning in the classroom. An implication emanating from them is the extent to which parents and teachers see children's literacy in the same (or different) ways.

The meaning of parent involvement

Walker (1994, 1996, 1997) developed a view of parental involvement which attempted to clarify its underlying assumptions and meanings. This view specifies different parental-involvement models which highlight different relationships existing between the home and the school in children's literacy and specific areas of activity in which parents' involvement takes place. These two dimensions of parental involvement are illustrated in Figure 4.1.

Areas of activity

The critical areas of activity identified in the Figure 4.1 are best considered in terms of the answers they provide to questions such as:

- To what extent are parents involved in planning (Chapman 1990) a school's literacy policy or classroom literacy programme?
- In which children's literacy practices (Rivalland 1989; Wheldall *et al.* 1987; Stevenson and Ralston 1985) are parents encouraged by teachers to be involved either at school or in the home?
- What is the nature of parent–school communication (Keogh 1992; Bastiani 1991; Maring and Megelky 1990; Trousdale 1990 and Kwarta 1988)?
- What provision is made by the school to involve parents in some form of parent training (Paratore *et al.* 1995; Cairney and Munsie 1992; Handel

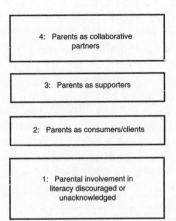

AREAS OF ACTIVITY

Planning	Practice in home/classroom	Communication	Parent training	Evaluation

MODELS

4: Parents as collaborative partners

3: Parents as supporters

2: Parents as consumers/clients

1: Parental involvement in literacy discouraged or unacknowledged

Figure 4.1 Models and areas of activity evident in parental involvement in literacy

1992; Hornby 1988; Spewock 1988; Raciti and Mathams 1987; Frede 1984) relating to children's literacy?

- To what extent do parents participate in the evaluation (Chapman 1990; Fredericks and Rasinski 1990) of a school's literacy policy or classroom literacy programme?

Parents may be encouraged to be involved in some of the areas of activity but not in others, and it is important to know when members of a school community talk about parental participation in children's literacy which specific areas or aspects they are considering.

Models of parental involvement

The second dimension identified in Figure 4.1 captures the nature of the relationship between the key adult agencies involved in children's literacy development (specifically, school administrators, teachers and parents). The following brief outline of the four models illuminates the different sorts of parent–school relationships that can be assumed to underlie how parental involvement is both viewed and practised in school communities.

Model 1: discouragement of parental involvement in children's literacy

In this model the relationship between parents and school personnel rests on either an active discouragement or a lack of acknowledgement by any one of the adult agencies of the role parents play in children's literacy, effectively marginalising parents in terms of their involvement. While the school or parents may recognise the value of parental involvement in children's literacy prior to a child's commencement in formal schooling, an assumption is made that, once a child starts school, teachers take over the responsibility for his or her literacy development. There is an implication that the school assumes the guardianship of literacy, and its view of literacy is not necessarily made explicit to parents.

Model 2: parents as consumer/clients

The view of parental involvement in literacy represented by the second model highlights the school as an educational producer and the parent as an educational consumer or client. This model is particularly evident in recent moves to devolve educational decision-making at the local school level (see, for example, Woods 1993; Townsend 1996). Key terms noted in this manifestation of the parent–school relationship are 'accountability' and 'marketability'. Parental involvement is, paradoxically, construed in both passive and active terms; parents as consumers may 'call the shots' by being assured that teachers are satisfying their children's literacy needs, but at the same time they have no identified or articulated participatory roles to play in children's literacy development.

Model 3: parents as supporters of school literacy

In contrast to the previous models, the parent is seen here as having a clear participatory function in the development of children's literacy at home and in the school. However, what is assumed in the relationship among the key adult agencies in this model is that the responsibility for children's literacy lies still predominantly with the school. Although the relationship between parents and teachers may be couched in 'partnership' terms, it is clearly one that favours a school's interpretation both of literacy and of any parental participation in it. The implied asymmetrical relationship between home and school in this form of partnership is reflected, for example, in cases where schools offer parent-training programmes which have as their agenda the need to ensure that parents are seeing children's literacy and their own involvement in it firmly in the school's terms. It could be argued that current parental-involvement practice suggests that the parent as supporter is the interpretation most commonly acknowledged or aspired to by school communities.

Model 4: parents as collaborative partners in children's literacy

This model represents an equal and reciprocal partnership between parents and teachers in the development of children's literacy. This form of partnership is clearly implied in socially constructed views of literacy and, in particular, the ethnographically focused research on 'family literacy' (see, for example, Barton 1989; Taylor and Dorsey-Gaines 1988; Heath 1983). In this model the authenticity of parental views of literacy and contributions to children's literacy learning is accepted alongside those views and contributions held or made by the school.

Consideration of both the specific areas of activity in which parents are involved and what amounts to notions of power which underlie relationships among the key adult agencies in the development of children's literacy makes a useful contribution to the clarification of what parental involvement in literacy means. At the same time it offers an opportunity to make links between the rhetoric about parental involvement, on the one hand, and how it operates in practice, on the other.

This analysis highlights a 'dominant culture' which influences how parental involvement in literacy tends to be conceived in school communities, where the involvement assumes the school as the major agency and authority. However, the fourth model presented above offers school communities the opportunity to explore what parental involvement in literacy could be like, a view which accepts equality between teachers and parents not only in parental participation but in how literacy itself is conceived.

Parent involvement in practice

In order for school communities to make progress in their implementation of parental-involvement policies and practices its members must question their own assumptions about children's literacy and, in particular, the role of parents participating in children's literacy development. One way to do this is for school communities to examine their school's profile of parental-involvement beliefs and practices using as a basis the models and areas of activity outlined above. This can be illustrated by reference to one of the specified areas of activity – parent training.

In a number of countries parent-training programmes are supported by governments and education departments as a means of developing more effective parental-involvement programmes. One view of this trend is to interpret them in terms of the official voice, ensuring control of the literacy agenda by training parents to support the school's view of literacy. In contrast to this view, a school community attempting a more participatory and collaborative model of parental involvement through parent training would need to expose important issues of parent participation and equality by seeking answers to such questions as:

* Are all parents invited to participate in the training programme or is it limited to a select number of parents?
* Will the school devise its own parent-training programme or adopt one that is being promulgated by education departments or governments?
* What parental input is there into the development and delivery of the parent-training programme?
* What is the opportunity for divergent school community views being incorporated into the training programme?
* Who will evaluate the programme?

Examination of a number of existing parent-training programmes suggests that often only tokenistic attempts are made to include parental views and experiences in them. An example of an attempt to give more equality to parental voices within a school community's development of a parent-training programme is the use of parent diaries, which provide a mechanism for parents to record and possibly reflect on literacy events as they occur in their own homes and communities (Paratore *et al.* 1995). If these are included in a parent-training programme parents become identified as ethnographers of their own literacy contexts and, as such, assume equality with teachers as ethnographers of classroom literacy.

Significant changes in the culture of schooling are occurring throughout the Western world. These socio-political changes threaten to undermine the fabric of school communities by imposing agendas on them which force them to reorganise their priorities away from fostering parental partnerships and towards meeting the bureaucratic and administrative demands of self-government (see, for example, Townsend 1996). Parental involvement in literacy can thus be contextualised within a wider power struggle in which teachers are becoming increasingly disempowered and parents are at risk of being locked into reductive consumer/client roles.

There is the possibility, however, of an alternative scenario in which school communities may achieve, even within negative social environments, more desirable and empowering partnerships through a recognition of the important contributory roles parents can play in children's literacy. School communities clearly must make a choice between these two scenarios. A school community clarifying its own views of literacy and parental participation by using the parental-involvement models and areas of activity presented in this chapter could eventually lead to a positioning of both teacher and parent as partners in the development of children's literacy. Given the speed with which socio-political changes are occurring and the impact they are having on 'good' practice, this collaborative task is not only timely but somewhat urgent.

Conclusion

Some of the demographic changes in our society considered above have been responded to by schools for some years. A few of these responses are the employment of language aides, translation of school newsletters into sometimes many different community languages, use of school funds to support students who might not otherwise be able to attend camps and excursions, and the involvement of parents and community members in school councils and other school activities.

However, the workload has intensified dramatically in the past few years. Now schools are involved in standardised testing of children's literacy and numeracy skills, mandatory reporting of possible child abuse, involving their school communities in the construction of school charters and asking parents to comment on the performance of the school, all of which are positive moves, but their effectiveness has been lessened because they have come at a time of substantial reductions in the educational budget. If we add to this the layer of administrative tasks related to accountability, staffing and budgeting, then the changes to the range of tasks falling on people in the school has been huge.

When this is added to the trend of lowering the levels of government resources allocated to schools, principals, teachers and parents have been left to pick up the increased range of activities with little or no resource support. Principals (Education Victoria 1997) and teachers, parents and school councillors (Townsend 1996) have all seen their workloads increase since the introduction of the self-managing school. This corresponds with evidence from other countries such as the United Kingdom (Campbell and Neill 1994; Rafferty 1994) and New Zealand (Bridges 1992; Livingstone 1994; Wylie 1994).

However, the most critical issue facing schools in the next decade is their ability to encourage parents to become more involved in school activities. Given the situation of many parents – in some families both parents work, in other families there is a language barrier and in yet other families there is a level of demoralisation because of financial, social (e.g. marriage breakdown) or employment problems – there will be some difficulty for schools in this task. Codding argued:

> As more and more young people come to school hungry, fearful and abused from homes with one or no parent, teachers can no longer expect that all of their students arrive at school ready to learn, and that once they are there they are all alert and engaged in their school work. This does not mean that schools need to take on the job by themselves of ensuring the health and well being of children and families; the mission of schools must remain educating young people to high levels. Nevertheless, schools must be part of the solution. The education system cannot make good on its promise of enabling all students to achieve at high levels until the issue of support for children and families is addressed. . . . Following the African proverb (somewhat a cliché), 'it takes a village to raise a child' – and addressing this issue requires collaboration among a host of agencies and organizations and the strong will of the people.
>
> (Codding 1997: 9)

As we head towards the third millennium, the changing nature of families and their ability to support their child at school may become the most critical factor that education, and perhaps the nation as a whole, will have to address.

References

Apple, M. W. (1988) 'Economics and inequality in schools', *Theory into Practice* 27(4): 282–7.

Armor, D., Conry-Oseguera, P., Cox, M., King, N., McConnell, L., Pascal, A., Pauly, E. and Zelleman, G. (1976) *Analysis of the School Preferred Reading Program in Selected Los Angeles Minority Schools*, Santa Monica, CA: Rand Corporation.

Austin, G. R. (1979) 'Exemplary schools and the search for effectiveness', *Educational Leadership* 37(1): 10–14.

Baldauf, R. B. and Luke, A. (1990) *Language Planning and Education in Australasia and the South Pacific*, Clevedon, Avon: Multilingual Matters.

Barton, D. (1989) 'Making sense of literacy in the home', paper presented at the Conference of the European Association for Research on Learning and Instruction, Madrid, Spain, May.

Bastiani, J. (1991) *Reporting Pupil Achievement: Survey of Teacher, Parent and Pupil Views*, Nottingham: University of Nottingham, School of Education.

Becher, R. M. (1984) 'Parent involvement: a review of research and principles of successful practice', paper presented to the National Institute of Education, Washington, DC, August.

Bridges, S. (1992) *Working in Tomorrow's Schools: Effects on Primary Teachers*, Canterbury, New Zealand: University of Canterbury.

Brookover, W., Beady, C., Flood, P., Schweitzer, J. and Wisenbaker, J. (1979) *School Social Systems and Student Achievement: Schools Can Make a Difference*, East Lansing, MI: Institute for Research on Teaching, Michigan State University.

Brookover, W. *et al.* (1982) *Creating Effective Schools: An In-service Program for Enhancing School Learning Climate and Achievement*, Holmes Beach: Learning Publications, Inc.

Brotherhood of St Laurence (1996) 'What is happening to "free" public education? Low income families' experiences of primary and secondary education', *Changing Pressures Bulletin* no. 3, Melbourne: Brotherhood of St Laurence .

Builder, P. (1986) 'Parental involvement', *Pivot* 13(4): 19–21.

Cairney, T. H. and Munsie, L. (1992) *Beyond Tokenism: Parents as Partners in Literacy*, Carlton, Victoria: Australian Reading Association.

Campbell, J. and Neill, S. (1994) *Curriculum at Key Stage 1: Teacher Commitment and Policy Failure*, London: Longman.

Chapman, C. (1990) 'The first twelve months', *Home–School Contract of Partnerships Newsletter* 2.

Clark, R. M. (1983) *Family Life and School Achievement: Why Poor Black Children Succeed or Fail*, Chicago, IL: University of Chicago Press.

Codding, J. (1997) 'Designing highly effective programs for successful schools', keynote presentation at the Successful Schools Conference, Melbourne, 3 June.

Coleman, J. S., Campbell, E., Hobson, C., McPartland, J., Mood, A., Weinfield, F. and York, R. (1966) *Equality of Educational Opportunity*, Washington, DC: US Government Printing Office.

Directorate of School Education (1993) *School Charters Information Package for Consultation and Promotion*, Melbourne: Directorate of School Education.

Dornbusch, S. (1986) *Helping Your Kid Make the Grade*, Reston, VA: National Association of Secondary School Principals (NASSP).

Eager, H. J. (1988) 'Quality schools index for private schools: instructions for use', paper presented at the First International Congress for Effective Schools, London, January.

Edmonds, R. (1979) 'Effective schools for the urban poor', *Educational Leadership* 37(1): 15–27.

Edmonds, R. and Frederiksen, J. (1978) *Search for Effective Schools: The Identification and Analysis of City Schools that are Instructionally Effective for Poor Children*, Cambridge, MA: Center for Urban Studies.

Education Victoria (1997) *Still More Work to Be Done But . . . No Turning Back, Co-operative Research Project Report*, Melbourne: Department of Education.

Edwards, P. A. and Jones Young, L. S. (1992) 'Beyond parents: family, community, and school involvement', *Phi Delta Kappa* 71(1): 72–80.

Frede, E. (1984) *Getting Involved: Workshops for Parents*, Washington, DC: Administration for Children, Youth and Families.

Fredericks, A. D. and Rasinski, T. V. (1990) 'Involving parents in the assessment process', *The Reading Teacher* 44(4): 346–9.

Graff, H. J. (1986) 'The legacies of literacy: continuities and contradictions in Western society and culture', in S. de Castell, P. Luke and K. Egan (eds) *Literacy, Society and Schooling: A Reader*, London: Cambridge University Press.

Gray, S. T. (1984) 'Increase productivity with volunteers', *School Business Affairs* 50(2): 18.

Handel, R. D. (1992) 'The partnership for family reading: benefits for families and schools', *The Reading Teacher* 43(2): 116–26.

Hayward, D. (1993) *Schools of the Future: Preliminary Paper*, Melbourne: Directorate of School Education.

Heath, S. B. (1983) *Ways With Words: Language, Life, and Work in Communities and Classrooms*, Cambridge: Cambridge University Press.

Hornby. G. (1988) 'Launching parent to parent schemes', *British Journal of Special Education* 15(2): 77–8.

Hunter, C. St J. (1987) 'Myths and realities of literacy/illiteracy', *Convergence: An International Journal of Adult Education*, 20(1): 1–18.

Keith, T. (1982) 'Time spent on homework and high school grades', *Journal of Educational Psychology* 74(2): 248–53.

Keogh, J. (1992) 'Identity, ideology and power: a study of parent–teacher interviews', unpublished Master of Education thesis, University of New England.

Kwarta, D. (1988) 'Parent/teacher communication: accepting both roles', *Exceptional Children*, September: 20–1.

Lezotte, L. Edmonds, R. and Ratner, G. (1974) *Final Report: Remedy for School Failure to Equitably Deliver Basic School Skills*, East Lansing, MI: Michigan State University.

Livingstone, I. (1994) *The Workloads of Primary School Teachers: A Wellington Region Survey*, Wellington, New Zealand: Chartwell Consultants.

Luke, A. (1992–3) 'Literacy and human capital: rethinking the equation', *Education Australia* 19–20: 19–21.

McLennan, W. (1997) *Yearbook Australia*, Canberra: Australian Government Publishing Service.

Maring, G. H. and Magelky, J. (1990) 'Effective communication: key to parent/community involvement', *The Reading Teacher* 43(8): 606–7.

Mayonbanks, M. and Epstein, J. L. (1987) 'Parent involvement in student learning', *Community Education Journal* 14(4): 8–10.

Michael, J. A. (1971) 'Conceptions of childhood and parent participation in schools', paper presented at the American Sociological Association Convention, Denver, USA, November.

Milburn, C. (1997) 'Looming welfare crisis as 1 in 3 adults collect payments', *The Age*, 26 June: 1.

National Education Goal Panel (1995) *Data Volume for the National Educational*

Goals Report: Volume One: National Data, Washington, DC: US Government Printing Office.

Paratore, J. R., Homza, A., Krol-Sinclair, B., Lewis-Barrow, T., Melzi, G., Stergis, R. and Haynes, H. (1995) 'Shifting boundaries in home and school responsibilities: the construction of home-based literacy portfolios by immigrant parents and their children', *Research in the Teaching of English* 29(4): 367–89.

Plowden Report (1967) *Children and Their Primary Schools*, London: HMSO.

Raciti, S. and Mathams, P. (1987) 'Training parents as effective listeners of their children's reading', *Queensland Journal of Guidance and Counselling* 1: 1–10.

Rafferty, F. (1994) 'Alarm at growth of 60-hour week', *Times Educational Supplement*, 5 August: 1.

Rauhauser, W. (1989) 'Design for implementing effective schools research', paper presented at the International Congress for School Effectiveness, Rotterdam, the Netherlands, January.

Rivalland, J. (1989) 'Parents helping in the classroom', *P.E.N. 71*, Rozelle: Primary English Teaching Association.

Rosenthal, R. and Jacobson, L. (1968) *Pygmalion in the Classroom: Teacher Expectation and Pupil Intellectual Development*, New York: Holt.

Schiff, H. (1963) *The Effect of Personal Contractual Relationships on Parents' Attitudes Towards Participation in Local School Affairs*, Evanston, IL: North Western University.

Spewock, T. (1988) 'Training parents to teach their preschoolers through literature', *The Reading Teacher* 41(7): 648–52.

Stallings, J. (1981) *What Research Has to Say to Administrators of Secondary Schools About Effective Teaching and Staff Development*, Eric Document number ED 209748, New York: Educational Resource and Information Clearinghouse.

Stevenson, B. and Ralston, F. (1985) 'Reading together: parents helping at school', *Best of SET: Reading Item 11*, Hawthorn, Victoria: Australian College of Educational Research.

Stoll, L. and Fink, D. (1996) *Changing Our Schools: Linking School Effectiveness and School Improvement*, Milton Keynes: Open University Press.

Street, B. V. and Wickert, R. (1991) 'Putting literacies on the political agenda and response to Street', *Australian Journal for Adult Literacy Research and Practice, 1* (1), pp 5–17.

Taylor, D. and Dorsey-Gaines, C. (1988) *Growing up Literate: Learning from Innercity Families*, Portsmouth, NH: Heinemann Educational.

Tizard, J. Schofield, W. N. and Hewison, J. (1982) 'Collaboration between teachers and parents in assisting children's reading', *Journal of Educational Psychology* 52(1): 1–15.

Townsend, T. (1996) 'The self-managing school: miracle or myth?', *Leading and Managing* 3(3): 171–94.

Trotter School (1977) *Trotter Educational Plan*, Boston, MA: William Monroe Trotter School.

Trousdale, A. (1990) 'Interactive storytelling: scaffolding children's early narratives', *Language Arts* 67: 164–73.

Walberg, H. J. *et al.* (1986) 'Walberg and colleagues reply: "effective schools use homework effectively"', *Educational Leadership* 43(8): 58.

Walker, I. (1994) 'Parental involvement in literacy, a fourth generation', in A. B.

Littlefair (ed.) *Literacy for Life*, Widnes, Cheshire: United Kingdom Reading Association.

—— (1996) 'Literacy in crisis families', in B. Neate (ed.) *Literacy Saves Lives*, Shepreth, Cheshire: United Kingdom Reading Association.

—— (1997) 'Parental involvement in children's literacy during the primary school years', unpublished doctoral thesis, Monash University, Australia.

Weber, G. (1971) *Inner City Children Can Be Taught to Read: Four Successful Schools*, Washington, DC: Council for Basic Education.

Wheldall, K. *et al.* (1987) 'Pause, prompt and praise for parents and peers: effective tutoring of low progress readers', *Support for Learning* 2(1): 5–12.

Woods, P. (1993) 'Parents as consumer-citizens', in R. Merttens *et al. Ruling the Margins: Problematising Parental Involvement*, London: IMPACT Project, University of North London Press.

Wylie, C. (1994) *Self Managing Schools in New Zealand: The Fifth Year*, Auckland: New Zealand Council for Educational Research.

Part III

CRITICAL ISSUES FOR THE RESTRUCTURED PRIMARY SCHOOL

5

THE EARLY YEARS OF
SCHOOLING

Anne Kennedy

The context

In Australia over the past decade the early years of schooling have been the focus for a plethora of national and state reviews, reports and task-force activity. Nationally, for example, the Schools Council of the National Board of Employment, Education and Training (NBEET) Compulsory Years of School project considered the early years of schooling and published five papers between 1991 and 1992.

In 1995 the Commonwealth Senate Employment, Education and Training Reference Committee announced its intention to examine early-childhood education in Australia using wide community consultation mechanisms. This enquiry was to be undertaken in the belief 'that a greater investment in the early years is more than offset by the savings later in the education process' (*Enquiry Information Leaflet*, February 1995).

At state level there have been numerous reviews and reports relating to early-years education. Some examples of this activity include the 1989 Tasmanian Department of Education and the Arts' Review of Early Childhood Education, the 1992 Victorian Ministerial Review of School Entry Age and the 1993 Western Australia Voluntary Full-time Pre-primary Education report.

Prior to this recent interest in the early years of schooling there was a period of dismantling or reduction of early-childhood units in nearly every state education ministry (Gifford 1992, 1993). This restructuring occurred in a climate of economic constraint and reflected the move away from specialist teachers and units to a more integrated school with generalist teachers.

In the 1990s those same ministries have seen fit to establish new early-schooling units or early-childhood consultative positions in order to respond to the international and Australian research and task-force activity; these have highlighted key notions relating to early-childhood education. The most consistent and influential research about early-childhood education (Sylva 1994) suggests that:

- learning begins from birth, with parents as the first and most important teachers of the child;
- the early years (0–8 years) are quantitatively and qualitatively a unique period of development;
- early intervention can reduce disadvantage and equalise opportunities for all children;
- there is a link between quality early-learning experiences and later school achievement.

While this chapter refers to Australian junior schools in a generic sense, it must be recognised that there is considerable diversity within these units. Public and private school systems, ethnic schools, isolated, rural or city schools, for example, provide different contexts for Australian children in their first years of school. In Australia the term 'junior school' is used to describe the first three grades of the compulsory school system. Although there are instances of separate junior schools in South Australia, for example, or in the private school system, this type of separate system is not as common as the fully integrated primary school. Junior school in this chapter, therefore, refers to the first three years of the compulsory school system.

School entry in Australia

Australian children enter the compulsory school system at different entry ages, via different enrolment procedures, and have different total numbers of years at school. Table 5.1 below illustrates the differences between the states and territories. Despite recommendations from the Australian Education Council (1990), the states have not agreed to a common school-entry age because of different philosophical positions related to the factors indicated in Table 5.1. South Australia, for example, believes continuous entry into school as children turn five allows for an individualisation of the transition-to-school process. New South Wales changed its enrolment procedures to allow children to enter school at a younger age (4.6 years), with a preferred single entry at the beginning of the school year. Moving away from a continuous entry system was believed to be in the children's best interest because it enabled all children to have an equal amount of schooling in the first year (Davies and North 1990).

School-readiness

Australian schools have generally preferred informal assessments to formal assessments, such as standardised tests, when determining a child's readiness

Table 5.1 Minimum entry age, enrolment procedures and total length of schooling

State	Minimum school-entry age	Grade entered	Enrolment procedure	Years of schooling
WA	5 by 31 December	Year 1	Single entry at beginning of year	12
NT	5	Year 1	Continuous entry until Week 1, Term 3	13
QLD	5 by 31 December	Year 1	Single entry at beginning of year	12
ACT	5 by 30 April	Kindergarten	Single entry at beginning of year	13
SA	5	Reception	Continuous entry	13
NSW	5 by 31 July	Kindergarten	Single entry at beginning of year is preferred; continuous entry until end of Term 2 a possibility	13
VIC	5 by 30 April	Preparatory	Single entry at beginning of year	13
TAS	5 by 1 January	Preparatory	Single entry at beginning of year	13

for school. Interviews with parents, questionnaires or checklists completed by pre-school, childcare staff and parents, and observations of the child in the pre-school setting and during orientation visits provide teachers with an overview of each child's ability across the developmental domains, as well as information about family background and the child's experiences within the family and in out-of-home care. The purpose of this data-gathering has not been to exclude children from school or to place them in a transition grade, but rather to assist schools in providing an appropriate transition-into-school programme for individual children.

A 1991 study by de Lemos and Mellor which investigated parent and teacher assessment of 700 pre-school children found general agreement between the parents' and the teachers' assessment of a child's school-readiness, and also that these two ratings generally agreed (86 per cent of the sample) with objective assessment measures. This research suggests that the use of informal measures to determine school-readiness is reasonably effective in an area of child development which is very difficult to define.

The American National Association for the Education of Young Children (NAEYC) published a 'Position statement on school readiness' in 1990 which shifts the *construct of readiness* from the child to the school: 'The NAEYC believes it is the responsibility of schools to *meet the needs of children as they enter* and provide whatever services are needed *in the least restrictive environment* to help each child reach his or her fullest potential' (National Association for the Education of Young Children 1990: 21). When schools attempt to meet this challenge issues such as school-entry age and determining school-readiness become less important.

While research in Australia (de Lemos 1988), the United Kingdom (Fogelman and Gorbach 1978) and the United States (Proctor *et al.* 1986; Shepard and Smith 1986) has shown that younger entrants are not disadvantaged academically or socially, particularly in the long term, teacher surveys (Griffin and Harvey 1995) and anecdotal evidence continue to demonstrate that teachers perceive younger entrants as less ready for school than their older peers. It may be necessary to persuade school staff to acknowledge the research evidence which refutes this belief if this perceived disadvantage is not to become reality for these younger entrants.

Transition to school

Young children are vulnerable to stress and anxiety when faced with moving from one setting to another, for example from pre-school or childcare to school. They may lack the social experience and cognitive capacity to employ appropriate coping strategies. As Stevens *et al.* suggest: 'Transitions in the life course are periods of particular opportunity and vulnerability that require new behaviours, often heavily taxing one's resources, skills and abilities' (Stevens *et al.* 1993: 340).

Successful transitions for young children require close and continuous communication and the active involvement of all concerned: the parents, pre-school/childcare staff, school staff and the children (Bredekamp 1987). In Australian states and territories where pre-schools are co-located with or are in close proximity to the primary school, or where there are close systemic links (all states except Victoria and, to some degree, New South Wales), the transition for children and families between services is easier to achieve (Mellor 1991). Practices such as extended orientation visits to the school involving both children and parents, 'buddy' systems which link an older child with the new entrant and comprehensive information sessions for parents are examples of strategies used by schools to assist with smooth transitions. Networks between staff who work in early-childhood settings have also helped improve the process. In multi-age classes new entrants may find the transition into school less difficult when they have the support and modelling of more experienced classmates. However, the most difficult task in achieving smooth transitions for young children is the provision of continuity between the types of programmes experienced. The Victorian *Ministerial Review of School Entry Age* (Department of School Education 1992) made four recommendations which were seen as essential requirements for schools trying to address this challenge:

- establishment of junior primary units within primary schools;
- adoption of flexible organisation structures within these units;
- improving the early-childhood knowledge base of teachers working in the junior primary years;
- implementing developmentally appropriate curriculum.

These approaches were to be introduced in a context which recognised and supported parents as the first teachers of their children and as partners with school communities when formal schooling begins.

The recommendations and the strategies suggested by the Review Committee have been influential in the restructuring which is occurring in Victorian junior schools and are similar to initiatives and programmes evident in other states and territories.

Flexible organisation structures

Flexible grouping, also called multi-age or vertical grouping, has been part of Australian rural school organisation since colonial times. The one-teacher bush school has been celebrated in verse and prose and documented in history-of-education texts (Turney 1975). The combining of two grades when numbers of children and staff shortages make it difficult to provide separate grades is a common practice in schools. These composite classes, as they are known, have not always been popular with teachers and parents because of concerns about meeting the curriculum needs of children in two grade levels.

A distinction needs to be made between these composite classes and multi-age classrooms: the former results from an organisational need and the latter from a pedagogical position.

Research which has demonstrated the uniqueness of the developmental period 0–8 years has focused attention on children's developmental level rather than their chronological age. Grade levels, by their lock-step nature, which traditionally links to chronological age, are therefore seen as barriers to meeting young learners' needs.

Multi-age classes provide opportunities for children to work/play with others who may match their developmental stage or who are in advance in particular areas and may therefore provide a competent role model. The work of Vygotsky (1962) and, later, Bruner (1983) demonstrated that learning is constructed in social contexts with either adults or peers. The interest, support and interaction by others contributes to the learning process. The social construction of learning theory provides theoretical support to schools adopting flexible age grouping.

Unlike the graded structure, where children change teachers annually, flexible grouping provides the possibility for a teacher to remain with a group of children over an extended period of time. This feature supports young children's need for continuity in their care and education, and assists teachers in establishing stronger links with families: 'Sustained development in young children, more meaningful student–teacher relationships and more effective use of time, particularly in the beginning of school years are claimed to be significant advantages' (Schools Council 1992a: 15). While the overseas research on multi-age classes is inconclusive, especially in relation to academic gains (Slavin *et al.* 1993), there is evidence to suggest the benefits may relate to more positive attitudes to school and higher self-esteem in children (Pavan 1992). There is agreement by researchers that restructuring junior schools into multi-age units will not provide learning improvements for children unless there is an understanding of the pedagogy behind multi-age grouping and a strong teacher/school commitment to implementing developmental approaches (Surbeck 1992).

South Australia and the Australian Capital Territory have multi-age units in many schools which are supported by their respective school ministries because they are considered to be an appropriate alternative to the graded structure. Victoria, Western Australia and the Northern Territory are currently trialling multi-age projects with evaluation mechanisms integral to the projects. The Victorian First Steps pilot project for the first three years of schooling has extensive evaluation procedures which include: a control group, standardised literacy and numeracy tests, profile monitoring, parent and teacher questionnaires, and children's self-evaluations. However, the evaluation of changes in school structures or curriculum is fraught with difficulties because of the complex nature of any classroom situation. Teacher motivation, beliefs and experience, parental expectations, children's family backgrounds and life experiences are all variables which complicate attempts to ascertain the benefits or disadvantages associated with a particular school or systemic initiative. Additionally, the use of standardised tests with young children has been seen by some as inappropriate when the focus on multi-ageing has been to promote a developmental orientation to programming.

Teachers researching in their own classrooms through action-research projects may provide an additional perspective on the possibilities and problems associated with introducing initiatives such as multi-age grouping.

Professional development needs to be an integral component of ministerial or departmental projects relating to early years of schooling. For example, the Victorian First Steps pilot project has professional-development initiatives which include state conference days, cluster meetings and dissemination of relevant material. The content of these professional-development programmes is best determined by the teachers rather than by external organisations.

Standardisation and accountability

The 1989 Hobart Declaration, which promulgated Commonwealth and state/territory-agreed National Goals of Schooling provided the impetus for the development of national curriculum documents (Allen 1993). From the ten goals in the declaration, eight key learning areas were designated for the development of national statements (content component) and national profiles (performance indicators). Despite the states' agreement on the goals of schooling, the national statements have not been mandated; instead, states and territories have used the documents to develop or modify their own curriculum packages (see, for example, Board of Studies 1995). These national statements emphasise the notion of 'learning outcomes' – 'what a child will be able to do' at any particular level of schooling – with scant recognition for the importance of the learner's attitude or motivation to learn if he or she is in fact to be 'able to do' anything. This emphasis on outcomes at the expense of pre-learning behaviours/attitudes provides a dilemma for Australian junior school teachers who believe in the broader, developmental approach. As Halliwell suggests, it is extremely difficult 'to achieve consensus about typical sequences in learning and development' in young children (Halliwell 1993: 9).

Closely connected to the development of national standards in education is the notion of *accountability*. Angus notes that the current devolution activity in Australia is combined with a greater emphasis on schools *being more directly accountable for their results* (Angus 1991: 82). State-wide testing in Australia is linked to these accountability measures. The growing acceptance in Australia of standardised testing for entire cohorts of Year 3 children, many of whom may be under eight years of age, is of concern to those who are promoting developmental approaches in teaching and learning. As Cahir suggests, 'these tests . . . discourage critical and creative thinking, potentially damage children's belief in their own ability and fail to take account of the very different rates in which children develop' (Cahir 1994: 16). Young children's performance in test situations can be influenced by external factors such as the time of day, where the test is given and who might be the test administrator. Children under 8 years of age may also find test situations difficult because they lack experience with test techniques and in maintaining interest and concentration (Powell and Sigel 1991).

Teachers in the Northern Territory were successful in having the 8-year-olds excluded from the state-wide standardised testing programme, but in other states, such as Victoria and New South Wales, testing programmes have been introduced for Years 3 and 5 as part of accountability measures. While the introduction of these tests has not yet been suggested for the junior grades, teachers have expressed concern that there may be pressure to prepare younger children for the Year 3 tests. Evidence of this type of pushing down of curriculum to meet the goals set for older children has been cited in the USA (Shepard and Smith 1988) and in the UK (Anning 1991).

Developmentally appropriate practice

Teachers working in Australian junior grades use the term 'developmental learning' to describe aspects of the curriculum or programme which they believe relate to young children's developmental needs. The provision of free play periods or learning centres within a classroom are examples of programme components designed to meet children's developmental levels. Following NAEYC's 1987 position paper on 'Developmentally appropriate practice' (DAP), there has been international usage of this term in the field of early-childhood education (Bredekamp 1987).

The philosophy of DAP has been challenged by, among others, Spodek (1991), Kessler (1991), Fowell and Lawton (1992), and Fleer (1992) on the basis that it is too simplistic and restrictive to practise, as well as failing to address the crucial role of the adult in the child's development of cognitive competence. NAEYC continues to defend DAP principles through the reiteration and expansion of the two key dimensions: age appropriateness and individual appropriateness (Bredekamp and Rosegrant 1992).

Despite the criticisms, the philosophy of DAP has influenced the practice of early-childhood teachers working in programmes for children from birth to 8 years. Research has been undertaken, especially in the United States, to determine the outcomes for children when programmes become developmentally focused.

Marcon's (1994) longitudinal studies of over 400 pre-school and kindergarten children (first year of school in Australia) in these early years, and later in transition from junior grades to grade four, compared the academic and developmental outcomes achieved in three different teaching approaches:

* the developmentally focused programme;
* the academically oriented programme;
* the middle-of-the-road model.

The results of these studies showed clearly that children attained consistent, long-term higher academic achievement and social/emotional competence in programmes with a developmental approach. Neither of the other models could provide these gains in either the short or the long term: 'children's academic and developmental progress through school is enhanced by more active, child initiated early learning experiences. Their progress is slowed by the "escalated curriculum" that introduces formal learning experiences too early for most children's developmental status' (Marcon 1994: 15).

Marcon's findings reinforce the importance of teachers understanding developmental approaches and then being able to articulate this knowledge into a philosophy which clearly informs their practice. Teachers' knowledge base relating to the uniqueness of early-childhood teaching and learning is critical to the implementation of a developmental approach. This factor was recognised in the Victorian *Ministerial Review of School Entry Age* (Department of School Education 1992) and the Schools Council paper *A Stitch in Time: Strengthening the First Years of School* (Schools Council 1992c). With an increasingly ageing teaching population in many states (for example, in Victoria only 15 per cent of teachers are under 30 years of age), there might be a considerable time lapse between teachers' previous developmental psychology studies and their current teaching positions. Munro suggests there can be up to fifty years difference between 'what is known about learning . . . and what is practised in schools' (Munro 1995: 8).

The prescribed content contained in curriculum framework documents and the focus on basic skills and competencies at specified stages seem to conflict with core elements of developmental approaches:

• meaningful and culturally relevant curriculum emerges from the children's needs and interests (Bredekamp and Rosegrant 1992);
• children's learning is not always sequential and higher-order thinking may in fact outpace basic skill acquisition (National Association for the Education of Young Children 1990).

The mechanistic view of teaching and learning which is expressed in many current curriculum documents does not reflect the real nature of young children's learning. As Malaguzzi, the driving force behind the exemplary pre-school programmes in Reggio Emilia, Italy, explains, 'What children learn does not follow as an automatic result from what is taught. Rather, it is in large part due to the children's own doing as a consequence of their activities and our resources' (Malaguzzi 1993: 59). Meeting the demands of the school system may therefore be difficult for teachers wanting to adopt a developmentally appropriate programme. Additionally, teachers may face criticisms from peers, parents and administrators who misunderstand the informal nature of a DAP classroom.

Play

The belief in the importance of play for young children is possibly the most fundamental value held by all those who have trained and worked in early-childhood education. The early-childhood theorists such as Comenius (1657), Pestalozzi (1898) and Froebel (1903) were different from other educational theorists of their time because they highlighted the importance of early childhood as a separate life-period and they recognised play as the 'work' of children. Froebel wrote: 'Play at this time is not trivial, it is highly serious and of deep significance' (quoted in Anning 1991: 10).

When a belief such as the importance of play for young children is developed and implemented over a long period it tends to become enshrined as something sacrosanct. Within the field the belief is not challenged or examined, and often the field cannot articulate to outsiders what it actually believes in and why. However, the sacrosanct nature of play has been challenged and threatened by the increasing focus on standardisation and structured curricula. Play researchers and early-years educators have not always been able to provide an adequate defence against this diminishment of the play ethos (Smith 1994; Anning 1994).

However, Anning (1994), Berk (1994) and others believe that more recent research into how children learn provides strong theoretical support for the inclusion of play in programmes for young children. The work of Vygotsky (1962), Bruner (1983) and Gardner (1995), for example, indicates how adults can support children's learning as they play and the type of learning environment which is conducive to learning through play. Gardner, in a recent interview, described the ideal learning environment for children as a place where they would 'have the opportunity to work with very interesting kinds of things, at their own pace, in their own way, in their own terms, using the kind of intelligence that they are strong in' (Gardner 1995: 24). Berk believes Vygotsky's theory 'highlights the critical role of make-believe in developing reflective thought as well as self-regulatory and socially cooperative behaviour' (Berk 1994: 38).

Discussions on how to achieve maximum benefits from play situations in classrooms refer to the importance of the adults in facilitating and extending the play. Adequate adult–child ratios, smaller class sizes, uninterrupted blocks of time and a variety of resources are mentioned as important factors in the provision of quality play environments (Sylva *et al.* 1980; Hutt *et al.* 1989; Berk 1994).

In Australian junior grades the inclusion of play periods on a regular or daily basis has been an individual teacher or unit decision which varies from ample provision to tokenism. The loss of early-childhood specialists in early-years units, with the preferred employment of generalist teachers, has been one of the reasons for this variation. Play which is meaningful and productive requires highly skilled teachers who are able to judge the play situation and know when and how to be involved, and how to observe and record the event for future planning. Bennett (1992) found that many teachers in English infant schools failed to provide quality interactions with the children as they played because they saw their role as a facilitator and not as a 'scaffolder' of meaning for children.

Teachers in junior grades need to understand the nature of children's play and its potential for learning opportunities, as well as their role in this activity. Some schools use learning centres set up around the classroom to enable children to explore materials more freely and to focus on their particular interests. Outside play environments in some junior schools lack the diversity of materials, activities and interest areas that are a feature of pre-school outdoor environments, and which are used by pre-school teachers to achieve individual and group objectives. Providing extended play periods in classrooms can be difficult for teachers, who may face criticisms from parents and administrators. As one teacher commented during an in-service programme, 'the principal times the children when they are playing and says things like, "are they still playing?"' Comments like this undermine a teacher's decision-making and reveal mistakenly held views about the way young children learn – '*still* playing' misses the point that a child's engrossment is suggestive of at least a learning threshold.

Parents as partners with teachers

There has been a gradual recognition in Australia and overseas of the impact on children's learning when parents are acknowledged as influential in this process and then actively encouraged to work in partnership with teachers. The results from pre-kindergarten/Head Start programmes in America indicate that early intervention, including parent education and involvement, has positive, long-term gains, especially for vulnerable children (Schweinhart *et al.*1993; Marcon 1994).

The social construction of learning theory, cited in support of peer tutoring, underpins the influential role parents play in the child's learning and development. Studies involving infants show how parent/adult playful interactions with the infant stimulate a response which in turn keeps the parent/adult involved. These dynamic episodes provide real learning opportunities for the infant (Belsky *et al.* 1980). Early intervention programmes for 'at-risk' children focus on teaching parents how to initiate and sustain these types of interactions.

While empirical research evidence on the benefits of parent involvement in children's schooling is somewhat limited, there are strong theoretical models which support this practice (Powell 1989). Promoting and supporting parental partnerships is most important in the early years of school, when foundations are laid for the type and quality of the relationship which will continue as the child proceeds through the school. Gifford (1992) notes the many formal and informal ways parents and schools can collaborate and support each other:

- open-door policies;
- participation in curriculum programmes;
- home visits;
- regular parent–teacher interviews;
- social events;
- communication diaries;
- newsletters;
- joint policy development;
- before- and after-school programmes.

Throughout Australia there is an array of school-based programmes to further parent's understanding of child development, and to foster active and shared participation with children in their education. The Victorian Opening Doors project, for example, has established district parent-education coordinators to act as a liaison between parents and schools. In New South Wales the Parent as Teachers pilot project for new parents has been initiated by the Department of School Education to provide parent education prior to and after a child's birth, and to strengthen new parents' confidence in their ability to provide appropriate stimulation and expectations (Amm and Juan 1994). Most Australian states/territories have developed parent and literacy programmes in junior schools in recognition of the influential role parents play in a young child's emerging literacy development (Spreadbury 1995). Numeracy/mathematics parent–school programmes have also been introduced. Family Maths Project Australia (Fampa) and Home Maths (Homa) are two examples which have been used extensively in schools.

Several challenges face schools trying to encourage and support parental partnerships in education. These include:

- the increasingly diverse nature of family structures and backgrounds;
- the growing number of vulnerable or marginalised families;
- the high proportion of families where both parents are working.

From the parents' perspective, the barriers to full and active participation in their child's education include the considerable time, emotional and energy demands made on them through out-of-home employment, family crises such as divorce and child-rearing commitments. Additionally, teachers and parents may have beliefs and attitudes about education, based on personal experiences, which may alienate one from the other.

New Zealand researchers Parr *et al.* (1993) confirmed there were significant differences between teachers' and parents' views on what was meant by partnerships. Teachers and parents in this study did not see a role for parents in pedagogical and curriculum decision-making. The researchers' caution regarding the need for schools with families from diverse cultural backgrounds to address this issue as a child enters school is relevant for Australian junior schools. The cultural conflict which can result from misunderstandings could be avoided if collaboration on significant matters such as curriculum content was actively encouraged.

Teacher training

Throughout this chapter there has been continued reference to the importance of preparing teachers for the demands of working with young learners. This issue has not been fully addressed at a national level and there remains considerable opposition to the notion of the specialist teacher.

Gifford (1993) makes a strong case for specialist training in early-childhood studies for teachers wishing to work in the first years of school. However, across Australia there are different requirements. In Victoria, for example, early-childhood specialisation is not mandated, although there was recognition for the need to improve teachers' knowledge in this area in the *Ministerial Review of School Entry Age* (Department of School Education 1992). Generalist teachers are also employed in Queensland, Northern Territory, the Australian Capital Territory (ACT), New South Wales and Tasmania, although some states/territories (for example ACT) see early-childhood qualifications as desirable. Only South Australia and Western Australia generally employ teachers with an early-childhood specialisation in their pre-primary or junior grades.

Increasing recognition and support for strengthening the first years of schooling in Australia may provide the impetus to explore the notion of specialisation. Determining the exact nature of this specialisation raises many questions. Should the early-years specialisation become a strand within existing primary-teaching programmes or should it be a new degree? What should be the age focus for this specialisation: 0–8 years; 3–8 years; 5–8 years?

Conclusion

It is beyond the scope of this chapter to explore all the issues relating to the first years of schooling in Australia. There remain several other important matters.

One of the areas which requires further analysis and research is the optimum class size and teacher–child ratio for young learners. There has been a tendency in Australia to have higher teacher–student ratios in secondary schools than in primary schools, when it could be argued that, developmentally, the older students may cope with less adult supervision and support than can younger children. Victorian statistics show that teacher–child ratios have worsened over the past few years, from 15.8 students for every teacher in 1992, to a predicted 19.1 students for every teacher in 1996 (Painter 1994: 3).

Blatchford and Mortimore (1994), in their synthesis of research on class size undertaken in Britain and the United States, found evidence to support a reduction in class size for junior grades, especially when vulnerable or disadvantaged children are attending. The high cost of this provision is acknowledged; however, this is offset by the cost of later intensive interventions and remediation when children fail to achieve basic skill levels, which would also be considerable. Mainstreaming children with special or additional needs in the first years of school when class sizes are rising and support services are being reduced results in a classroom environment which may not be conducive to meeting these children's needs.

The nature of best-practice teaching and learning for children in their first years of schooling has received considerable attention by Australian education ministries; however, the recognition of teacher knowledge in this field and the provision of opportunities for this knowledge to be voiced and disseminated need to become a priority. Teachers reflecting on their own practice and researching in their own classrooms are essential components in the development of effective teaching strategies and environments.

Currently in Australia there are two movements shaping the curricula in the early years of school. On the one hand, there is international, national and state concern for the early years of schooling at both a research/theoretical and policy/systems level which reflects an awareness of these years for their intrinsic merit and uniqueness and the influence they will have on a child's subsequent school and life experiences. On the other hand, there are standardisation and accountability movements which frequently work against the understandings we have developed about the nature of young children and their learning. This polarisation of views results in considerable tension for school communities. Making educationally sound decisions in a system which is unsure of the direction it wants to take – uniformity versus diversity, content versus process, state regulation versus local determination – is not an easy task.

Children entering compulsory school systems in Australia today bring with them a more diverse range of family backgrounds and life experiences than previous generations. This diversity provides both challenges and opportunities for school communities. The challenges include the difficulty of determining the nature of a culturally relevant curriculum and how to address the pastoral-care needs of marginalised families. The diversity of backgrounds provides the opportunity to weave a richer tapestry of classroom life, as well as the chance for children to grow in tolerance and, indeed, to celebrate the differences they encounter.

Junior schools, because they provide a child's and a family's first encounter with the compulsory school system, have a key role to play in establishing the foundations for effective learning: children's confidence in their ability to learn and their enjoyment of learning, and supportive social contexts within the classroom and between home and school. School systems, school organisation and environments, and teachers' professionalism are the significant factors in ensuring that these strong foundations and bridges are established.

References

Allen, S. (1993) 'National curriculum: a parent perspective', *Australian Journal of Early Childhood* 18(4): 3–8.

Amm, R. and Juan, S. (1994) 'A parent education success story: the parents as teachers program in the US and Australia', *Australian Journal of Early Childhood* 19(2): 10–15.

Angus, M. (1991) 'Award restructuring: the new paradigm for school reform', *Unicorn* 17(2): 78–84.

Anning, A. (1991) *The First Years of School*, Milton Keynes: Open University Press.

—— (1994) 'Play and legislated curriculum. Back to basics: an alternative view', in J. Moyles (ed.) *The Excellence of Play*, Milton Keynes: Open University Press.

Australian Education Council (1990) *Mobile Students: A Guide for Schools*, Canberra: Australian Government Printer.

Belsky, J., Goode, M. and Most, R. (1980) 'Maternal stimulation and infant exploratory competence: cross sectional, correlational and experimental analyses', *Child Development* 51: 1168–1178.

Bennett, N. (1992) 'The quality of educational provision for 3–5 year olds in Britain', in J. Cullen and J. Williamson (eds) *The Early Years: Policy, Research and Practice*, West Perth: Meerilinga Young Children's Foundation.

Berk, L. (1994) 'Vygotsky's theory: the importance of make believe play', *Young Children* 59(1): 30–9.

Blatchford, P. and Mortimore, P. (1994) 'The issue of class size for young children in schools: what can we learn from research?', *Oxford Review of Education* 20(4): 411–28.

Board of Studies (1995) *Victorian Curriculum and Standards Framework*, Carlton, Victoria: Board of Studies.

Bredekamp, S. (ed.) (1987) *Developmentally Appropriate Practice in Early Childhood Programs Serving Children from Birth Through Age 8*, vol. 1, Washington, DC: National Association for the Education of Young Children.

Bredekamp, S. and Rosegrant, T. (1992) *Reaching Potentials: Appropriate Curriculum and Assessment for Young Children*, Washington, DC: National Association for the Education of Young Children.

Bruner, J. (1983) *Child's Talk: Learning to Use Language*, London: Oxford University Press.

Cahir, P. (1994) 'Standardised mass testing of eight year olds', *Every Child* 1 (spring): 16–17.

Comenius, J. (1657) *The Great Didactic*, Amsterdam: de Geer Family.

Davies, M. and North, J. (1990) 'School entrance: NSW kindergarten teachers' attitudes to changes in policy', *Australian Journal of Early Childhood* 15(2): 9–13.

de Lemos, M. M. (1988) 'Longterm effects of early school entry', *The Australian Educational and Developmental Psychologist* 5(1): 6–11.

de Lemos, M. and Mellor E. (1991) 'A study of the assessment of school readiness', summary report (photocopy), Monash University.

Department of School Education (1992) *Ministerial Review of School Entry Age in Victoria*, Melbourne: Department of School Education, Victoria.

Fleer, M. (1992) 'From Piaget to Vygotsky: moving into a new era of early childhood education', in B. Lambert (ed.) *Changing Faces: The Early Childhood Profession in Australia*, Watson, ACT: Australian Early Childhood Association.

Fogelman, K. and Gorbach, P. (1978) 'Age of starting school and attainment at 11', *Educational Research* 21(1): 65–6.

Fowell, N. and Lawton, J. (1992) 'An alternate view of appropriate practice in early childhood education', *Early Childhood Research Quarterly* 7: 53–73.

Froebel, F. (1903) *The Education of Man*, New York: Appleton–Century–Crofts.

Gardner, H. (1995) 'Time to talk turkey', *Education Quarterly* 3 (spring): 23–5.

—— (1993) *Early Childhood Education: What Future?*, Occasional Paper No. 21, Curtin, ACT: Australian College of Education.

Government of Western Australia (1993) *Voluntary Full-time Pre-primary Education in Western Australia: A Report*, Perth: Government of Western Australia.

Griffin, M. and Harvey, D. (1995) 'When do principals and teachers think children should start school?', *Australian Journal of Early Childhood* 20(3): 27–32.

Halliwell, G. (1993) 'Will national curriculum statements and profiles replace "child study" with "assessment"?', *Australian Journal of Early Childhood* 18(4): 9–15.

Hutt, S. I., Tyler, S., Hutt, C. and Christopherson, H. (1989) *A Natural History of the Preschool: Exploration, Play and Learning,* London: Routledge.

Kessler, S. (1991) 'Alternative perspectives on early childhood education', *Early Childhood Research Quarterly* 6(2): 183–97.

Malaguzzi, L. (1993) 'History, ideas and basic philosophy: an interview with Lella Gandini', in C. Edwards, L. Gandini and G. Forman (eds) *The Hundred Languages of Children: The Reggio Emilia Approach to Early Childhood Education*, Norwood, NJ: AblexPub.

Marcon, R. (1994) 'Doing the right thing for children: linking research and policy reform in the District of Columbia public schools', *Young Children* 50(1): 8–20.

Meisels, S. J. (1992) 'Doing harm by doing good: iatrogenic effects of early childhood enrolment and promotion policies', *Early Childhood Research Quarterly* 7(2): 155–74.

Mellor, E. (1991) 'Improving transition from preschool to primary school: a matter of principle as well as practice', *Unicorn* 17(4): 216–20.

Munro, J. (1995) 'Teaching is lagging behind the learning', *The Age*, 18 March: 8.

National Association for the Education of Young Children (1990) 'Position statement on school readiness', *Young Children* 41(1): 21–3.

Painter, J. (1994) 'Victoria's student–teacher ratio on the increase', *The Age*, 25 July: 3.

Parr, J., McNaughton, S., Timperley, H. and Robinson, V. (1993) 'Bridging the gap: practices of collaboration between home and the junior school', *Australian Journal of Early Childhood* 18(3): 35–42.

Pavan, B. (1992) 'The benefits of nongraded schools', *Educational Leadership* 50(2): 22–5.

Pestalozzi, J. (1898) *How Gertrude Teaches Her Children* (no publishing details).

Powell, D. R. (1989) *Families and Early Childhood Programs*, Washington, DC: National Association for the Education of Young Children.

Powell, D. R. and Sigel, I. E. (1991) 'Searches for validity in evaluating young children and early childhood programs', in B. Spodek and O. Saracho (eds) *Issues in Early Childhood Curriculum*, New York: Teachers' College Press.

Proctor, T. B., Black, K. N. and Feldhussen, J. F. (1986) 'Early admission of selected children to elementary school: a review of the research literature', *Journal of Educational Research* 80(2): 70–6.

Schools Council (1992a) *Developing Flexible Strategies in the Early Years of Schooling: Purposes and Possibilities*, Canberra: Australian Government Printer.

—— (1992b) *A Snapshot of the Early Years of Schooling*, Canberra: Australian Government Printer.

—— (1992c) *A Stitch in Time: Strengthening the First Years of School*, Canberra: Australian Government Printer.

Schweinhart, L., Barnes, H. and Weikart, D. (1993) *Significant Results: The High/Scope Study Through The Age 27*, Ypsilanti, MI: High Scope Press.

Shepard, L. and Smith, M. (1986) 'Synthesis of research on school readiness and kindergarten retention', *Educational Leadership* 44(3): 78–86.

—— (1988) 'Escalating academic demand in kindergarten: some nonsolutions', *Elementary School Journal* 89(2): 135–46.

Slavin, R., Karweit, N. and Wasik, B. (1993) 'Preventing early school failure: what works?', *Educational Leadership* 50(4): 10–18.

Smith, P. (1994) 'Play and the uses of play', in J. Moyles (ed.) *The Excellence of Play*, Milton Keynes: Open University Press.

Spodek, B. (1991) 'Early childhood curriculum and cultural defintions of knowledge', in B. Spodek and O. Saracho (eds) *Issues in Early Childhood Curriculum*, New York: Teachers' College Press.

Spreadbury, J. (1995) 'Why parents read to children', *Australian Journal of Early Childhood* 20(1): 1–6.

Stevens, J., Hough, R. and Nurss, J. (1993) 'The influence of parents on children's development and education', in B. Spodek (ed.) *Handbook of Research on the Education of Young Children*, New York: Macmillan.

Surbeck, E. (1992) 'Multi-age programs in primary grades: are they educationally appropriate', *Childhood Education*, fall: 3–7.

Sylva, K. (1994) 'The impact of early learning on children's later development', in C. Ball (ed.) *Start Right: The Importance of Early Learning*, Royal Society of Arts, Manufacturing and Commerce, London.

Sylva, K., Roy, C. and Painter, M. (1980) *Child Watching at Playgroup and Nursery School*, London: Grant McIntyre.

Tasmanian Department of Education and Arts (1989) *Review of Early Childhood Education*, Hobart: Tasmanian Department of Education and Arts.

Turney, C. (ed.) (1975) *Sources in the History of Australian Education: A Book of Readings*, Sydney: Angus & Robertson.

Vygotsky, L. (1962) *Thought and Language*, New York: MIT Press.

6

BUILDING A SCHOOL CULTURE

John Williamson and Maurice Galton

What is a school culture?

A visitor from the northern hemisphere making a whirlwind tour through countries on and near the Pacific rim, from Myanmar to Japan and then on to Australia, would, if he or she ventured into schools, find much that was familiar but also much that was strange and puzzling. At primary level, in particular, there would be variations in the size of schools and of classes. Many schools in Australia, particularly those in rural settings, have fewer than fifty pupils. In Singapore over 2,000 pupils would be the norm, with classes of over forty pupils. Generally these pupils sit in rows facing the teacher, while in Australia the room arrangement follows the pattern of English and American schools, with groups of boys and girls sitting around tables or desks pushed together (Williamson and Fraser 1991). In countries with large schools, classes are streamed by ability. Elsewhere, setting for certain subjects such as mathematics and language is more typical. Much more common is the trend for one teacher to cover the whole curriculum apart from some specialist areas such as music and physical education.

However, if our visitor probes below these structural features he or she will begin to identify more subtle variations in the way each classroom operates. Most important is the nature of the relationship between the teacher and the pupils. Do pupils view their teacher as 'the fountain of all knowledge', a policeman, a facilitator, or a nursemaid? Does the teacher regard the class as friends, empty vessels which need filling, tender plants needing nurturing or a rabble which needs careful watching if it is not to gain the upper hand. Such perceptions will manifest themselves in the way question-and-answer sessions are conducted, the form of classroom control exercised, the system of rewards and punishments, and the degree to which pupils exercise choice over their learning. This is often referred to as the *classroom ethos* (Rutter *et al.* 1979) or, more narrowly, the *classroom climate* (Halpin and Croft 1962).

Part of this classroom ethos or climate derives from the structural features described earlier. Empty vessels tend to sit in rows, and to answer questions put to them by the teacher rather than ask them. Tender plants will be encouraged to seek support from their peers, will exercise a degree of autonomy over what they learn and will be more likely to be praised than criticised. These teacher behaviours, however, will also stem, in part, from the individuals' personal belief-systems, their view of themselves and their openness to other people's ideas.

It is this interplay between ideas and structure which creates the life of the primary school and its classrooms – what we term its culture. In this we follow Raymond Williams's definition of culture as depicting 'a way of life' of any group, be it a nation or a profession or 'the way we do things around here' (Williams 1963). Others such as Robin Alexander describe the primary-school culture in terms of its beliefs, concerns and distinctive language (Alexander 1992). This view, from the UK, is similar to that described in the US by Deal and Kennedy (1982). At this level the idea of culture appears, therefore, to be similar in different English-speaking countries.

Alexander argues that there is an 'inescapable relationship' between ideas and structure within a culture since:

> they do not exist independently of each other. Ideas generate structures; but structures also generate ideas in order to explain and sustain structures. In conjunction, ideas and structure secure collective cohesion and continuity, and confer identity and security on the individual.
>
> (Alexander 1992: 171)

This picture of culture as reflecting tangible and intangible elements is summarised in the description of culture 'as the shared philosophies, ideologies, values, assumptions, beliefs, expectations, attitudes, and norms that knit a community together' (Kilmann *et al.* 1985). The power of the culture to shape behaviour, however, should not be underestimated. Sarason described the relationship between the thinking and actual behaviour in the situation as follows: 'The problem [of change] inheres in the fact that history and tradition have given rise to roles and relationships, to interlocking ideas, practices, values, and expectations that are the "givens" not requiring thought or deliberation' (Sarason 1971: 227). Thus a culture not only serves to identify but also to 'define, justify and control' its members (Alexander 1992: 169). This is because as ideas, beliefs and values become identified with the group rather than the constituent individuals, as a manifestation of its cultural identity, they provide the ideological basis for action. In order to demonstrate membership of the cultural group an individual is forced to enact the ideology, chiefly because the system of rewards, promotions, etc. is likely to be dependent on such demonstrations of 'cultural purity'. Hargreaves

(1992) supports this view in making a distinction between the *content* of a culture and its *form*. The former he defines as the system of shared beliefs within, in this case, the teacher community. The latter he describes as 'the pattern of relationships and forms of association between members of the culture' (*ibid.*: 219). It is these cultural forms which are most resistant to change.

Recognising the complex nature of this interplay between structure and ideas is crucial to any understanding of the process of curriculum change. Too often in recent years politicians and administrators have sought to change educational structures in the expectation that school improvement would follow through a shift in teaching strategies. In most cases, however, teachers adopt the least line of resistance and 'bolt' the innovation on to their existing practice. This appears to have happened in the United Kingdom with the national curriculum (Pollard *et al.* 1993; Galton *et al.* 1995) and in Australia (Williamson and Fraser 1991). Many studies by the Council of Europe (CDCC 1982, 1987) and by the Organization for Economic Cooperation and Development (OECD) confirm a similar trend (OECD 1974, 1982, 1990). The picture of national innovation is similar to attempts at school level to enact change. But before going on to consider the strategies most frequently used by school principals when seeking to innovate, we shall briefly look at some aspects of primary-school culture that seem to encourage teachers' resistance to change.

Manifestations of the primary-school culture

In most countries, primary schooling, as it exists today, grew from the need to provide mass education to a standard that allowed for the shift away from an agrarian to an industrialised economy. In its minimalist form, this elementary education required pupils to be able to read, write and count. Although, during the course of the twentieth century, standards have been continually raised in meeting technological advances and concomitant societal expectations, this elementary tradition remains strong. Even in developed countries, the bulk of curriculum time is still given over to these 'core' activities, which nearly always take place at the beginning of the school day when pupils are believed to be most attentive. Those responsible for early developments in mass primary education saw the teaching of language, in particular, as the key which opened up the cultural inheritance, in the sense that the term was used by Matthew Arnold in *Culture and Anarchy* to represent all that was known to be best in our civilisation. Arnold's argument for inducting as many citizens as possible into this culture was that only through the experience gained from the study of the achievements of past societies could people be persuaded to turn away from the path of revolution as the solution to the grave social problems that had arisen as the result of industrialism. The view, as it developed, had important implications for pedagogy in that it presupposed a 'transmission' model of teaching and a belief in the power of the educated mind to make decisions on behalf of individuals whose education mainly consisted of acquiring practical knowledge and skills. This led, very early on, to the creation of different types of schools and a search for ways of selecting each child for the education to which he or she was best fitted.

Industrialism, however, also brought about a reaction which sought to retain the perceived benefits of the agrarian way of life, particularly the feelings and emotions resulting from close contact with natural surroundings. A crucial period in developing this awareness of nature was seen to be early childhood, perceived as an age of innocence. From this approach has flowed what Blyth (1989) has termed the developmental tradition in primary education, giving rise to various stage theories of learning and culminating in the child-centred approaches which, in different countries, have been grouped within labels such as, 'progressive', 'informal' and 'open education'. Central concepts within these approaches have been 'learning through doing', 'readiness', and a view of knowledge as 'integrated and personally constructed' rather than as a collection of distinct disciplines consisting of universally agreed bodies of knowledge.

But as Kliebard (1986) notes in his study of *The Struggle for the American Curriculum*, ideas, as they trickle down into the classroom, rarely retain their pure form. Partly because, as we have already seen, teachers tend to 'bolt' innovation on to existing practice, and partly because many classroom decisions are driven by pragmatism rather than theory, as a 'coping' response to immediate problems, a new set of ideas tends to get mixed up with existing ones. Kliebard refers to this mixing process as one of *hybridisation*, which frequently results in a gap between 'rhetoric' and 'reality'. Thus numerous studies of primary teaching in Australia, the UK and elsewhere have found that, often, those teachers who claim to believe in experiential learning as part of a child-centred philosophy nevertheless spend considerable amounts of time teaching didactically, albeit in a classroom environment which emphasises individual learning (Galton 1989; Williamson and Fraser 1991).

Curriculum hybridisation therefore serves to reinforce the common public perception of primary teaching, since the outwardly shared set of beliefs, often perceived as self-evident truths, creates a barrier which prevents too close an inspection of the disjunction between an individual teacher's aims and his or her practice. Alexander (1984) notes, for example, that research evidence is often reinterpreted to match the ideological perspective and that those who challenge such views are accused of damaging teacher morale. Instead, critics are urged to celebrate what is good rather than dwell on weaknesses. It is for this reason that Hargreaves argues that:

> physically, teachers are often alone in their own classrooms, with no other adults for company. Psychologically, they never are: what they do, their classroom styles and strategies – is powerfully affected by

the orientations of the colleagues with whom they work now and
have done in the past.

(Hargreaves 1992: 217)

The above analysis accounts for the strong resistance to change among
primary teachers which has caused one commentator to describe the profession as characterised by *'presentism'*, *conservatism* and *individualism* (Lortie
1975). Teachers prefer to concentrate on short-term planning in their own
classrooms, where their efforts can be seen to bring immediate results (*presentism*); avoid discussing fundamental issues concerning teaching and learning,
for fear it might raise fundamental questions about their practice (*conservatism*); and shy away from forms of collaboration with colleagues, such as
team teaching (*individualism*). For all these reasons, it would seem that
schools, like living cells, seem largely impervious to outside pressures to
change well-established existing practices. As a result, more and more
emphasis has been placed on the school leader as the major change agent.
This is particularly true of post-industrial societies, where there are many
more conflicting ideologies offering competing rationales for curriculum-
building. School leaders now face demands from a variety of sources that
their pupils should be educated for 'employment', 'life', 'self-development'
and 'leisure', to name but a few possibilities. In many countries this trend of
emphasising the key role of the school principal in managing innovation has
led to increasing the degree to which resources are devolved directly to
schools through local management schemes. Principals are no longer just
managers of the curriculum and people, but now act as financial controllers
and public relations executives (Caldwell and Spinks 1992). It is in this
context that we now turn to the styles of leadership most frequently found in
primary schools and consider the capacity of each style to innovate successfully in ways which bring about fundamental changes in a school's culture.

Contemporary styles of primary-school management

Primary schools, for reasons we have set out in earlier sections, give an
outward appearance of operating within a culture of collaboration. Unlike
secondary schools, they have no separate departments with distinct identities
and competing agendas. In most secondary schools, for example, science staff
will often prefer to have their own tea and coffee facilities in the laboratory
preparatory room, rather than join arts colleagues in the staff room at break
times. Human movement staff rarely appear in anything but tracksuits and
pride themselves on being able to keep even the most disruptive pupils under
firm control. In most primary schools this degree of compartmentalisation is
rare and schools tend to be characterised by a network of informal communication structures. For example, much information in the primary school is
exchanged at break and lunch times rather than during formal staff meetings.

Alexander refers to the mechanism by which these informal structures operate as 'familial complementarity' (Alexander 1984: 167).

Within this approach the principal acts as head of the family, and decision-making operates by means of establishing *consensus* whenever possible. Discussion takes place in much the same way as between adult members of a family when important issues arise. The process is often an extended one since all points of view have to be considered. The approach operates on the principle that when staff feel a sense of 'ownership' in a collective decision they will be more strongly committed to its subsequent implementation.

In practice, it is doubtful that a true consensus is often established. As Alexander (1984) notes, the power and responsibility of the principal often mean that all viewpoints do not carry equal weight. Often staff feel manipulated and can be heard to say things like: 'We spent all that time discussing things only to end up doing what the principal wanted to do anyway.'

Furthermore, consensus – when it is established – is often couched in words which are interpretable in more than one way or are sufficiently broad to gain general assent. As a result, the danger of open conflict breaking out between staff because of different beliefs, values, and so on is avoided. All teachers can sign up to a statement which promises to educate all children in the school according to 'their needs' rather than 'their abilities' to ensure that they reach 'their fullest potential'. Just what this means in practice within the classroom will rarely, if ever, be explored. Galton has referred to this consensus approach as 'the common market model' (Galton 1989). In the same way, government ministers in the European Union meet together, draw up agreements after prolonged discussion, in ways which allow countries with vested interests to interpret the rules so that they can continue to operate as before. In Australia a similar situation can be found in such bodies as the Asia Pacific Economic Consortium (APEC), which recently released a consensus report on trade between Asia-Pacific countries after several days of meeting.

There are two further practical constraints that render this model ineffective: increased curriculum demands and the corresponding time pressures that result from them. In recent years, nearly every country involved in the transition from an industrial to a post-industrial society has engaged in large-scale 'top-down' curriculum development in which governments have required schools to meet certain statutory requirements concerning curriculum coverage and learning targets. In Australia the National Statements and Curriculum Profiles produced by the Australian Education Council (AEC) have produced a statement and a profile in each of the eight key learning areas: English, mathematics, science, technology, languages other than English (LOTE), health and physical education, studies of society and environment, and the arts. The statements provide a framework for curriculum development by education systems and schools. But these are not understood by teachers, as indicated by a South Australian teacher:

There's nothing to say, 'Well this is how you go about doing it'. Nobody really knows yet exactly what the uses will be and I think that's probably what is scaring people – it makes it very difficult to get implementation because you get blockers thinking, 'Oh, they are going to use this against us if a student hasn't achieved to a certain level'.

In the UK teachers are now required to follow specific programmes of study in three core (English, mathematics and science) and four foundation subjects (history, geography, art and physical education). In this situation it makes sense for the school principal to delegate responsibility for curriculum development to experienced teachers with expertise in a particular subject. These subject coordinators then take responsibility for a team of other teachers representing different stages (e.g. early years). Subject coordinators then meet with the principal from time to time, together with other staff responsible for areas such as special needs. Campbell (1993) has labelled this approach *managerialism*, since it smacks of the corporate management approach, with the principal acting as chief executive of a senior team.

There are a number of obvious disadvantages to this approach. First, it cuts across the 'familial complementarity' which is an long established element of primary-school culture. As a result, some teachers who are not part of the key decision-making process may become resistant to attempts by the subject coordinator to influence practice. Alexander (1992), in his study of primary education in the city of Leeds, describes a situation where some teachers obstructed colleagues efforts to work with them collaboratively through team teaching. Furthermore, these subject structures, similar to those operating in secondary schools, give rise to similar tensions. Hargreaves (1992: 223) refers to this trend as *balkanization*. Teachers begin to attach their loyalties to and to identify with a particular group of colleagues with whom they work most closely. The existence of these groups can denote different outlooks on teaching and learning so that agreed whole-school policies are difficult to secure. Even before the advent of recent curriculum reform, teachers with special responsibility for children with learning difficulties tended to experience this isolation. More recently, as Hargreaves (1992) and Campbell (1993) argue, the effect is spreading across the curriculum and between teachers of early (5–7 years) and later (7–11 years) years.

Perhaps more damaging is the effect of managerialism on the principal's role as the main change agent. A study by Churchill *et al.* (1995) looked at primary teachers in Tasmania and South Australia. The teachers described an acceptance of inevitable change over which they had little control. In turn, this gave rise to feelings of nostalgia for the past, a sense of survival and coping and considerable feelings of cynicism about the real reasons for the innovation. Typical of the reaction was the following comment:

I just want to be a teacher for a while. Just leave me and the children alone for a while: let us be comfortable. We have been trying so hard over the last five years we really haven't let anything settle. Sometime, somewhere, they have got to stop banging the side of the chookshed [chicken coop].

Recent studies in the UK, for example by Webb (1993), reveal that many primary-school principals have a very poor understanding of the new curriculum, having delegated its management to subject coordinators. As non-teaching executives they have become preoccupied with financial administration and public relations under a 'market forces' system where schools compete against each other for pupils from inside and outside their natural catchment area. In contrast, Galton *et al.* (1995) found that principals of small rural primary schools who retained a two-thirds teaching commitment were very familiar with the new curriculum and continued to take an active lead in promoting change at classroom level. Williamson and Cowley (1995) found a similar result when they surveyed maths, science and technology education innovation in a number of Tasmanian schools; that is, in those schools where the principal stayed involved as a participant in the innovation he or she was perceived as exercising a change-agent role at the classroom level.

The third favoured strategy for the management of change is often termed *collegial* and is based on a culture of collaboration. Instead of promoting the false sense of agreement often observed with the consensus approach, the principal acknowledges the power that derives from the office. The approach is therefore one of offering teachers opportunities to partake in decision-making within a clearly defined framework. According to Nias *et al.* (1989), in such a culture of collaboration an individual teacher's weaknesses are not overlooked but shared and discussed with colleagues. Trust and openness operate on a routine moment-by-moment, day-by-day basis. Collaborative or collegial cultures require broad agreement on values but also openly tolerate disagreement and, in part, encourage it within certain limits. Hargreaves argues that, 'like good marriages', such relationships have to be worked at, and he concludes:

Leadership is important here – particularly leadership through example; through frequent praise; through helpful, personal notes placed in staff mailboxes; through indulging their staff with little treats like cakes or flowers which show caring and thoughtfulness; and through principals having high visibility around the school, revealing an interest in what is going on and pleasure in making contact with students and teachers alike.

(Hargreaves 1992: 227)

127

It would appear, however, that collegiality of this kind is fairly rare and is becoming even rarer against the external demands for greater accountability. In the UK, certain forms of school inspection and statutory publication of examination results – designed to compare one school against another – tend to mean that collaborative activity concentrates on short-term goals to the exclusion of long-term planning. When this happens, a form of *contrived collegiality* ensues. It is characterised, according to Hargreaves, by a set of bureaucratic procedures to increase the attention being paid to joint teacher planning and consultation (Hargreaves 1992: 229). It can be recognised by such features as the initiation of formal mentoring schemes, demands for clear job descriptions and compulsory training programmes.

While Hargreaves concedes that certain aspects of these contrived forms of collaboration can be a prelude to the richer form of collegiality which he advocates, he is pessimistic that this transition can be negotiated within the current climate of 'legal statute or administrative contrivance' (Hargreaves 1992: 217). For example, minuting meetings of subject coordinators so that they are available to other ad hoc working parties not only adds to the work-load but, more importantly, appears to deny the value of the more informal kinds of collaboration that already exist. Furthermore, space for such meet-ings is usually taken out of those times when the culture of collaboration is developed through the 'acceptance and intermixture of personal lives with professional ones' (Nias *et al.* 1989). Thus the informal exchanges at tea and lunch breaks – consisting of humorous accounts of a classroom incident or a helpful comment from a teacher who had the same problem with the class in a previous year – become more infrequent as colleagues grab a sandwich and rush off to yet another planning meeting. It seems clear that Hargreaves is arguing that arrangements of this kind, while appearing on the surface to foster a spirit of collaboration, can rapidly develop into what we have termed managerialism.

The limitations of contemporary management styles

Although the authors have some sympathy for Hargreaves's argument, we also wish to express a number of reservations about his enthusiastic endorse-ment of the approach described by Nias *et al.* (1989). First, as he observes, the number of schools displaying the qualities of informal collaboration that are the mark of true collegiality seems to be remarkably small. We think this situ-ation is not accidental, but structural, and that it arises because of the lack of explanations within the culture of teaching concerning how teachers learn to teach or, more importantly, how experienced teachers learn to teach better. Faced with an example of expert teaching, colleagues do not shy away from imitation because of 'presentism', conservatism and individualism, as Lortie (1975) argues, but because they lack confidence as they believe that it is the expert's superior personal characteristics rather than any specific pedagogic action that determine success. We will argue later in the chapter that a clear theory of teacher development coupled with an understanding of how children learn is an essential feature of any management strategy designed to change the culture of teaching within the primary school. Here, however, we wish to observe that this view is at variance with one of the central principles of the collegial model and, indeed, all the other approaches discussed so far. This principle is that a central feature of the culture of teaching concerns the autonomy of the individual to decide the best way to teach for a particular outcome. Put simply, there is widespread acceptance that there is more than one way to achieve any particular learning outcome and that each teacher should be free, within very wide limits, to choose the method with which he or she feels most comfortable. Such limits might include a ban on streaming or ability grouping but they would certainly not restrict the choice of a teacher's use of individualisation, despite the overwhelming research evidence concerning its disadvantages for teaching certain outcomes involving mathematical computation, formal grammar and reading (Brophy and Good 1986).

The autonomy of the classroom teacher to decide on matters of pedagogy is an essential part of the collegial approach; although, as Hargreaves observes, this approach requires 'broad agreement on educational values, [it] also tolerate[s] disagreement and to some extent actively encourage it within those limits' (Hargreaves 1992: 226). In different ways, both the consensus and managerial models of school leadership also adhere to this principle of the teacher's autonomy on pedagogic matters. In both these approaches there is an assumption that what Fullan and Hargreaves (1992) label the 'if-then' approach to innovation operates, namely that if the correct structures are put in place, then those processes which follow logically from adopting such structures will be incorporated into classroom practice. Thus a school-development plan which highlights the value of collaboration is believed to lead, self-evidently, to an increase in the use of cooperative group work in the classroom. However, in the consensus model the definition of group work is not explored, so that some teachers interpret this as sitting in groups but working individually on the same task, while others see it as a licence to sit pupils at particular tables by ability. In managerial settings the debate, if it takes place at all, is likely to lead to balkanisation as different interest groups argue about the value of group work, so that no overall whole-school strategy is likely to emerge. Fullan and Hargreaves also note that 'if-then' approaches often change to 'if-only' ones, where innovators look for sources outside their own control to account for failed implementation (*ibid.*). For example, administrators tend to blame those responsible for teacher training for the failure to shift classroom practice, wrongly arguing that trainers concentrate on theory rather than offering practical advice. Galton (1995) has described this process in relation to the implementation of the English national curriculum and has argued that subsequent policy decisions, based on this false 'if-only' premise, have led to a crisis in primary teaching.

Hargreaves (1992), however, seems to have ignored his own analysis in moving to the argument that if only curriculum innovation was not imposed by legal statute, and if only administrative frameworks of accountability were not in place, true collegiality could flourish and the culture of teaching would change. We doubt this conclusion, not only because of the general neglect of pedagogy within the culture of teaching, but also because as more and more countries shift to post-industrial economies the demand for national curriculum frameworks with their associated targeted assessment schemes is more likely to increase, as will the demand for schools to develop bureaucratic quality-assurance procedures. Indeed, elsewhere, when arguing that such developments are inevitable, Fullan advises school principals that 'it is no use waiting around for things to get better – they won't' (Fullan 1992).

The task of the school principal is therefore to manage collegiality within a framework of public accountability in ways which have a consistent and coherent impact at classroom level throughout the whole school. We believe that at the centre of this approach, which we term *consequential collegiality*, should be a theory of pedagogy, that which Gage (1981) defined as the science of the art of teaching. Furthermore, we believe that there now exists a reasonable body of research, some based upon theoretical studies, some on empirical observation and some on analysis of expert teacher's craft knowledge, which provides a base for this scientific approach. In the remaining parts of this chapter we indicate the main strands of this theory and then go on to describe how such knowledge should be incorporated into a principal's collaborative strategy for engineering a change in the culture of teaching.

The need to know how young children learn to think

Over the last thirty years or so there have been persistent calls for schools and teachers to help students learn to think more critically, construct and solve problems, synthesise information and become independent lifelong learners. The force of exhortations such as these varies with school level, but it is possible to see them having an influence in the primary school. In Australia in the 1960s the influence of Piaget was evident and his theory began to displace the more behaviourist explanations of children's learning. In part this was because teachers saw in Piaget's work better explanations for such classroom activities as 'self-directed problem-solving'. Over time the influence of Piaget began to wane, as researchers became more critical of his methodology and some of his findings – particularly his downplaying of the importance of language and the social situation in learning (Meadows 1993). The assumption that children actively 'construct' their learning, a key feature in Piaget's theory, is still widely accepted (Resnick 1987).

The history of the wax and wane of the influence of Piaget's theory is instructive for those in education. Read at a particularly narrow level, some teachers took the theory to be saying that teaching was dependent upon an appropriate stage in the child's development having been reached: 'the child's own existing understanding, based on his commerce with nature, is an appropriate state of readiness for change' (Wood 1988: 16). This very restricted view of readiness led to a lack of interest in pedagogy, as it allowed children's failure to learn to be attributed to a stage of development rather than to teaching methods.

Recent work in information processing (Pintrich *et al.* 1993; Nuthall, 1997; Putnam and Borko, in press) has emphasised the importance of student mediation of learning, including the role of 'classroom contextual factors' and the student's 'motivational beliefs' as major contributors to their 'level of engagement and willingness to persist at a task' (Pintrich *et al.* 1993: 167). An approach such as this implies a goal of 'teaching for understanding' where teachers are focused on student learning and outcomes. In the classroom they 'scaffold' knowledge in a way, to assist understanding and also to provide the skills for increasing independent learning. The notion of 'scaffolding' is an important one as it enables us to understand how for 'an individual child [there is a gap] between what he is able to do alone and what he can achieve with help from one more knowledgeable and skilled than himself' (Wood 1988: 25). The role of the teacher is to assist in the change from *other regulation* (by a peer or adult) to *self-regulation* (Brown and Palincsar 1986).

What does this mean for the principal?

In the 1990s the fields of 'teaching for understanding' and 'subject-matter learning' can be seen to be drawing together. There is general agreement about a number of issues: that knowledge is constructed; that knowledge networks are structured around powerful ideas; that prior knowledge influences how students integrate new knowledge; that knowledge structures and concepts are changeable; that knowledge is socially constructed; that learning is facilitated when it is tied to the real world; and that teachers should progressively transfer responsibility for managing learning from themselves to the learner (Good and Brophy 1994). While the principal needs to work with his or her staff to promote teaching for understanding within a constructivist perspective, it is obviously a very time-consuming task to do this classroom by classroom. How might the principal and teacher gain insights more quickly into what is happening in the classrooms? Williamson and Cowley (1995) investigated science, maths and technology education curricula innovation at the primary and secondary levels. In this project not only were there interviews, questionnaires and document analysis, but use was also made of student journals. In each of the three curricula areas a simple journal format was developed for use by the student. Following a typical primary-school science lesson five questions were asked in the journal. For example: what did you learn or do today in science? (Answer: study and build a volcano; investigate the workings of an ant colony.) What were the links between what you learned today in science and other subjects you have studied? (Answer: designing a bridge in technology; colours in art; energy in physical education.) Some of the students' comments were:

- 'It was good because we got to do our own thing – we don't get to do our own thing in other classes' (Grade 7).
- 'I liked setting up the apparatus and doing the actual experiment as it is interesting' (Grade 4).
- 'We measured ourself and two of our friends that told us our weight and height and it was fun' (Grade 4).
- 'We had a lot of freedom because it was our ideas for the experiment, not no one else's' (Grade 7).

The richness of the data from the classrooms these students were in provides insights into the teaching–learning process, the nature of the teacher–student and the student–student interaction. The data allow the principal to have insights into the educational life in the classroom. From this practically grounded classroom data the principal can build what we call *consequential collegiality*.This is a complex procedure and involves several phases.

Understanding teacher development

A visitor to a number of classrooms, after a time, will observe that the teachers are operating in different ways and at different levels. These differences have been referred to as teacher expertise (Berliner *et al.* 1988; Berliner 1994). Berliner (1994) outlined five specific stages in the development of a teacher from what he termed, 'novice' to 'expert'. These are:

1 Novice level (deliberate).
2 Advanced beginner level (insightful).
3 Competent level (rational).
4 Proficient level (intuitive).
5 Expert level (arational).

Berliner does not assert that teachers move through these in linear fashion or that experience equates to expertise.

Berliner (1994) postulates twelve behaviours displayed by an expert teacher. These include:

- Experts excel mainly in their own domain and in particular contexts.

132

- Experts often develop automaticity for the repetitive operations that are needed to complete the task.
- Experts are more sensitive to the social situation and task demands when solving problems.
- Experts are more flexible and opportunistic in their teaching.
- Experts perceive meaningful patterns in their domain of experience.
- Experts attend to the atypical or unique events in their domain.

Williamson (1994) refers to the behaviour of these more skilled practitioners as 'quality teaching'. Based on data from a thirteen-country study for the OECD, Williamson proposed five dimensions of quality teaching. These dimensions were content knowledge, pedagogic skills, reflection, empathy and classroom management. Table 6.1 shows how these propositions and dimensions interact.

Our argument, as outlined above, is that the culture of the school – at the macro-level – will only be changed when there is a change in pedagogy, student–teacher relationships, and so on at the classroom, or micro-, level. To facilitate this change the principal must acknowledge the strengths and weaknesses of his or her staff, and work to match the training and professional needs of the teachers to their present stage of development. The goal, in short, is to work with the teachers to help them move along the continuum from novice to competent or expert practitioner. How might this be done? Consider an example where the principal has a relatively new member of staff at Berliner's (1994) competent level. Using data gathered from the classroom by either the teacher or the students, the principal or another mentor can develop, in true collegial manner, any of the five dimensions described by Williamson (1994). So, for example, if the teacher and the principal were working together to change teaching strategies from fairly direct or teacher focused to more activity or learner focused, then use of

Table 6.1 Interaction between Berliner's (1994) twelve propositions of teacher expertise and Williamson's (1994) five dimensions of teacher quality

Williamson's dimensions	i	ii	iii	iv	v	vi	vii	viii	ix	x	xi	xii
						Berliner's propositions						
Content knowledge	X				X	X	X					X
Pedagogic skill		X		X		X		X				X
Reflection						X	X	X	X	X	X	
Empathy			X					X				
Classroom management		X				X						X

133

classroom data would allow the positive benefits of consequential collegiality to be enjoyed, rather than the typical managerial or contrived
collegiality approaches so evident today.

Consequential collegiality: short term and long term

The shift in thinking and in approach required to adopt a consequential
collegiality mode of operating is significant. It requires not only recognition
of the simplistic nature of the use of external criteria such as school logos
and mobiles outlining the seven characteristics of leadership in the staff
room, but also an understanding that change must be internal to the teacher
and to his or her own classroom. Yet unless this shift happens widespread
teacher concerns about managerialism and contrived collegiality will
continue to grow and, with them, teacher negativity and cynicism. The
approach to consequential collegiality described above accepts that the principal and the school staff work within a long-term framework. There is the
opportunity to develop a plan of action which is realistic for both the
teacher and the expectation of change.

In some situations this extended time-frame is not necessary as other
factors intervene. For example, if there is a large turnover of staff because of
a particular transfer policy the principal can combine this approach with
one which is better able to select staff for the school on the basis of their
existing commitment to a preferred culture.

Teachers' perceptions of change in Australia

In recent years a number of studies have sought to assess the impact of
curriculum change on Australian teachers (Churchill et al. 1995; Williamson
and Cowley 1995). Churchill reports that most teachers in his sample, drawn
from elementary teachers in Tasmania and South Australia, accepted the
inevitability of change over which they felt they had little control. This gave rise
to feelings of nostalgia for the past, a sense of survival and coping and considerable feelings of cynicism about the real reasons for the innovation. Typical of
the reaction was the comment of one South Australian teacher:

> They are either only about saving money or they jump onto the
> latest jargon-led bandwagon. I wish that they would truly believe in
> the principle of providing quality education.

There was also evidence of the growth of practices resulting in managerialism:

> I spend too much time hassling with the paperwork instead of actually
> teaching. . . . Absorption in things other than I would call straight

teaching is significant, and therefore energy levels and interests are not there.

Furthermore, workloads increased disproportionately, because, according to one Tasmanian teacher:

> You spend a lot more free time at home working on your classroom planning and marking because it just can't be done in the school day and it can't be done in the time before school or the time after school or at any time you would be in school for staff meetings and professional development sessions.

Nevertheless, despite the fears expressed by Hargreaves (1992) about the effects of contrived collegiality on opportunities for informal teacher collaboration, these Australian teachers claimed that they received the greatest help in coping with these changes from informal discussions with colleagues:

> You become dependent on colleagues. If you want help you turn to them rather than whoever the consultant used to be.

> People have seen the need to share their work – to share ideas and materials. Before that, everyone was teaching what they wanted to teach when they wanted to teach it – but now we are thinking more professionally together.

This last quotation aptly describes a situation where what we have termed the consensus model of management applied. It may be that in such cases the switch to managerialism occasioned by pressures from outside produces an opposite reaction among class teachers, causing them to collaborate more closely as an antidote against their personal feelings that 'things are sliding out of control'. One of the researchers in Williamson and Cowley's (1995) OECD study of a programme of innovation in science, mathematics and technology education summed up the situation using the metaphor of the 'wave':

> Innovation and change may be perceived as a wave. It can be a long roller which one prepares students to ride and those who ride it best may be the ones who have been trained to handle exactly this one type of wave to its greatest potential. But it could change shape or be a dumper, in which case the student needs skills in recognition and prediction and decision making as to whether to go for it, stay with it, back off, or dive under it. . . . Many teachers are not swimmers and have no confidence in fast moving big seas. Some perceive the wave as a potential tidal wave and fear their inability to cope and to prepare students to survive, or float let alone surf with it.

School managers can perceive the waves as threatening to crash down and demolish their organisational structures. Yet others see the wave as offering an inspirational and energetic ride to both old and new places.

(Williamson and Cowley 1995: 33)

References

Alexander, R. (1984) *Primary Teaching*, London: Holt, Rinehart & Winston.
—— (1992) *Policy and Practice in Primary Education*, London: Routledge.
Arnold, M. *Culture and Anarchy*, Murray.
Beare, H., Caldwell, B. J. and Millikan, R. H. (1989) *Creating an Excellent School: Some New Management Techniques*, London and New York: Routledge.
Berliner, D. C. (1994) 'Expertise: the wonder of exemplary performances', in J. N. Mangieri and C. Collins (eds) *Creating Powerful Thinking in Teachers and Students: Diverse Perspectives*, Fort Worth: Harcourt, Brace College.
Berliner, D. C., Stein, P., Sabers, D., Clarridge, P. B., Cushing, K., and Pinnegar, S. (1988) 'Implications of research on pedagogical expertise and experience for mathematics testing', in D. A. Grouws and T. J. Cooney (eds) *Perspectives on Research on Effective Mathematics Teaching*, Vol. 1, Reston, VI: National Council of Teachers of Mathematics.
Blyth, W. (1989) *Development and Experience in Primary Education*, London: Routledge.
Brophy, J. E. and Good, T. L. (1986) 'Teacher behaviour and student achievement', in M. C. Wittrock (ed.) *Handbook of Research on Teaching*, 3rd edn, New York: Macmillan.
Brown, A. and Palincsar, A. (1986) *Guided Cooperative Learning and Individual Knowledge Acquisition*, Technical Report 372, Cambridge, MA: Bolt, Beranak & Newham, Inc.
Caldwell, B. J. and Spinks, J. M. (1992) *Leading the Self-managing School*, Bristol: Falmer Press.
Campbell, R. (1993) 'A dream at conception: a nightmare at delivery', in R. Campbell (ed.) *Breadth and Balance in the Primary Curriculum*, London: Falmer Press.
CDCC (1982) (Council for Cultural Cooperation) *Primary Education in Western Europe: Aims, Problems, Trends*, report of a Council of Europe Project No. 8 Seminar held at Vaduz, Liechtenstein. Strasbourg: Council of Europe (DECS/EGT [83] 647).
—— (1987) *School Development in Practice. Report on Education Centres as a Means of Introducing Innovation in Primary Education* by A. Strittmatter (Switzerland) Strasbourg: Council of Europe (DECS/EGT [87] 18).
Churchill, R., Williamson, J. and Grady, N. (1995) 'Educational change and the new realities of teachers' work lives', paper presented at the Annual Conference of the Australian Association for Research in Education, Hobart, Tasmania, November.
Cowley, T. (1995) 'Teacher expertise and teacher transfer: implications for teacher educators', in T. Cowley and J. Williamson (eds) *Four Aspects of Change: The Challenge for Teacher Education*, Launceston: School of Education, University of Tasmania.

Deal, T. E. and Kennedy, A. (1982) *Corporate Cultures: The Rites and Rituals of Corporate Life*, Reading, MA: Addison-Wesley.

Fullan, M. (1992) *What's Worth Fighting for in the Headship*, Milton Keynes: Open University Press.

Fullan, M. and Hargreaves, A. (1992) *What's Worth Fighting for in Your School*, Milton Keynes: Open University Press.

Gage, N. L. (1981) *The Scientific Basis of the Art of Teaching*, New York: Teachers' College Press.

—— (1985) *Hard Gains in the Soft Sciences: The Case for Pedagogy*, CEDR monograph, Bloomington, Indiana: Phi Delta Kappa.

Galton, M. (1989) *Teaching in the Primary School*, London: David Fulton Publishers.

—— (1995) *Crisis in the Primary School*, London: David Fulton Publishers.

Galton, M., Hargreaves, L. and Comber, C. (1995) *Implementation of the National Curriculum in Rural Primary Schools*, final report to the Economic and Social Science Research Council (ESRC), Report No. R00023 3383, Slough: ESRC.

Good, T. and Brophy, G. (1994) *Looking in Classrooms*, 6th edn, New York: Harper-Collins.

Halpin, A. W. and Croft, D. B. (1962) *The Organizational Climate of Schools*, St Louis, MO: Washington University.

Hargreaves, A. (1992) 'Cultures for teaching: a focus for change', in A. Hargreaves and M. Fullan (eds) *Understanding Teacher Development*, London: Cassell in association with Teachers' College Press, Columbia University, New York.

Kilmann, R., Saxton, M. and Serpa, R. (1985) *Gaining Control of the Corporate Culture*, San Francisco, CA: Jossey-Bass.

Kliebard, H. (1986) *The Struggle for the American Curriculum 1893–1958*, New York: Methuen.

Lortie, D. (1975) *Schoolteacher*, Chicago, IL: University of Chicago Press.

Meadows, S. (1993) *The Child as Thinker: The Development and Acquisition of Cognition in Childhood*, London: Routledge.

Nias, J., Southworth, G. and Yeomans, R. (1989) *Staff Relationships in the Primary School*, London: Cassell.

Nuthall, G. (1997) 'Many faces of student thinking and learning', in B. J. Biddle, T. L. Good and I. F. Goodson (eds) *The International Handbook of Teachers and Teaching*, Dordrecht, The Netherlands: Kluwer.

OECD (1974) *The Teacher and Educational Change: A New Role*, OECD: Paris.

—— (1982) *In-service Education and Training of Teachers: A Condition for Educational Change*, OECD: Paris.

—— (1990) *The Teacher Today: Tasks, Conditions and Policies*, OECD: Paris.

Pintrich, P., Marx, R. and Boyle, R. (1993) 'Beyond cold conceptual change: the role of motivational beliefs and classroom factors in the process of conceptual change', *Review of Educational Research*, 63(2), 167–200.

Pollard, A. with Osborn, M., Abbott, D., Broadfoot, P. and Croll, P. (1993) 'Balancing priorities: children and the curriculum in the nineties', in R. Campbell (ed.) *Breadth and Balance in the Primary Curriculum*, London: Falmer Press.

Putnam, R. T. and Borko, H. (1997) 'Teacher learning: implications of new views of cognition', in B. J. Biddle, T. L. Good and I. F. Goodson (eds) *The International Handbook of Teachers and Teaching*, Dordrecht, The Netherlands: Kluwer.

Resnick, L. (1987) *Education and Learning to Think*, Washington: National Academy Press.

Rutter, M., Maugham, B., Mortimore, P., Ouston, J. and Smith, A. (1979) *Fifteen Thousand Hours: Secondary Schools and Their Effects on Children*, Cambridge, MA: Harvard University Press.

Sarason, S. (1971) *The Culture of the School and the Problems of Change*, Boston, MA: Allyn & Bacon.

Webb, R. (1993) *Eating the Elephant Bit by Bit: The National Curriculum at Key Stage 2*, final report of research commissioned by the Association of Teachers and Lecturers (ATL), London: ATL Publishers.

Williams, R. (1963) *Culture and Society*, London: Penguin.

Williamson, J. (1994) 'Teacher quality in Australia: Australian concerns in an international perspective', in F. Crowther, B. Caldwell, J. Chapman, G. Lakomski and D. Ogilvie (eds) (1994) *The Workplace in Education: Australian Perspectives*, Sydney: Edward Arnold.

Williamson, J. and Cowley, T. (1995) *Windows on Successful Practice: Innovations in Science, Maths and Technology Education*, Hobart: Tasmanian Department of Education and the Arts.

Williamson, J. and Fraser, B. J. (1991) 'Elementary education in Australia', *The Elementary School Journal* 92(1): 5–23.

Wood, D. (1988) *How Children Think and Learn*, Oxford: Blackwells.

7

CURRICULUM DEVELOPMENT IN THE RESTRUCTURED SCHOOL

Colin Marsh

Introduction

Multiple demands continue to be thrust upon primary schools, and it is little wonder that many of the teachers and administrators are feeling stressed and exhausted. Primary teachers are being coerced into working within student outcome and learning area frameworks; to adopt new arrangements for reporting and assessment; to develop closer links with parents and community; and to be accountable to various groups through student performance standards and teacher appraisal schemes. Small wonder that there is low morale among teachers. Parents are justifiably concerned about the possible negative effects upon their children.

An understanding of curriculum planning techniques and skills involved in managing curriculum is a necessity for primary teachers if they are to survive current pressures. Further, the acquisition of curriculum planning skills enables teachers to work cooperatively together rather than working independently in their solitary classrooms. School-based, cooperative planning of curriculum enables teachers to benefit from different perspectives and to learn from each other (Richards 1995).

It can be argued that school-based curriculum development has the potential to be a powerful vehicle for coping with head office requirements and yet maintaining the exciting, creative aspects of primary schools – enabling teachers 'to exhibit all the sense of wonder, fun, enjoyment, creativity, dedication and professionalism' (Woods 1996: 12).

Some important terms

Curriculum developers

There is no agreement about what people who make curriculum decisions should be called, and various terms have been used to describe them, such as *curriculum planners, curriculum designers, curriculum improvers* and *curriculum developers*. The last term has been adopted here because it is widely used in the literature.

Generally, curriculum developers are persons charged with the responsibility of planning, designing and producing a curriculum, whether it be in the form of a brief document or an elaborate curriculum package. In their final product, the developers may provide specific guidelines for implementing the written curriculum (with or without having first tried it out in schools) and evaluating the effects on students and teachers. The range of activities of curriculum developers depends, of course, on such things as the scale of the curriculum they are producing, the time available and the level of funding.

In primary schools, individual teachers, pairs of teachers or sub-school groups may be involved in curriculum development. The level of activity will depend upon the funding available and the degree of prescription, in terms of frameworks required by head office.

Curriculum change

Curriculum change is a generic term that subsumes a whole family of concepts such as *innovation, development* and *adoption*. It includes changes that are planned or unplanned (unintentional, spontaneous or accidental).

Fullan (1989) maintains that for teachers there are four core changes. When a teacher participates in a curriculum development project 'he or she faces (1) some form of regrouping or new grouping (structure), (2) new curriculum materials, (3) changes in some aspects of teaching practices (that is, new activities, skills, behaviour), and (4) change in beliefs or understandings vis-a-vis curriculum and learning' (*ibid.*: 8).

Innovation

The term *innovation* may mean either a new object, idea or practice, or the process by which a new object, idea or practice comes to be adopted by an individual group or organisation. Much emphasis is placed on innovation as a process, the planned application of ends or means new to the adopting educational system and intended to improve the effectiveness and/or efficiency of the system. The process of innovation includes not only an awareness of alternatives but a definite intention to implement one or more alternatives. Many early studies of innovations tended to focus on knowledge, awareness and decisions about adopting alternatives, but few explored the crucial area of implementation to find out how teachers were actually using a curriculum innovation.

Educators do not always agree with the contention that a change must be an improvement to qualify as an 'innovation'. Whether an innovation is regarded as an improvement or not depends, of course, on the judgement of whoever makes the decision about adoption, with the judgement usually made in terms of aspirations and past experiences. If an innovation seems different from what existed before, then it may be perceived as likely to bring about improvement. Innovations are not objective and unchanging; they are constantly being changed and redefined as a result of experience.

The inclusion of the idea of 'improvement' within the concept of 'innovation' emphasises the political nature of curriculum innovations. While other educational terms such as 'child development' or 'instructional level' tend to be regarded as referring to something intrinsic in the educational process, curriculum innovations are often initiated because certain authorities are not satisfied with what they believe is going on in schools and want to do something different. The tremendous explosion in recent years of studies on school improvement, school effectiveness and national standards is a sure sign of the political nature of innovations (Apple 1982). These studies have attempted to identify behaviours or school characteristics that lead to beneficial change, such as 'teacher commitment', 'strong leadership by the principal', and an 'orderly and safe school environment'.

Diffusion and dissemination

Diffusion and *dissemination* are two terms crucial to understanding how innovations spread. Diffusion is the spontaneous, unplanned spread of new ideas. Diffusion therefore involves the spread of information and ideas which were previously unfamiliar and which may result in the adoption of an innovation.

The term dissemination has a narrower focus and applies to intentional efforts to inform individuals or groups about an innovation and to gain their interest in it. Emphasis falls on arousing interest in the innovation in order that potential clients will adopt it.

The curriculum continuum

One way of depicting the process of curriculum development that incorporates many of the ideas and terms discussed above is as a continuum, as shown in Figure 7.1. Pressures for change and incentives to try out innovative practices might emanate from local perceptions (for example the perceived need to improve student achievement in mathematics) or from newly proposed principles or models (for example a particular approach to reading). The planning and development of a new curriculum, depending on the scale of the activity, might then occur over a period of a few months or extend over several years. If a new curriculum 'package' is developed externally, the developers might next attempt to disseminate it directly to individual schools and teachers, although some schools might already have learned of the innovation indirectly, through diffusion. Evaluation studies might be used to provide evidence of the desirability of the curriculum and to further the likelihood of its adoption. Once a school has made a decision to adopt an innovative curriculum, actually implementing it can be extremely complicated, often taking two or three years and requiring the support of external agencies, as well as the persistence of those teachers acting as implementers. If these efforts continue successfully over a sufficient period of time, however, the innovation will be translated from a planned curriculum to an enacted curriculum, hence becoming a permanent part of the total offerings of the school.

Figure 7.1 is based on the premise that the development of an innovative curriculum is undertaken by a team external to the school which eventually adopts and institutionalises it. If the new curriculum is a local, school-based endeavour the activities of dissemination, evaluation and implementation merge into a single, ongoing process of development.

Levels of curriculum development

Four levels at which curriculum development takes place can be readily identified:

1   At the *national* level in Australia curriculum development is undertaken by teams, the composition of which may vary but which usually include both subject specialists and experts in curriculum design. Teachers may also be active members of these teams or observers who provide advice at times. During the period 1991–3 a number of national curriculum teams were funded and organised by the Australian Education Council to develop national statements and profiles (C. J. Marsh 1994; Langrehr 1994). All project teams included experienced, practising teachers as well as university personnel and administrators. Given recent political developments, it is unlikely that further national curriculum development will occur in the immediate future.

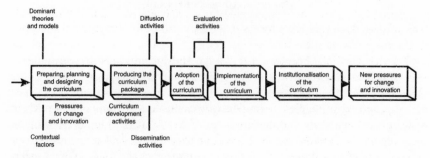

Figure 7.1 The curriculum continuum

2   At the *state* level curriculum development appears to have ebbed and flowed over recent decades. During the early 1990s state education systems drastically reduced their curriculum development activities due to declining budgets and the emphasis on the national curriculum project. More recently, state-level initiatives to fine-tune and/or redefine national statements and profiles has led to increased activity in some states and territories.

3   At the *school* level teachers often work cooperatively deciding how to coordinate subject matter, both within academic areas (such as mathematics, reading, music and art) and among years or grade levels. State-level frameworks may provide numerous examples, guidelines or constraints, or teachers in a particular school may collectively make most curriculum decisions for themselves.

4   At the *classroom* level individual teachers may be relatively free to make numerous curricular decisions, both about what they teach and about how they teach it. It is here that the planned curriculum becomes both the enacted curriculum and the experienced curriculum. Though officially restricted by state frameworks concerning what must be taught and what cannot be taught, almost all teachers can make enough curriculum decisions to give what they teach its own distinctive texture.

The activities of curriculum developers

Kinds of activities

It is worth reflecting on the major goals that curriculum developers might have in mind as they go about their tasks. There are three broad kinds of activities, which can be described as:

*   activities that are designed to maintain and reinforce existing syllabuses, resources, and practices;
*   activities that are designed to produce innovative curricula and concrete experimentation;
*   activities that are predominantly speculative and 'think-tank' approaches to possible future curricula.

The first kind of activities – those designed to maintain existing practices – involves developers in making only minor modifications to an existing curriculum, perhaps because the curriculum has been found satisfactory and merely needs updating, or perhaps because time constraints or the political climate are such that nothing more than slow, gradual change is likely to succeed. The third kind of activities – the speculative ones – involves developers in creative lateral thinking, speculating on how and in what combination different learning activities might be organised. Very few, if any,

143

actual curricula would be developed by speculative activities, since they are directed towards conceptualising new approaches to be applied in the future.

In contrast, the second kind of activities – ones promoting innovative curricula and concrete experimentation – covers the middle ground of innovation and change: new and different curricula are conceptualised, and actual concrete programmes are produced, tried out and made available for use in schools.

Some authors, such as Popkewitz (1985), argue that little change comes out of most curriculum-development activities. He asserts that typical activities simply secure compliance with elite agendas – a practice of social legitimation. In other words, although most such activities give the appearance of thoughtful reappraisal of existing values and practices, they actually reiterate them, thereby in effect contributing to their continuing unexamined acceptance. Kirst and Meister (1985) observe that few educational reforms involving curriculum development continue for more than a few years and that secondary schools have remained remarkably stable. When supposedly innovative curricula are carefully examined they usually seem to be little more than old curricula in new forms.

The site of activities

Although large-scale curriculum-development activities occur from time to time, as evidenced by the national curriculum project in Australia in 1991–3, they are becoming increasingly infrequent. Rather than these generic activities, increased attention is now being given to site-specific activities, which typically occur at single schools.

Site-specific curriculum-development projects can usually be identified by four characteristics:

- They are undertaken by a small group of teachers, almost always working on the project part time.
- Their assessments of what needs to be done are brief and informal.
- Their activities tend to focus on the production of materials.
- They may use generic materials as guides, sometimes even incorporating such materials into their final products.

School-based curriculum development

School-based curriculum development (SBCD) is the term frequently used in the literature to describe site-based decision-making in Australia and the UK, and to a lesser extent in Canada and the USA. Major reasons which are often advocated for accepting it in education systems include the following:

- 'Top-down' modes of curriculum development do not work.
- SBCD allows schools to have increased autonomy.
- Schools need to be responsive to their environment and this requires the freedom, opportunity, responsibility and resources to determine and direct their affairs.
- Schools are best fitted to plan and design the curriculum, and to construct the teaching and learning of specific programmes.
- Teacher self-actualisation, motivation and sense of achievement are integrally bound up with curriculum decision-making, which is the staple of teachers' professional lives.
- The school is a more stable and enduring institution for curriculum development than regional and national bodies.

Some major factors relating to SBCD are depicted in Figure 7.2. Three factors – motivations of stake holders, awareness of innovative approaches and ownership – are given a central focus but there are also many other interrelated factors.

Motivations of stakeholders

If a school principal and his or her teachers are relatively satisfied with what is happening at their respective school there is little likelihood that serious SBCD activities will be initiated unless there is an externally generated initiative. Most teachers strive for stability, routines and practices that work – it is a source of sanity for the myriad of conflicting activities and turmoil that can occur during the course of a school day. It is often the school principal who jolts staff out of these accepted routines. The motivations may be diverse. They can involve personal ambitions and goals or they might be part of a long-term goal of development for school staff as a whole.

Research studies provide some interesting insights and caveats about the motivations of stakeholders (Stannard 1995; Webb 1996). For example, Huberman and Miles (1986) noted as a result of their involvement in the study of Dissemination Efforts Supporting School Improvement that persons who are highly motivated to initiate SBCD activities can enthuse, but they can also destabilise staff because of their subsequent career shifts. During their period of time at a school these leaders can establish enthusiastic work groups only abruptly to leave them leaderless at short notice.

An SBCD project can provide the opportunity for teachers and principals to undergo extensive self-criticism. This process can become most enlightening and motivating to the individuals concerned, even though the extent of this development might not be anticipated prior to their involvement. The emancipatory opportunities resulting from school-based activities can be a major benefit for school staff.

The development of appropriate policies and practices as a result of

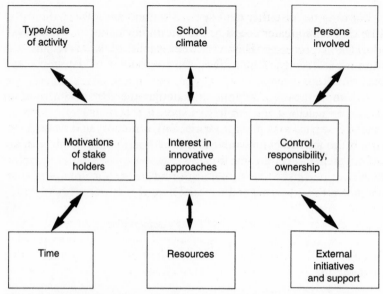

Figure 7.2 A conceptual map of school-based curriculum development

private and public reflections might be termed 'practical theories'. It is evident that SBCD projects can provide powerful opportunities for teachers to enquire deliberately and systematically about their practical theories. But not all teachers are willing participants – there can be considerable reluctance from staff at primary schools (Llorens 1994).

Interest in innovative approaches

If teachers or principals are dissatisfied with their present effectiveness they may decide to use a specific innovative process or product to alleviate the problem. Taking an altruistic stance, they may opt to use an educational innovation because they anticipate benefits for their students. However, there may also be some self-interested motives involved to the extent that an innovation is used to give individuals higher levels of visibility and to increase their prospects of promotion. In real-life situations it is difficult, if not impossible, to separate the genuine altruistic motives from those of self-interest as most individuals are probably affected by both considerations.

Teachers and principals are very susceptible to innovations because there is still no unequivocal evidence about the superiority of specific methods of teaching. The pressures of accountability from various organisations, especially the government and the media, all have the effect of persuading school principals (and teachers to a lesser extent) to demonstrate that they are willing to consider.

It is likely that principals have more opportunities to initiate innovative practices, not only because they are expected to perform a leadership role, but because they have greater access to the latest information about innovative products and processes. However, well-established practices are not easily jettisoned in favour of new ideas and products. Furthermore, some innovations which are asserted at the time to be a major advance never get beyond a very short period of adoption. Examples of innovations that have been ephemeral include 8mm projectors, voucher systems, programmed learning and Cuisenaire rods in mathematics. Innovations which are selected by a central office for all schools run the risk of being used by only a small number of teachers. The contents of many storerooms provide evidence of items which were deemed to be an innovative advance by a head office but which were not accepted by classroom teachers and were subsequently relegated to a dusty shelf.

Control, responsibility and ownership

There will be a number of stages in developing the commitment of participants in SBCD to the project/tasks/activities. Motivation and interest in innovations are only the first – albeit important – steps on the path towards commitment to learning and change. Initial motivation may well become soured or decline if, for example, there is little support, time, energy and resources, if the task is too large or if the school climate is not right.

A major factor is perceived ownership and control. Whether the project is initiated by the principal, an individual or a group of teachers, where others who were not the originators become involved it is important to ensure that they feel able to exercise control and ownership of the processes of the tasks, and responsibility for these and the outcomes.

Type and scale of activity

SBCD activities can be classified into many types/forms and this will depend in turn upon such factors as time availability, funds and purpose. One way of categorising SBCD activities is in terms of whether the focus is on creating new curriculum products or on selecting or adopting existing ones. Clearly, the creation of new products is a far more time-consuming and complicated project than merely adapting them. The three orientations of 'transformation', 'transaction' and 'transmission' are useful to highlight the differences. The first of these terms, 'transformation', can be related to SBCD activities which involve creating new products, structures or processes for a school. The emphasis is on personal and social change. The other two terms of 'transaction' and 'transmission' can be linked to SBCD activities which emphasise more effective ways of teaching with given content, skills or values. There is little interest in any problematics of 'why'. Rather, the emphasis is on the 'how'.

However, SBCD activities can also be concerned with processes rather than the creation or adaptation of products. SBCD activities are often undertaken to improve aspects of organisational health: communication adequacy, the ability of the staff to solve problems collaboratively, cohesiveness and morale.

Because SBCD activities are concerned with advancements for the total school staff, or at least departments or sections, it is most important to consider processes that will facilitate this rather than merely advantage individuals.

In undertaking these SBCD activities, whether they are product- or process-oriented, there will be some sequences of events, or procedures. These procedures are neither linear nor prescriptive. Enormous variations can occur. Some school staffs might spend inordinate amounts of time on needs analysis (assessment and goal-setting). Others might undergo rigorous evaluation exercises using internal as well as external personnel. The contextual factors will affect the extent to which procedures will be followed in any SBCD activity.

School climate

The concept of school climate/organisational climate has been recognised by many writers as a major factor in school change. Halpin and Croft (1963) introduced their Organisational Climate Description Questionnaire (OCDQ) in the early 1960s. Many studies have been completed since then using the OCDQ and modifications of this instrument. The studies have highlighted such dimensions as principal supportiveness, motivating teachers by example and social cohesiveness among teachers. Brady (1988) examined the relationship between organisational climate and aspects of SBCD and concluded that 'principal supportiveness' was the most consistent predictor of successful SBCD activities.

Other writers have used an ecology metaphor to explain the importance of school climate, for example Butterworth and Weinstein (1996) and Goodlad (1987). Goodlad refers to the school as an ecosystem. He extends this analysis to consider how a school can become healthy and renewing. School communities need constantly to examine the functions they perform. A healthy school is one which realises that it is an incomplete culture, and that it is necessary to articulate and confront problem areas.

Lieberman and Miller examine the school culture in terms of 'routinisation and regularities of school life and the strong informal norms that grow up among teachers and which govern their working life' (Lieberman and Miller 1986: 56). They argue that SBCD activities have to build on the school norms that are in operation. Initiators of SBCD projects should not underestimate the complexity of these relationships and the tensions that often occur in schools that are either structurally loose or tight (Gipps 1995; Campbell 1996).

Huberman and Miles (1986) provide some rather different, if not provocative, arguments about certain aspects of school climate. They suggest that a positive school climate for SBCD is one in which there is

> administrative decisiveness bordering on coercion, but intelligently and supportively exercised . . . because powerful people tend to be able to exert directional control over the environment – to shape the surround, to reduce the uncertainties, to reduce the degree of freedom of actors having countervailing plans – and to offer assistance resources.
>
> (Huberman and Miles 1986: 89)

Leadership

The number of persons involved and their type of involvement are important aspects of any SBCD activity. Numerous studies on school principals over recent years attest to their role as a key agent in SBCD at primary-school levels and to the important skills they need to use. Butterworth and Weinstein (1996) emphasise the vision and rich motivational activities that a school principal can bring to SBCD activities. Griffin (1995) refers to the support and resources that a principal can bring to an SBCD project. School principals are also able to monitor the degree to which SBCD projects are succeeding (Heller and Firestone 1995). Various principal styles have been advanced in the literature, especially by Hall and Rutherford (1983) and Leithwood and Montgomery (1986). The former suggest that there are three typical styles of 'responder', 'manager' and 'initiator'. The latter suggest that there are four discernible levels that principals progress through over a period of years, namely 'administrator', 'humanitarian', 'programme manager' and 'problem-solver'. It would appear that 'initiator' and 'problem-solver' principals would be particularly successful at facilitating SBCD activities.

However, it is too simplistic to place all the leadership burden for SBCD upon school principals. Other key figures can also undertake leadership roles in a school. Some of these figures may have achieved respect from others because of their past accomplishments or special personal qualities. Others might undertake leadership roles because they occupy formal staffing positions or because special authority has been delegated to them.

Marsh and Bowman (1988) report that many key players in the Californian School Improvement Plan (SIP) programme have been class teachers. Hall *et al.* (1984) and Hord (1986) refer to Second Change Facilitators (Second CFs) as also being key actors in SBCD activities. They can be assistant principals, an appointed teacher from within the school, curriculum coordinators or external district-level advisers. The Second CF tends to take a complementary leadership role to the principal. Hord maintains that 'principals provide planning, guidance, reinforcement, and supervision directed to the individual teachers and teacher groups, while the Second CF does more training and problem solving work with individual teachers' (Hord 1986: 46).

Caldwell and Spinks (1993) have demonstrated how organisational structures can be developed (Collaborative School Management Approach (CSM)) which enable class teachers to become leaders in SBCD activities. They advocate a policy group of administrators, teachers and parents, and various programme teams whose task it is to review current programmes and to produce viable plans and budgets for school improvement. As a result of their involvement in such project teams, class teachers can develop important leadership and interpersonal skills. It is these kinds of experience that enable teachers to become valuable key actors in SBCD activities.

Time

Having sufficient time is a major factor for all SBCD endeavours. It can be considered from several different perspectives, namely 'project' time in terms of schedules and target dates, and 'personal' time in terms of commitment required by participants.

Most schools are governed by tight schedules such as term dates, daily timetables, monthly tests and many more requirements. Typically, SBCD activities need to be undertaken within one school year, as staff mobility and other changes make it extremely difficult to extend a project for longer periods. Sometimes the project has to be of much shorter duration, perhaps a term or a number of weeks. Caldwell and Spinks (1993) suggest procedures for keeping SBCD activities within reasonable time limits. For example, they advocate that project teams should consist of only six to eight persons; that no school should become involved in more than three to five projects per year; and that policy recommendations from a project team should be kept to a maximum of two pages per team. These authors have a very task-oriented focus for SBCD activities and this may be appropriate on many occasions, but there may be other situations where such efficiency-oriented priorities do not allow sufficient time for self-reflection and discussion sessions for participants.

For individual teachers, time spent on non-teaching activities can be a very real cost. There are, of course, the attractions of involvement in a group project, with all the bonhomie, excitement and camaraderie that can develop, as well as it being a welcome relief from isolation, but this is only the positive side. On the negative side there is the very real danger that a person will overextend him- or herself and become fatigued. It is also possible that earlier convivial meetings can be transformed into sessions of friction and conflict. Fullan (1991) refers to the personal time costs of doing SBCD in terms of actual time lost, energy expended and perceived threats to a person's sense of adequacy. Teacher stress and burnout are frequently featured in the media and may be related to unrealistic expectations about how much SBCD activity can be undertaken by teachers in addition to their normal teaching loads. Professional development programmes which provide teacher release time are an obvious solution, but it is becoming increasingly difficult to provide them in a period of restricted education budgets (Stannard 1995; Drummond 1996).

Resources

The provision of appropriate resources is, of course, a major concern in any SBCD project. Resources can take various forms. Grants of money paid direct to a project team might be perceived by recipients to be the most ideal solution but they are becoming far less prevalent in the current period of budget downturns and concerns about accountability. Grants of money tied to the purchase of materials can be of considerable assistance to a project team. Then again, consultants with subject-matter expertise or process skills can be hired to work with a project team. These experts can give demonstrations and workshops or be used in the role of group leader or project evaluator. Some of the resources that may be made available include:

- money grants;
- materials, for example teacher readings, activity sheets, curriculum kits, class sets, equipment;
- expert advice/modelling, for example presentations by external experts, demonstrations, visits to attend workshops;
- timetabling assistance, for example a reduced number of teaching periods, rearranged classes, teacher relief;
- information retrieval/circulation, for example answering requests for information, circulation of information to others, exchange of tips/solutions.

There are also many other avenues by which a principal or deputy principal can provide human resources. For example, project members can be given reduced teaching loads if the principal has access to a fund for teacher-relief days (Wallace and Wildy 1994). Even without such funds, the administrator responsible for the school timetable can reallocate duties so as to optimise the block times or free periods available to SBCD project members.

The school principal and other experienced teachers can be a resource to a project team by providing moral support – offering advice, assisting with the location of sources, or simply being willing to react to proposals and to discuss their reactions in some detail (Hamilton and Richardson 1995).

However, there can be problems with the provision of resources to project teams. Too often, funds are depleted before a project is completed and so team members are not able to get the resources they need for the lifetime of the project. Sometimes the resource providers lose interest in the project or they become committed to other more immediate problems.

An equally serious problem is that resource provisions are often tied to specific conditions. Pressure may be applied to ensure that resources are used for specific purposes, whether these are congruent with the intentions of the SBCD project team or not. In these circumstances it is likely that the provision of resources could lead to resentment by project team members, with resultant negative outcomes for all concerned.

External initiatives and support

External agencies such as state, province and local education authority systems have the resources to initiate various changes in schools. Farrar (1987) adds to the list by including state legislatures, a most important force on educational matters over recent years. Various British authors, such as Lawton and Chitty (1988) and Reid *et al.* (1988), Campbell (1985), Simons (1987), refer to the powers of the secretary of state for education and science and the Department of Education and Science. These external agencies are increasingly applying pressure to schools by establishing policy priorities and linking funds to each. They also have the capacity to redistribute staff and provide consultants to facilitate the implementation of these policies.

The literature is replete with assertions and counter-assertions about the benefits and/or problems of top-down and bottom-up curriculum initiatives (see, for example, Berman and McLaughlin 1977; Datta 1980; Crandall *et al.* 1983; C. J. Marsh and Huberman 1984; Sabar *et al.* 1987; D. D. Marsh and Bowman 1988). Berman and McLaughlin (1977) argue that a grass-roots approach is the most successful. In an ideal, closed system most would agree that a school community should initiate its own SBCD efforts. In actual practice it is virtually impossible to avoid political interventions by external agencies. Some top-down initiatives will invariably occur – and occurred in most countries during the later years of the 1980s – whether they are from general policies or specific programmes.

Participants in SBCD activities may not be overly concerned about the source of the initiative so long as the funding is not closely tied to specific priorities and is sufficient for them to undertake their respective projects. There is some recent evidence in the literature to support this stance. For example, Huberman and Crandall conclude that 'locally adaptive, demo-cratic enterprise is a caricature' (Huberman and Crandall 1982). The source of innovations is quickly blurred once local implementation begins.

Politics and SBCD

The overwhelming feature of primary schooling over recent decades has been its politicisation. Political activity occurs at all levels, from politicians and bureaucrats, through community and parent groups, to teachers and students. Each interest group endeavours to use its power to achieve certain ends.

Prideaux (1988) reports on the disparity between the rhetoric extolling SBCD in Australian states and the actual support structures provided to participants. Most education authorities in Australia issued formal statements and bulletins during the 1970s and 1980s couched in terms such as 'school-based', 'devolution of control' and 'decentralised decision-making'. SBCD, however, requires new levels of skills for participants and time to practise the skills. To a large extent, education systems did not provide the support structures needed. Little information was disseminated about decision-making models, professional development workshops were few in number and no major increases in non-teaching time were allocated to teachers to enable them to undertake planning activities. The economic restraints of the late 1980s and early 1990s meant that there were few opportunities to fund some of these provisions.

Support is needed for the development of collaborative curriculum decision-making (Llorens 1994). Few teachers have an opportunity to learn and practise group skills during their pre-service education. Some teachers were able to develop such skills through professional development programmes funded by the Commonwealth government in the 1970s and 1980s but, unfortunately, the entire professional-development programme was terminated in 1986. The states did not have the resources to continue these programmes. Declining resources also affected staffing levels from the late 1980s onwards, and it is difficult for some schools to maintain a stable group of staff to provide continuity in collaborative decision-making.

There are some important structural factors which limited the development of SBCD. These arose from the very nature of SBCD and its mode of introduction in Australia. One such factor was the 'suddenness' with which SBCD changes were thrust upon schools. 'Top-down' legislative changes were enacted in Victoria. Sudden policy changes also occurred in other states such as Western Australia and South Australia (Angus). Change can cause confusion and stress, and may lead to the rejection of new policies.

One of the most important influences which restricted the development of SBCD in Australia was its limited scope. It was generally not extended beyond the school to include participation by the community. Not all states embraced SBCD to the same degree. In South Australia, Prideaux (1993) notes, SBCD was 'partial' in that it was limited to the school context, 'consensual' in that it ignored conflict and conflict resolution, and 'piecemeal' in that it did not challenge the overall structure of the curriculum, especially its function in social selection and reproduction. Pusey (1981) has claimed that SBCD was associated with the decreasing importance of bureaucratic control through inspection systems, external examinations and imposed curriculums.

Some of the suddenness of the changes was caused by politicians and senior administrators reacting to criticism of education in the media and in the community. As economic downturn took hold in Australia the curriculum in schools was criticised both for contributing to the downturn by supposedly neglecting the 'basic skills and knowledge' deemed important in maintaining economic competitiveness, and for failing to lead recovery by teaching new 'more relevant' skills and competencies. As a consequence, senior officials tended to introduce more stringent guidelines for all schools relating to such aspects as literacy tests and secondary-school graduation requirements. There was far less inclination to encourage school communities to develop their own approaches and solutions to curriculum issues and problems, although there are strong advocates of this approach (Chrispeels 1996; Rapoport 1997;).

SBCD activities commenced in Israel at around the same time. In the early 1970s education officials began to examine some of the benefits of matching school experiences to different learning levels. According to Sabar (1987), this led to a major move in 1984 towards fuller autonomy for schools. This occurred as a result of specific contextual factors such as:

- the greater independence of local education authorities from the Ministry of Education;
- a revival of allegiance to cultural and ethnic 'roots' among local groups;
- a social polarisation between religious and non-religious groups.

Rather than being about whole-school curriculum planning, SBCD in Israel has focused upon site-based planning of part of the school curriculum. That is, required courses are still developed centrally (mathematics, native language, foreign language, Bible studies and natural sciences), but elective courses and optional courses are developed locally. SBCD activities in Israel are facilitated by school-based support centres or 'tracks'. A group of teachers who teach the same subject or same classes at the one school can form a team and are given support, as outlined below:

- School administrators allocate additional resources to these teachers.
- Other teacher experts are contracted to assist in the preparation of materials.
- Resource centres have been established in schools containing a variety of learning materials and teaching aids.
- School-based in-service training courses are provided for the teachers in the team.
- Meetings are established from time to time with teachers from other schools who are established as an inter-institutional support team.

As has been noted by Eden *et al.* (1987), these activities and additional resources place additional burdens on each school, but the activities are close to the needs of the specific students and are generally very successful.

In their review of SBCD practices, Ben-Peretz and Dor (1987) conclude that teachers in Israeli schools feel a strong responsibility for the school curriculum. Teachers are concerned about their own professional fulfilment, and SBCD enables them to develop new skills and abilities. Sabar and Silberstein are equally positive about SBCD developments in Israel: 'Recognition of the importance of school autonomy is spreading throughout Israel. School autonomy is being increasingly perceived as a way to fulfil a school's own ethos, to nurture staff growth and development, and to enhance responsiveness to local needs' (Sabar and Silberstein 1987: 17).

Where Australia is heading in terms of school-based/site-based curriculum development is problematic. Braithwaite (1996) refers to 'second-wave' reforms occurring in New South Wales, whereby clusters of schools have been formed into regions and budgets are provided for non-staff resources. Caldwell (1993) extols the virtues of Schools of the Future in Victoria – which have responsibility for selecting and dismissing staff; responsibility for a budget including staff, and a three-year planning and budgeting frame; and the negotiation of a school charter to guide planning and accountability.

Yet others argue that decentralisation of curriculum development has stalled, with a counter-move towards centralisation or recentralisation. Seddon et al. (1990) refer to the contradictions which are now occurring in various states between school-based decision-making and management, and central demands for accountability and control. While there have been moves in some states to promote more local involvement in school management, this has concentrated on financial and administrative management rather than curriculum matters.

Smyth argues that events in the 1990s in Australia revolve around a rhetoric of devolution in a context of centralism: 'These ideas, while they are dressed up to look democratic, are basically being pushed around by the New Right largely as a way of enabling central educational authorities to increase rather than decrease their control over schools' (Smyth 1993: 23).

National standards and curriculum

The national goals developed by the Australian Educational Council (AEC) in 1989, and the subsequent development of national statements and profiles, constituted a major initiative. Although in the mid-1990s it appeared that a truly national curriculum would be produced for all primary schools in Australia, subsequent actions by individual states and territories now make this unlikely.

Nevertheless, the outcomes-based approach which is incorporated into each of the eight learning areas has been adopted by all states and territories, along with a profiles approach to assessment (Wilson 1994). According to Boomer:

The profiles approach comes out of a strongly teacher-centred, classroom-oriented understanding of how judgment works on a day to day basis in our schools. Profiles are a vertical map of performance territory from lower to higher performance upon which a student's cumulative performance as assessed can be placed – to allow each student, in relation to standards, to keep going for their next 'personal best'.

(Boomer 1992: 63–4)

Profiles, as developed for the eight learning areas, emphasise:

- bands of schooling;
- subject elements (later termed 'strands');
- student outcomes in relation to each subject element;
- assignments which richly describe and illustrate the outcomes (later termed 'pointers');
- exemplifications (later termed 'work samples').

The results to date are encouraging. A survey of all states and territories in July 1995 (C. J. Marsh 1995) revealed that a number of teachers were recognising many benefits from using a profile/outcomes approach (see Table 7.1), especially the availability of a common language, access to more diagnostic information and the reaffirmation of the importance of teacher judgements. Yet there are also a number of problems still to be resolved (see Table 7.2). Of these issues the most vexatious ones relate to teacher time to talk through problems with colleagues and the matter of moderating (triangulating) teacher judgements. A recent development has been the announcement by the federal minister that national literacy testing for Years 3 and 5 and retesting in Years 7 and 9 will commence in all states and territories. Although some form of benchmarking may be a laudable goal (McGaw 1995), whether national testing is a desirable vehicle for achieving it is a problematic question.

Conclusion

The development of curriculum planning skills is an essential requirement for busy primary-school teachers coping with teaching in the present difficult times. It also involves teachers working with colleagues in making workable curriculum plans which are relevant to the local context.

Teachers have to establish priorities rather than doing all the things that are pressed upon them. These decisions have to be discussed openly and vigorously. In a postmodern world teachers must have the opportunity to contest ideas and beliefs (Campbell 1996).

SBCD, or variations under different titles, is developing steadily in most

Table 7.1 Benefits of using nationally developed profiles

1	They provide a common language and common purpose for monitoring and recording student achievement.
2	Students are demonstrating they can achieve many of the outcome statements.
3	Teachers have more diagnostic information now to review and modify their teaching programme.
4	Teachers can identify with confidence current levels of achievement by students and plan for future learning.
5	Teachers use outcome statements as a guide to how they use syllabuses and other support materials.
6	This reaffirms the importance of teacher judgements in assessing students and their role as professionals.
7	Teachers quickly demonstrate an ability to make comparable judgements about student levels.
8	Teachers have found that wholesale change is not needed to use profiles.
9	Teachers are very positive about a developmental approach to learning and vertical maps of progression.
10	They provide a stable and consistent reporting framework.
11	They emphasise positive aspects of student attainment.
12	They will encourage teachers to use a wide range of content and processes in their planning and teaching.
13	They will increase the public accountability of schools.
14	Parents appreciate the common language and framework.
15	Teachers are gaining new insights into how students think and learn.
16	Students get feedback and opportunities to plan their own progress, and are recognising this as an improvement.

Table 7.2 Problems still to be resolved in using nationally developed profiles

1	Teachers need a very detailed understanding of outcome statements and strands to use them effectively.
2	Teacher judgements are only reliable if taken over a period of time and in a variety of contexts to triangulate the evidence.
3	Teachers are not conversant with a range of assessments/assessment tasks.
4	Teachers need time to talk with colleagues about outcome statements to develop and clarify their understanding.
5	Teachers need time to examine student work and to work out judgements collaboratively with other teachers.
6	Some of the outcome statements/substrands need further refinement and there can be problems with evenness across profiles.
7	If insufficient support is obtained at a school from staff (key teachers, principal) limited progress occurs.

Western countries, despite head office demands which are often restricting the professionality of teachers. SBCD enables site-based teachers and administrators to create an effective school curriculum – one that supports the growth of foundational learning of basic skills and attitudes but also maintains the 'fun' activities of primary schools where teachers can capitalise on the positive emotions of students, the teachable moments (Woods 1996).

References

Apple, M. W. (1982) *Education and Power*, Boston, MA: Routledge & Kegan Paul.

Ben-Peretz, M. and Dor, B. Z. (1987) 'The autonomous school: a long term perspective on school-based curriculum development', in N. Sabar, J. Rudduck and W. Reid (eds) *Partnership and Autonomy in School-based Curriculum Development*, Sheffield: University of Sheffield.

Berman, P. and McLaughlin, M. W. (1977) *Federal Programs Supporting Educational Change*, Santa Monica, LA: US Office of Education, Department of Health, Education and Welfare/Rand Corporation.

Boomer, G. (1992) 'The advent of standards in Australian education', *Curriculum Perspectives* 12(1): 61–6.

Brady, L. (1988) 'The principal as a climate factor in Australian schools: overview of studies', *Journal of Educational Administration* 26(1): 13–19.

Braithwaite, R. J. (1996) 'Teacher willingness to participate in school-based decision-making', unpublished paper, University of Tasmania.

Butterworth, B. and Weinstein, R. S. (1996) 'Enhancing motivational opportunity in elementary schooling: a case study of the ecology of principal leadership', *Elementary School Journal* 97(1): 57–80.

Caldwell, B. J. (1993) *Decentralising the Management of Australia's Schools*, Melbourne: National Industry Education Forum.

Caldwell, B. J. and Spinks, J. M. (1993) *Leading the Self-managing School*, London: Falmer Press.

Campbell, R. J. (1985) *Developing the Primary School Curriculum*, London: Holt, Rinehart & Winston.

—— (1996) 'Educational reform and primary teachers' work: some sources of conflict', *Education 3 to 13* 24(2): 13–22.

Chrispeels, J. H. (1996) 'Evaluating teachers' relationships with families: a case study of one district', *Elementary School Journal* 97(2): 179–200.

Crandall, D. *et al.* (1983) *The Study of Dissemination Efforts Supporting School Improvement (DESSI)*, Andover, MA: The Network.

Datta, L. E. (1980) 'Changing times: the study of federal programs supporting educational change in the case of local problem solving', *Teachers' College Record* 82: 1.

Drummond, M. J. (1996) 'Teachers asking questions: approaches to evaluation', *Education 3–13* 24(3): 8–17.

Eden, S., Mozes, S. and Amiad, R. (1987) 'Multi-track curriculum planning', in N. Sabar, J. Rudduck and W. Reid (eds) *Partnership and Autonomy in School-based Curriculum Development*, Sheffield: University of Sheffield.

Farrar, E. (1987) 'Improving the urban high school: the role of leadership in the school, district and state', paper presented at the Annual Meeting of the American Educational Research Association, Washington, DC.

Fullan, M. G. (1989) *Implementing Educational Change: What We Know*, Washington, DC: Population and Human Resources Department, World Bank.

—— (1991) *The New Meaning of Educational Change*, London: Cassell.

Gipps, C. (1995) 'Teacher assessment and teacher development in primary schools', *Education 3–13* 23(1): 8–12.

Goodlad, J. I. (ed.) (1987) *The Ecology of School Renewal*, Chicago, IL: University of Chicago Press.

Griffin, G. A. (1995) 'Influences of shared decision-making on school and classroom activity: conversations with five teachers', *Elementary School Journal* 96(1): 29–46.

Hall, G. E., Rutherford, W. L. and Huling-Austin, L. B. (1984) 'Effects of three principals' styles on school improvement', *Journal of Educational Leadership* 41(5): 39–47.

Hall, G. E. and Rutherford, W. L. (1983) *Three Change Facilitator Styles: How Principals Affect Improvement Efforts*, Austin, TX: Research and Development Centre for Teacher Education, University of Texas; also presented at the Annual Meeting of the American Educational Research Association, Montreal.

Halpin, A. W. and Croft, D. B. (1963) *Organisational Climate of Schools*, Chicago, IL: University of Chicago Press.

Hamilton, M. L. and Richardson, V. (1995) 'Effects of the culture in two schools on the process and outcomes of staff development', *Elementary School Journal* 95(4): 367–85.

Heller, M. F. and Firestone, W. A. (1995) 'Who's in charge here? Sources of leadership for change in eight schools', *Elementary School Journal* 96(1): 65–86.

Hord, S. M. (1986) 'Implementing excellence in schools: rhetoric and reality', paper presented at the Annual Conference of the South Pacific Association for Teacher Education, Perth, July.

Huberman, A. M. and Crandall, D. P. (1982) 'A study of dissemination efforts supporting school improvement (DESSI)', *People, Policies and Practices: Examining the Chain of School Improvement*, vol. IX, Andover, MA: The Network.

Huberman, A. M. and Miles, M. (1984) *Innovation Up Close: How School Improvement Works*, New York: Plenum Press.

—— (1986) 'Rethinking the quest for school improvement: some findings from the DESSI study', in A. Lieberman (ed.) *Rethinking School Improvement*, New York: Teachers' College Press.

Kirst, M. W. and Meister, G. R. (1985) 'Turbulence in American secondary schools: what reforms last?', *Curriculum Inquiry* 15(2): 37–49.

Langrehr, J. (1994) 'The national curriculum: new courses? New methods', *Primary Education* 25(1): 13–15.

Lawton, D. and Chitty, C. (eds) (1988) *The National Curriculum*, Bedford Way Papers 33, London: University of London Institute of Education.

Leithwood, K. A. and Montgomery, D. J. (1986) *Improving Principal Effectiveness: The Principal Profile*, Toronto: Ontario Institute for Studies in Education (OISE) Press.

Lieberman, A. and Miller, L. (1986) 'School improvement: themes and variations', in

A. Lieberman (ed.) *Rethinking School Improvement*, New York: Teachers' College Press.

Llorens, M. B. (1994) 'Action research: are teachers finding their voice?', *Elementary School Journal* 95(1): 3–10.

McGaw, B. (1995) 'Benchmarking for accountability or for improvement?', *Unicorn* 21(2): 7–12.

Marsh, C. J. (1994) *Producing a National Curriculum: Plans and Paranoia*, Sydney: Allen & Unwin.

—— (1995) 'Putting the profiles to work: real gains or real problems', paper presented at the Biennial Conference of the Australian Curriculum Studies Association, Melbourne, July.

Marsh, C. J. and Huberman, A. M. (1984) 'Disseminating curricula: a look from the top down', *Journal of Curriculum Studies* 16: 1.

Marsh, D. D. and Bowman, G. A. (1988) 'Building better secondary schools: a comparison of school improvement and school reform strategies in California', paper presented at the Annual Meeting of the American Educational Research Association, New Orleans.

Popkewitz, T. S. (1985) 'Educational reform rhetoric, ritual, and social interest', unpublished paper presented at the University of Salamanca, Spain.

Prideaux, D. (1988) 'School-based curriculum decision-making in South Australian primary schools', unpublished PhD dissertation, Flinders University, South Australia.

—— (1993) 'School-based curriculum development: partial, paradoxical and piecemeal', *Journal of Curriculum Studies* 25(2): 169–78.

Pusey, M. (1981) 'How will governments strive to control education in the 1980s', *Discourse* 1: 3–9.

Rapoport, R. N. (1997) 'Families as educators for global citizenship: five conundrums of intentional socialisation', *International Journal of Early Years Education* 5(1): 67–78.

Reid, K. *et al.* (1988) *An Introduction to Primary School Organisation*, London: Hodder & Stoughton.

Richards, C. (1995) 'Curriculum leadership: challenges for primary head teachers', *Education 3–13* 23(3): 3–10.

Sabar, N. (1987) 'School-based curriculum development: the pendulum swings', in N. Sabar, J. Rudduck and W. Reid (eds) *Partnership and Autonomy in School-based Curriculum Development*, Sheffield: University of Sheffield.

Sabar, N., Ruddock, J. and Reid, W. (eds) (1987) *Partnership and Autonomy in School-based Curriculum Development*, Sheffield: University of Sheffield.

Sabar, N. and Silberstein, M. (1987) 'Training for curriculum coordination in a school-based curriculum development', paper presented at the Annual Conference of the American Educational Research Association, Washington, DC, April.

Seddon, T., Angus, L. and Poole, M. E. (1990) 'Pressures on the move to school-based decision-making and management', in J. D. Chapman (ed.) *School-based Decision-making and Management*, London: Falmer Press.

Simons, H. (1987) *Getting to Know Schools in a Democracy*, Lewes: Falmer Press.

Smyth, J. (1993) (ed.) *A Socially Critical View of the Self-managing School*, London: Falmer Press.

Stannard, J. (1995) 'Managing the primary curriculum after Dearing: a rationale', *Education 3–13* 23(1): 3–7.

Wallace, J. and Wildy, H. (1994) 'The national school project: school site experiences at restructuring', *Unicorn* 20(1): 63–72.

Webb, R. (1996) 'Changing primary classroom practice through teacher research', *Education 3–13* 25(3): 8–17.

Wilson, B. (1994) 'Profiles: the changing role of assessment', *Primary Education* 25(1): 9–12.

Woods, P. (1996) '"The good times": creative teaching in primary school', *Education 3 to 13* 24(2): 3–12.

Young, J. H. (1990). 'Teacher participation in curriculum development: a study of societal and institutional levels', *Alberta Journal of Educational Research* 36(2): 141–56.

Zaltman, G., Florio, D. H. and Sikorski, L. A. (1977) *Dynamic Educational Change*, New York: Free Press.

8

ASSESSMENT IN PRIMARY SCHOOLS

John Ainley

Introduction

Primary schools have undergone many changes in the past decade, in management strategies, in funding arrangements and in curriculum development and implementation. Perhaps the area that has had the most impact on the work of the school is the stronger focus on state-wide accountability for student outcomes, which has passed from the system as a whole to individual schools and teachers. This has brought about an intensification of effort in terms of assessing students, recording their progress and then reporting the outcomes of this progress, to parents, to the education authority and to the wider community. Regular testing based on procedures and instruments that are comparable across schools, computer-based recording of student progress and publicly available information derived from assessments are all new considerations for the modern primary school.

The purposes of assessment in primary schools are wide-ranging, and the emphases on its different purposes vary according to circumstance and change over time. In general, assessment serves the purpose of providing and interpreting evidence about student learning. Assessment intended to inform students and their parents about what has been learned, to provide a basis for improving student learning or to reach a summarising judgement about achievement for certification is long established in education. Most teachers regularly assess what their students have learned. In recent years various forms of student assessment have also been used to evaluate the performance of school systems, and even schools. Sometimes a different terminology is used when measurements of performance are used to provide information about individuals (assessment) and when similar measures are used to provide information about a programme or school (evaluation).

Even though it is common to think of assessment as being synonymous with traditional written tests, this is not necessarily the case. A variety of forms of assessment are used in Australian primary schools. These forms differ in a number of characteristics, including the evidence that is used, the ways in which measures relate to that evidence, the intended purpose of the assessment and the ways in which assessments are reported.

Breadth of evidence

A central feature of assessment is the use of evidence to indicate the extent to which learning has taken place. Assessment attempts to detect the extent of learning progressively over time or at the end of a sequence of study. Since learning cannot be measured directly, assessment procedures seek to identify indicators of learning through various forms of evidence. In a traditional approach to assessment, evidence of learning is obtained from students' written performance in response to a set of questions constituting a 'test'. Those responses are typically processed as measures (or scores), which form the basis of the assessment of an individual's level of achievement. Modern approaches to assessment make use of a wider variety of evidence of student achievement. The *Assessment Resource Kit* (Masters and Forster 1996) stresses the variety of relevant evidence that can be used, and is used, by teachers in primary schools to assess student learning. This evidence includes teacher observations and judgements about student work, portfolios (collections of student work assembled over a period of time), projects, products, performances, and paper and pen tests completed in a limited period of time under specified conditions.

The collection of evidence for assessment involves the recording of observations and the forming of judgements. Teachers use a variety of methods for this purpose, including general comments recorded on record sheets, indications as to whether a particular task has been completed satisfactorily, records of attempts that were partly correct, ratings of different aspects of a piece of work or overall ratings of the quality of a piece of work. The extent to which an assessment is based on evidence relevant to what is being assessed is reflected in its validity. The matching of assessment methods to curriculum goals is fundamental to effective assessment. In this sense, assessment methods should embrace the range of knowledge, skills and understandings that constitute an area of learning. Reliability or accuracy of assessment is also an important criterion of good assessment and refers to the extent to which the collected evidence reflects an individuals' knowledge, understandings and skills (rather than such things as the idiosyncratic views of the marker). Objectively scored (often multiple-choice) tests became popular because they were considered to be reliable (and because they were considered to be cost-effective). In recent years considerable effort has been expended on developing procedures to improve the reliability of assessments based on other types of evidence. Reliability can be improved by specification of criteria and evidence, training assessors, using work samples as guides, and making adjustments for differences between assessors in standards and in the details of tasks completed by students.

Points of reference

Interpretation is an important aspect of assessment since assessment is not just about recording information such as test scores for its own sake. If assessment is to inform one's knowledge about the extent of learning, this involves interpretation. Part of the process of interpretation requires reference to other information such as the performance of other students, a criterion to be achieved, the student's own previous best or progress along a continuum of growth. Recent years have seen the emergence of a more sophisticated use of points of reference for assessments in Australian primary schools.

Norm-referenced assessment

In the recent past many approaches to assessment were based on the principle of comparing the performance of an individual (or a group of individuals) with a wider reference group: a *norm-referenced* approach. This approach was common for tests of general abilities (such as the Australian Council for Educational Research (ACER) Intermediate G) and tests of some specific curriculum areas (such as the Class Achievement Tests in Mathematics (CATIM)). Performance is typically measured as the percentage of the items answered correctly and reported as a score or mark. The reporting of results from such an approach to assessment tends to emphasise relative performance: the achievement of a given student compared to others in a class, or compared to others of the same age and grade in the population. For example, results could be reported in terms of standardised scores or position in a distribution (e.g. as a stanine). Norm-referenced assessment has become less common as teachers seek to provide assessments which are more powerful in terms of monitoring progress and can more readily make use of a wider range of evidence.

Criterion-referenced assessment

Criterion-referenced assessment refers to assessment where the performance of an individual (or group of individuals) is compared with a desired level of mastery or a standard. For example, a student may be expected to spell correctly certain types of words (a skill that is operationalised as a word list). Criterion-referenced and norm-referenced assessments make a similar assumption about the validity of the evidence that is used but differ in the ways in which inferences are drawn and interpretations constructed. For assessments designed to provide comparisons among students the essential property required is that of discrimination; in other words, they need to spread the students out. For assessments designed to judge students in terms of a criterion it is not important to spread the students out; it does not matter if the majority are in the category 'achieved the criterion'. Therefore, in criterion-referenced assessment traditional notions of reliability defined as consistency of discrimination are not appropriate, and are replaced by coefficients of efficiency and of reproducibility. The 1975 and 1980 Australian Studies in School Performance (Keeves and Bourke 1976; Bourke *et al.* 1981) were important as the first major examples of criterion-referenced assessment in Australia. In these studies definitions of minimum competence in literacy and numeracy for 10-year-olds and 14-year-olds were developed and tests were designed to determine whether or not students had achieved the minimum competence levels. Performances were expressed primarily in terms of the percentage of the relevant population achieving the defined levels.

Scale-referenced assessment

In recent years a new approach to measurement has emerged which blurs the dichotomy between norm-referenced and criterion-referenced assessment. The approach has various names, such as the 'Rasch model' or 'item-response theory' (Wright and Stone 1979). It begins with an analysis of the interactions of individuals with items, and allows the definition of a measurement scale on which people can be located in terms of achievement and items can be located in terms of difficulty. The approach is sometimes called 'latent-trait theory' because the scales can be thought of as underlying dimensions. A practical outcome of the approach is the development of a scale that has clear units and the potential to measure a readily interpretable difference. In this sense the scale is analogous to that on a thermometer. The positioning of the items on the scale facilitates the interpretation of points on the scale in terms of what students could be expected to do on the basis of a given score. The reason this approach blurs the distinction between norm-referenced and criterion-referenced approaches is that the interpretation in terms of a scale does not depend on comparisons among students, even though it allows those comparisons to be made.

This approach to assessment was used in the Tests of Reading Comprehension (Torch) (Mossenson *et al.* 1987), a series widely used in primary schools across Australia. Each test in the series is based on a piece of prose (fiction or non-fiction) for students to read. Students are then asked to respond to a retelling of that prose which contains gaps that they are required to complete using one or more of their own words. Filling each gap requires a non-unique response and the scoring key allows for a range of acceptable responses. Teachers make a judgement about what is an appropriate response. The total score obtained is a measure of the student's achievement in reading comprehension and can be converted to Torch scores using tables based on Rasch scaling procedures. The full Torch scale covers a set of 14 tests from Years 3 to 10, all calibrated on a common scale. Points on the scale correspond to skills which range from 'provide the subject of a story given multiple references', through 'complete simple rewording' and 'provide a detail in the presence of distracting ideas', to 'provide evidence of having understood the motive underlying a series of actions' and 'reconstruct the writer's general message from specific statements'.

The *scale-referenced* approach to assessment was also used in the New South Wales Basic Skills Testing Program (BSTP) (Masters *et al.* 1990). Central to the analysis of the BSTP results was the idea of a skill continuum, with development in each aspect of literacy or numeracy being seen as a continuous process through which students progress from low to advanced levels of understanding and skill. Advantages of this approach for a state-wide monitoring programme are that it enables each successive year's test to be calibrated (using some common items) on the same scale (and thus facilitates the monitoring of trends) and that it enables reporting in terms of identifiable skills. From a detailed analysis of the items, descriptions of performance bands were developed and each student received a personalised report in which his or her performance was located on a set of scales. Each student was located in a performance band for which a description was printed (*ibid.*: 1990). This approach to scaling has now become the basis for most state-wide assessment programmes in Australian primary schools.

Other approaches

Other approaches to assessment are less structured than these and are based on descriptive statements about categories of work (descriptive assessment) or the completion of defined tasks (work-based) (see Withers and Batten 1990). These attempt to report intentions, quality and content of the learning that has taken place in a narrative form. They are characterised by not having an explicit single continuum of growth underpinning the assessment. This form of assessment is extremely widely used by teachers in Australian primary schools when they compile summary reports for parents. These forms of assessment make it possible to identify and describe new developments in learning that have taken place.

Profiles

One of the most important recent developments affecting assessment in Australian primary schools has been the emergence and application of profiles. A profile is a description of the progression of learning outcomes typically achieved by students during a period of education (e.g. their school years). Some writers have referred to profiles as 'progress maps' that enable teachers to record and interpret a wide variety of evidence about student learning (Masters and Forster 1996). What has provided an important impetus to the development and use of profiles has been their emergence from the twin concerns of better curriculum definition and the application of modern methods of assessment.

Curriculum frameworks

Over the latter part of the 1980s there emerged in Australia considerable pressure for consistency in curriculum across its various education systems. Out of some curriculum-mapping exercises there arose collaborative efforts to develop curriculum and assessment frameworks in English and mathematics. Then, at a meeting in 1989, the Commonwealth and State Ministers for Education decided to act jointly to assist Australian schools and agreed on ten national goals for schooling (Australian Education Council 1989). Although these goals were expressed in generic forms the ministers subsequently established a Curriculum Corporation as a jointly owned company to facilitate collaborative development on curriculum and identified eight key learning areas as the overall structure of the curriculum. These areas were English, health and physical education, languages other than English, mathematics, science, studies of society, and environment and technology. For each area the council commissioned the development of a statement of what was to be taught and a profile of what students were expected to learn.

The statements define learning areas in terms of sub-areas called 'strands' (which reflect the major elements of learning in each area) and bands corresponding to different stages of schooling. For example, in mathematics the strands are attitudes and appreciations; mathematical inquiry; choosing and using mathematics; space; number; measurement; chance and data; and algebra. The strands specify both content and process, and suggest a sequence for developing skills and knowledge in that area. In that sense they are sometimes referred to as a framework since they are not as specific as a syllabus. The bands are common to all the learning areas, with Band A referring to the lower primary years (Years 1 to 4) and Band B referring to the upper primary years (Years 4 to 7).

For each learning area corresponding profiles describe outcomes and show typical progression in the achievement of outcomes. By describing what students are expected to achieve at each level the profiles provide a common language for assessment, for reporting, and for the development of teaching and learning. The profiles are sequenced as eight levels, which correspond roughly to the first ten years of schooling. They provide details for subdivisions of the strands (strand organisers), within which student learning outcomes are defined for each of the eight levels. In English there are three strands (speaking and listening, reading, and viewing and writing) divided into four strand organisers (texts, contextual understanding, linguistic structures and features, and strategies). For each level there is a general description of student performance at that level and a set of pointers which are indicators of the achievement of an outcome. There are also annotated examples of student work which demonstrates the achievement of one or more outcomes at the particular level.

Even though the national statements and profiles were eventually not adopted on a national basis by the council of ministers, many aspects were incorporated by the states in their own curriculum statements. In this way these formal statements of what students are expected to learn have become a powerful influence on the way assessment is conducted and the way students' achievements are reported.

An assessment perspective

The clear definition of curriculums in terms of intended learning outcomes for students was one of the influences on the emergence of profiles as an important part of assessment. However, there were simultaneous developments in methods of assessment that also resulted in profiles becoming such an important aspect of assessment in the modern primary school. The emergence of scale-referenced approaches (variously called Rasch, item response or latent trait) provided the technology to analyse data on student performance to establish standards in profiles empirically. Two early examples of this application illustrate this perspective.

One early example of the empirical establishment of standards was a light-sampling-based evaluation of literacy and numeracy levels in Victorian schools (McGaw *et al.* 1989). The evaluation was intended to establish how many students were completing school with inadequate levels and to compare current with past levels of performance. The tests devised were specific to the Year 5 and Year 9 levels but contained some items common to both tests and some items common to the tests that had been conducted in 1975 and 1980. All the items could then be mapped on to a common scale and items could be inspected to determine the point on the scale that represented the minimum acceptable performance (for functioning in adult society). The percentage of students at each year level could then be estimated and reported in a manner that enabled others to debate whether the definition of competence was too stringent or too relaxed. The use of a common scale also enabled the question of whether standards had improved or declined to be addressed. In this case the scale points were entirely based on empirical evidence. The evaluation preceded the elucidation of profiles related to an intended curriculum.

The Western Australian Monitoring Standards in Education project commenced at a time when statements of outcomes had been developed for the Western Australian school system (Titmanis *et al.* 1993). Consequently, it was possible for the monitoring programme to be built around these outcome statements with levels of achievement defined in relation to these statements and test items designed to assess these levels of achievement. Student data was then analysed in a way that enabled an empirical validation of the assignment of items to levels of achievement. For example, the 'space' strand of the mathematics area had four levels of development: Level 1 referred to drawing (inaccurately) and naming two-dimensional shapes in an everyday scene; Level 2 referred to identifying a circular and a rectangular shape in a scene where several shapes are shown; Level 3 referred to selecting the net of a three-dimensional box from its two-dimensional representation; and Level 4 referred to recognising that a turning angle in a figure was 90 degrees. Anomalies in the analysis provide important information on whether an item is inappropriate or (more importantly) whether the specified outcome should be allocated to a different level. The authors point to the possibility of gradually adjusting the detail of the profile with which they began.

Extending the principle

The principle of using a profile related to student development as a basis for assessment has found significant application and extension beyond the development and analysis of tests. This approach has provided a basis for the systematic use of a variety of evidence as part of assessment. It has enabled the use of a wider range of student work and allowed teachers' professional judgements to be incorporated formally in assessment processes. This has been possible because of the establishment of profiles in which those judgements can be keyed.

Griffin (1990) describes the process of developing profiles of literacy development in the Victorian school system. Griffin used a range of teacher judgements or ratings of samples of student work and related these to performance on a series of tests (the Torch tests). Sets of seven bands in reading and nine in writing were established, with each band being described in terms of the skill levels that it represents. The result is a system of levels in which a range of assessment information (worksheets, tests, checklists and performance tasks) can be incorporated and against which reporting with defined criteria can be facilitated. Subsequent developments have modified the Victorian profiles and enabled them to be used to study the intellectual growth of students over successive years (Rowe and Hill 1996a).

The emergence of profiles has stimulated resources for developmental assessment by teachers. Masters and Forster define developmental assessment as 'the process of monitoring a student's progress through an area of learning so that decisions can be made about the best ways to facilitate further learning' (Masters and Forster 1996). Masters and Forster describe profiles as 'progress maps' that teachers can use to monitor the development of students on an established continuum. This continuum provides a basis for using a variety of assessment evidence in a common framework. The resources that can be used within such a framework allow a rich variety of tasks and provide the possibility of giving meaning to statements in areas where clarity has traditionally been difficult. For example, the Developmental

Assessment Resource for Teachers (DART) (Forster *et al.* 1994) has yielded a more detailed continuum of the development of skills in speaking and listening than was possible in the absence of empirical testing. Masters and Forster (1996) also elaborate on how performances, portfolios and projects can be incorporated into an assessment framework that has a developmental orientation.

Assessment as part of monitoring

Over recent years a new emphasis on monitoring the achievement levels of students has been fuelled, at least partly, by anecdotal and non-systematic claims of a decline in standards. In the absence of systematic data about student achievements it was difficult to refute such claims. Similarly, within the processes of government programmes, learning areas were increasingly being asked to provide evidence that programmes across a range of areas were meeting the goals that were set for them.

National assessment programmes

The first national effort to document student achievement was designed to estimate the proportions of each age group performing below defined levels of minimum competence in literacy and numeracy (Keeves and Bourke 1976). It was based on two nationally representative samples of 6,600 students at the age of 10 years and 14 years, respectively. Although the study concluded that significant numbers of children were failing to reach adequate levels, data on a single occasion could not reveal anything about changes in levels of performance. A repeat survey in 1980, commissioned by the Australian Education Council, demonstrated no decline in performance levels since the 1975 survey (Bourke *et al.* 1981). For a considerable period no further national surveys were undertaken because of opposition from both teachers' organisations and education authorities. It was argued that such surveys were inevitably narrow in their scope and thus likely to distort the curriculum.

In 1996 a National Schools English Literacy Survey (NSELS) was conducted on the basis of a sample of 4,000 students in each of Years 3 and 5 in a nationally representative sample of 400 schools (Masters and Forster 1997). The survey involved assessment materials in the five strands of the English profile: reading, writing, listening, speaking and viewing. Analyses and the development of the assessment materials were based on scale-referenced approaches known as Rasch modelling or item-response theory. In its operation the survey involved the training of teachers so that teachers in classrooms were actively involved in its administration and in making judgements. The results show the extent of growth that takes place between Year 3 and Year 5 and relates student achievement to a range of student and school characteristics. However, its basis was so different from the study conducted in 1975 that it is not possible to compare the two sets of results.

In 1997 the federal, state and territory Ministers of Education agreed that state-wide testing programmes in the primary school years would focus on Years 3 and 5, and that there would be some coordination of the tests so that some common elements would be included in each.

Information about achievement levels in mathematics and science has also been obtained from surveys conducted by the International Association for the Evaluation of Educational Achievement (IEA). These studies have typi-cally involved national samples of students selected from the upper years of primary school, the early years of secondary school and the end of secondary school. Australia participated in the First International Mathematics Study in 1964, the First and Second International Science Studies in 1970 and 1983 (Rosier and Banks 1990) and in the Third International Mathematics and Science Study in 1995 (Lokan *et al.* 1997). There have been a number of other international studies in which Australia has not participated.

State-wide assessment programmes

In recent years most Australian states have introduced, revived or continued assessment and monitoring programmes, especially at primary-school level. Some of these programmes began as sample studies, but in recent times most have shifted to adopt population assessment programmes at designated years, most commonly Year 3 and Year 5. Sample programmes of moni-toring are considered to be less intrusive on school curricula and to allow the possibility of testing over a wider range of curriculum areas in a system-atic way. On the other hand, population testing provides individual reports on each student with the prospect of identification of, and attention to, diffi-culties. Population testing programmes also provide the opportunity for monitoring the progress of disadvantaged minorities in the school system.

Sample surveys

Victoria introduced sample surveys of student achievement in 1988. It commissioned a survey of literacy and numeracy in 1998 (McGaw *et al.* 1989), followed by studies of science achievement in 1990 (Adams *et al.* 1991) and social education in 1992 (Doig *et al.* 1994). Those studies focused on students in late primary (Year 5) and early secondary (Year 9) schools and were limited to government schools. Since 1990, Queensland has conducted surveys of the performance of students, with tests of English and mathematics involving random samples of students in Years 5, 7 and 9. Western Australia introduced sample testing involving students in Years 3, 7 and 10 through its Monitoring Standards in Education (WAMSE) from 1990 onwards (Titmanis *et al.* 1993). Some 1,500 students are sampled but the samples are different for each of the tests involved. Results are provided in the form of state-wide results and schools are encouraged to use the tests to monitor the achievement levels of their own students. Although this programme began with tests in literacy and numeracy, it now involves assessments across the range of learning areas rather than being confined to the areas of English and mathematics.

Population testing

In order to report on individual students' performances to parents and schools, population testing was introduced in the Northern Territory at primary level in 1983 and mid-secondary in 1989. Tasmania has had testing of all students aged 10 years and 14 years in literacy and numeracy since 1976, but on a four-year cycle with one test and one age group each year. New South Wales introduced population testing in 1989 at Years 3 and 6 but soon shifted the focus to Years 3 and 5. South Australia adopted the New South Wales tests from 1995. Victoria introduced population testing at primary level (Years 3 and 5) in 1995, and Queensland adopted Year 6 as the focus for its programme of population testing.

Some results

Monitoring programmes have provided evidence about student performance levels over time. One of the results of the 1980 national study was to point to a significant improvement in the newspaper-reading items in the five years since the first study. In Victoria, data from the 1988 study could be compared with data from 1975 and 1980, and the conclusion was reached that there had been no decline in standards of performance (see, for example, McGaw et al. 1989). Similarly, for Tasmania there was no change in basic reading skills since 1975 and, until the appearance of a decline in the early 1990s, no change in basic numeracy skills (Evaluation and Assessment Unit 1993). Both the Western Australian and Queensland programmes have been used to monitor changes over more recent times, from 1990 to 1992. Often it is changes in particular items rather than general global changes which can be the most informative.

Most of the Australian testing programmes include some items common to tests at the different year levels. This allows calibration of the tests at different year levels onto a single scale and direct comparisons of performance across year levels. Such a process provides an indication of how much growth takes place from one year level to the next. It also provides an indication of the extent of overlap between year levels. In the Victorian study of literacy and numeracy there was substantial overlap of the distributions of Year 5 and Year 9 students (McGaw et al. 1989). A similar result was found in science (Adams et al. 1991).

Monitoring programmes can yield comparisons of achievement levels for subgroups of students and thereby address equity issues. The report of the New South Wales programme for 1989 showed females performing better than males in literacy and numeracy at Year 3, and in literacy and numeracy at Year 6, but males performing better in measurement and space at Year 6 (Masters *et al.* 1990). Students of non-English speaking background and students from the indigenous Aboriginal and Torres Strait Islander populations had lower performance levels than the overall student population. The Aboriginal Education Policy Task Force relied on a meta-analysis of data from state testing programmes to establish the extent of the educational disadvantage of those groups.

Interpreting results at school level

One of the important conclusions to emerge from research on school effectiveness is that some schools are more effective than others and that the differences among schools might be as substantial as differences in social background in shaping some important outcomes of schooling (McGaw *et al.* 1992). As a consequence there is renewed interest in using achievement data to identify factors associated with the effectiveness of schools. The inference to be drawn from much of the research in recent years is that achievement data can provide an important perspective when analysed carefully in conjunction with other information. Some of the considerations which need to be taken into account are outlined below.

Allowing for differences in student characteristics

One of the important issues in examining between-school differences in achievement has been that of adjustment for the influence of the characteristics of the school population. Results achieved by students depend upon factors associated with their background characteristics (e.g. socio-economic status, non-English speaking background) as well as on what their school experience contributes. Therefore results need to be considered in the context of the kind of students who attend the school. It is possible to make statistical adjustments to compare the actual results for a school with those which would be predicted. If the actual exceeds the predicted score it is taken as an indication that the school has maximised the achievement of its students.

Change rather than static measures

More recent studies have suggested that a statistical allowance for differences in social background is not sufficient to provide an indication of the contributions of schools to student learning. Allowance needs to made for differences in prior levels of achievement. Indeed, one of the most important developments in the methodology of school-effectiveness research has been the use of achievement growth (the change in achievement over time), rather than a single static achievement score at a particular time, as a criterion of school effectiveness (Mortimore *et al.* 1988; Ainley and Sheret 1992). It has come to be accepted that the assessment of achievement outcomes needs to be based on a concept of growth if a study is to identify school contributions to outcomes. One of the benefits of modern approaches to assessment is that they provide a better basis for the assessment of growth provided that longitudinal data are available. For an individual school it may well be that an assessment of change from year to year will be of greater value than the results from a single year.

Differences within schools

A number of studies have indicated that school influences are not distinct from classroom and teacher influences, and that classroom and teacher differences are generally greater than school differences. This was evident in a study of mathematics and reading achievement in primary schools in Victoria (Ainley *et al.* 1990). Similar results have been found using more sophisticated multi-level statistical analysis in studies within Australia and overseas (Rowe and Hill 1996b). This implies that within any school there will be more effective and less effective classrooms, and that improvement will come from improvements at classroom level.

Assessment and the quality of primary schools

Recent years have seen advances in approaches to assessment in primary schools. It is of considerable interest, and of great benefit, that the use of broader evidence of learning and attention to more informative forms of reporting have been supported by developments in the technology underpinning the assessment process. These have provided teachers with the basis on which to incorporate more appropriate forms of assessment in their school programmes.

At the same time there has been wider use of large-scale student testing programmes, so that these have become a common part of many education systems. Although the details of these programmes vary somewhat there are many common features and many similar purposes. At their best these programmes can provide valuable additional information about education systems that can inform future development and improvement. Properly interpreted, they can provide schools with information which will assist in the development of their programmes. However, such information will always refer to a sample of the goals of school systems and should be part of a wider network of information. How it interacts with that wider network and how schools and teachers can make best use of the information provided are areas about which much remains to be learned.

References

Adams, R. J., Doig, B. A. and Rosier, M. (1991) *Science Learning in Victorian Schools: 1990*, Melbourne: Australian Council for Educational Research.

Ainley, J., Goldman, J. and Reed, R. (1990) *Primary Schooling in Victoria: A Study of Students' Attitudes and Achievements in Years 5 and 6 of Government Primary Schools*, Melbourne: Australian Council for Educational Research.

Ainley, J. and Sheret, M. (1992) *Progress Through High School: A Study of Senior Secondary Schooling in New South Wales*, Melbourne: Australian Council for Educational Research.

Australian Education Council (1989) *Annual National Report on Schooling*, Carlton, Victoria: Australian Education Council.

Bourke, S. F., Mills, J. M., Stanyon, J. and Holzer, F. (1981) *Performance in Literacy and Numeracy: 1980*, Canberra: Australian Education Council.

Doig, B., Piper, K., Mellor, S. and Masters, G. (1994) *Conceptual Understanding in Social Education*, Melbourne: ACER.

Evaluation and Assessment Unit (1993) *1992 Survey of Basic Numeracy Skills of 10-year-old Tasmanian Students*, Hobart: Department of Education and the Arts.

Forster, M., Mendolovits, J. and Masters, G. (1994). *Developmental Assessment Resource for Teachers*, Melbourne: Australian Council for Educational Research.

Griffin, P. (1990) 'Profiling literacy development', *Australian Journal of Education* 34(3): 277–89.

Keeves, J. P. and Bourke, S. F. (1976) *Literacy and Numeracy in Australian Schools: A First Report*, Australian Studies in School Performance, vol. I, Canberra: Australian Government Publishing Service.

Lokan, J., Greenwood, L. and Ford, P. (1997) *Maths and Science on the Line: Australian Middle Primary Students Performance in the Third International Mathematics and Science Study*, Melbourne: Australian Council for Educational Research.

McGaw, B. (1994) 'Standards from a curriculum and assessment perspective: Directors comment', *ACER Annual Report 1993–94*, Melbourne: ACER.

McGaw, B., Banks, D., Piper, K. and Evans, B. (1992) *Making Schools More Effective*, Melbourne: Australian Council for Educational Research.

McGaw, B., Long, M. G., Morgan, G. and Rosier, M. J. (1989) *Literacy and Numeracy in Victorian Schools: 1988*, Melbourne: Australian Council for Educational Research.

Masters, G. and Forster, M. (1996) Mapping Literacy Achievement: Results of the 1996 National Schools English Literacy Survey, Canberra: Department of Employment, Education, Training and Youth Affairs.

—— (1997) *Bridging the Gap: The National Schools English Literacy Survey*, Melbourne: Australian Council for Educational Research.

Masters, G., Lokan, J., Doig, B., Khoo, S. K., Lindsey, J., Robinson, L. and Zammit, S. (1990) *Profiles of Learning: The Basic Skills Testing Program in New South Wales 1989*, Melbourne: Australian Council for Educational Research.

Mortimore, P. Sammons, P., Stoll, L., Lewis, D. and Ecob, R. (1988) *School Matters: The Junior Years*, Salisbury: Open Books.

Mossenson, L., Hill, P. and Masters, G. (1987) *Tests of Reading Comprehension*, Melbourne: ACER.

Rosier, M. J. and Banks, D. K. (1990) *The Scientific Literacy of Australian Students*, Melbourne: Australian Council for Educational Research.

Rowe, K. and Hill, P. (1996a) 'Assessing, recording and reporting students' educational progress: the case for subject profiles', *Assessment in Education* 3(3): 309–52.

—— (1996b) 'Multi-level models in school effectiveness research: how many levels?', *School Effectiveness and School Improvement* 7(1):1–34.

Titmanis, P., Murphy, F., Cook, J., Brady, K. and Brown, M. (1993) *Profiles of Student Achievement: English and Mathematics in Western Australian Government Schools*, Perth: Ministry of Education.

Withers, G. and Batten, M. (1990) 'Defining types of assessment', in B. Low and G. Withers (eds) *Developments in School and Public Assessment*, Melbourne: Australian Council for Educational Research.

Wright, B and Stone, M. H. (1979) *Best Test Design*, Chicago, IL: Measurement Evaluation and Statistical Analysis (MESA) Press.

9

THE IMPACT OF COMPUTER TECHNOLOGY ON PRIMARY EDUCATION

Geoff Romeo

Introduction

A major component of the restructuring activity taking place in most Australian states is the exploitation of technology to improve school administration and to enrich the curriculum. The purpose of this chapter is to look at the part computer technology is likely to play in the restructured school's curriculum, and to discuss some of the issues involved to help principals, teachers, parents and students of education better to understand what the technology is offering and likely to offer in the future.

Computers and the curriculum

Background

There is a lot of confusion, both inside and outside the educational community, about the exact role of computers in the primary classroom. This is despite, over the last ten to fifteen years, the expenditure of millions of dollars on professional development and despite a concerted effort by organisations such as the various Computers in Education Groups around the country, the Australian Council for Computers in Education (ACCE) and the Commonwealth Schools Commission to get the message across that there is more to computers in education than simply teaching children about computers and how to use particular pieces of application software.

If educators and the wider community are to understand more fully what is trying to be achieved with the technology then they must be able to distinguish between computer studies, or what is more commonly referred to as information technology, and computers in education. Basically, computer studies is the study of the computer itself, its applications, its social implications and the issues surrounding its use. One could describe computer studies as learning about computers, an essential element of which is developing computer literacy and awareness. Computers in education, on the other hand, is about exploiting the machine's power, versatility, flexibility and uniqueness to help the teacher establish powerful learning environments. This does not mean that computer literacy and computer awareness are not important, just that these two elements should be part of an integrated programme which emphasises:

> developing inquiry and problem solving skills so . . . information technology will not be seen as applicable to any one curriculum area, but as a tool for establishing meaning and communication, for classifying and ordering data and experiences and for opening up new approaches to learning.
>
> (NACCS 1985: 25)

One could describe computers in education as learning with computers.

In the Australian context, the development of this dichotomy of learning with computers and learning about computers is linked to the early-educational initiatives of the various state education departments, academics and computer education groups around the country. It was given a substantial boost, however, with the establishment of the National Program.

The National Program

By the early 1980s the use of computers in education had become a national concern. Both political parties at the federal level were seriously considering the question of computers in education, and the Commonwealth Schools Commission had taken the first steps in policy development. This interest at the national level was fuelled by considerable community concern with regard to technological change. Walker states: 'By 1982, the major political parties were responding to the pervasive interest and anxiety in the Australian community about computers and recognised that a commitment to support educational computing would be advantageous in the forthcoming election' (Walker 1991: 303). Upon taking office in March 1983 the Labor Government established the National Advisory Committee on Computers in Schools (NACCS). It wanted to establish a national policy framework for computing and support it with a considerable injection of funds.

The first report of NACCS, *Teaching, Learning and Computers* (NACCS 1983), recommended that a national programme, run in conjunction with the states, be established. Funds of A$18 million were made available over the subsequent three years. The report, while not explicitly stating its teaching/learning philosophy, advocated the use of computers for inquiry, analysis and problem-solving. It consolidated the trend towards learning with computers.

This trend was further consolidated with the release of *Teaching, Learning and Computers in Primary Schools* (NACCS 1985). The overriding aim of this second report was to enhance and improve educational practice in primary schools through the use of computers. It devoted a whole chapter to highlighting valuable aspects of contemporary classroom practices which lent themselves favourably to the use of computers in primary classrooms. These aspects included the view of the child as an active learner. The authors firmly believed that computers could assist teachers in promoting active engagement in learning by allowing students 'access to a wide range of high quality software which provides motivation, opportunities or contexts in which students read, write, think, discuss, or interact with peers and teachers' (*ibid.*: 6). A second aspect highlighted was the achievement of active engagement through the provision of a variety of learning experiences. The authors identified the potential of the computer to provide flexible learning environments which would allow students 'to travel through various pathways of learning, dependent on their cognitive styles or modes of learning and matched to their levels of cognitive ability' (*ibid.*: 8). A third aspect highlighted was the enquiry-learning approach, with its emphasis on processing information, developing problem-solving and investigation skills, and its relationship with the development of language.

The authors stressed that the potential existed for simulations, information-handling programmes and writing programmes to be developed which would allow students to handle information in different ways, to try out different solutions, pose and test hypotheses, and express their own ideas (NACCS 1985: 9).

The final aspect highlighted was the holistic approach to child development, which takes into account the development of both the affective and cognitive domains. The approach favours curriculum integration with the teaching of skills and understandings that reach across traditional subject boundaries, and focuses on the development of the child rather than concentrating on content. The authors viewed the computer as an important resource for student use in holistic approaches to learning (NACCS 1985: 9ff.).

Chasing the 'computers in education' dream

The rationale underpinning the national programme, the preferred teaching/learning philosophies of the various education departments around the country, and the fact that all education departments were expected to submit proposals for funding based on the assumptions underpinning the NACCS reports ensured that Australian states and territories attempted to develop programmes which merged the ideas of active, flexible learning environments, and enquiry and holistic approaches, with the technology. One of the main processes for doing so was School-based Curriculum Development (SBCD) combined with action research.

Many successful programmes were developed, but for many individual teachers and schools the merging of the technology with contemporary learning theories, the use of SBCD and action research was a substantial headache for a number of reasons.

First, the constructivist, humanistic, child-centred learning environment based on enquiry learning and the integration of the curriculum – which the NACCS seemed to believe was the dominant philosophy of state primary schools across the country – was, in practice, somewhat alien to many teachers. Despite millions of dollars being spent on projects such as Frameworks (see Ministry of Education 1985) and despite the promise of SBCD, teaching practices and procedures in a great many classrooms were still very traditional.

Second, the idea of using the computer in the classroom was new; there were no well-established instructional strategies to fall back upon. There was an expectation that teachers would carry out school-based research and develop their own instructional strategies. Many teachers lacked experience and training in the SBCD process, and were unfamiliar with the principles of curriculum development and design.

In some schools this was compounded by an unstable teacher base, lack of resources – especially time and energy – and inadequate support mechanisms at school and regional levels. There was also a natural resistance to change, with many teachers and administrators feeling threatened by the altered role of the teacher which SBCD and action research brought with them (Print 1991: 13ff.). The situation was further complicated by a lack of computer literacy and an unfamiliarity with the basic assumptions and rationale underpinning the emerging computers in education movement.

Some direction was coming from the academic community. Academic research into the use of computers in the classroom was being conducted all over the world. However, since it was a relatively young and diverse discipline, debate often focused on research methodology and on hardware and software issues, at the expense of pedagogical and curriculum issues. Also, teachers were traditionally circumspect about academic research, which they saw as accentuating the gap between theory and practice.

Finally, the merging of the technology with the perceived teaching and learning philosophy relied on teachers' willingness and opportunity to develop computer literacy skills and simultaneously develop procedures and practices for the use of the machines in the classroom. It is hard to tell how many were willing and how many were not. Certainly, over a number of years a lot of good work was done, a lot of knowledge was generated, collated and disseminated, but there was a significant number of teachers who were unwilling, or did not have the opportunity, to participate. Lack of funding, lack of direction and lack of expert knowledge probably contributed to the missed opportunities, and the nature of the technology itself contributed to the unwillingness.

Substantial as these problems may have been, they did not stop some creative and committed people from developing an astonishing array of programmes and projects based on the philosophy of learning with computers. In Victoria alone, the State Computer Education Centre (SCEC) and the regional computing centres were supporting projects such as the Inclusive Computing Project (see Ministry of Education and Training, Victoria 1991), the Computing History Project (see Allitt and Hellier 1987), the Sunrise School Project (see Ryan *et al.* 1991), as well as individual school initiatives (see Alder and Guss 1985). Some schools were using laptops and LogoWriter; some were using adventure games; some were using electronic communications; some were using Lego/Logo; some were doing desktop publishing, others databases and spreadsheets.

This was probably the original aim, diversity and variety, but the diversity and variety were also a problem. For some, it was a very confusing state of affairs. New schools, schools just embarking on a computer programme and schools still looking for solutions did not know where to turn for a role model. Should they do Logo, should they do word processing, what about keyboarding and adventure games, what about desktop publishing, spreadsheets, problem solving, simulations?

There was also confusion about organisation and logistics: how many computers should be bought? Where should they be located? What about site licences and copyright? Do we need a computer specialist? And so on. Complicating the equation was the technology itself, whether is should be PC or Macintosh, Pentium 120 or 166, Performa or Powermac, standalone or network, desktop or notebook, inkjet or laser, modem, CD-ROM, and so on?

The Australian community had invested millions of dollars in pursuit of the computers in education dream, but by the mid-1990s there was still a great deal to be done.

The current situation

Computers in the classroom

It is difficult to summarise what the current situation is in Australia. As mentioned, over a decade of SBCD and action research has ensured variety and diversity. What can be said for certain, thanks to federal and state funding programmes, Coles Supermarket schemes and generous parent bodies, is that schools have invested heavily in software and hardware. Whether this technology is being used effectively, or even used at all, is more difficult to answer.

Anecdotal evidence suggests that the predominant use of computers in primary classrooms is for word processing and various classroom publishing activities. Many schools would also be using adventure games, problem-solving, and drill and practice software, while some schools would be using databases, spreadsheets, Microworlds and Hypercard.

In 1994 the Victorian government published a report by the State Government Working Party on the use of technology as an education and communication facility in Victorian Schools (Smith 1994). The authors investigated various information technologies then being used in educational settings. The report, which has become known as the Smith Report, gives some insight into the current situation.

In an effort to analyse computer use in schools, the working party scrutinised the Department of Education assets register. From the data the working party was able to report that schools in Victoria were equipped with a range of computer technology from late-model Macintosh and DOS machines, to early BBC, Microbee and Apple IIe machines. The register did not inform the working party, however, of how many computers were being used, for what purposes, by whom, how often or for how long. Still, the working party was, through alternative means, able to highlight a number of individual schools which were successful users of computer technology.

One such case was the use of laptop computers by students at Methodist Ladies' College (MLC) in Melbourne. Students use the computers for recording work in most subject areas and carry the machines between home and school. Most students from middle primary to upper secondary are required to purchase their own laptop. Although not on the scale of MLC, some Victorian government primary schools, such as Jells Park Primary School, have also introduced laptop computers to their senior grades, with pleasing results. The report also highlighted other programmes: at Keilor Downs Secondary College the computer is used as a tool in physics; at Greythorn Primary School a Digicard network links Apple IIe, Macintosh and DOS machines to a file server; and students at Broadford and Mansfield Secondary Colleges use global networking to correspond with students in other states and internationally (Smith 1994: 19ff).

A broader, more national picture of computer use in schools is painted by the Australian Capital Territory (ACT) Department of Education and Training and Children's, Youth and Family Services Bureau's (DEETYA 1996) report on the use of information technologies in the learning process. The report details the employment of a variety of computer applications to enhance learning in the eight key learning areas (KLAs). Examples include the use of multimedia CD-ROMs for research and for learning languages other than English (LOTE), electronic mail to correspond with keypals and experts, multimedia authoring tools to produce talking books and electronic projects, Web authoring tools to publish student work on the World Wide Web, simulations in chemistry, spreadsheets in mathematics and composition tools in music.

Both reports (Smith 1994; DEEYTA 1996) and anecdotal data provide evidence that computer technology is being used in some schools to help establish challenging and exciting learning environments. Apart from the ones mentioned, both reports could probably have highlighted more schools and individual teachers across the country who are using computers in education in an exemplary way. Unfortunately, however, there would be many more schools where the computers in education programme is not well established, and within individual schools there would be classrooms not taking advantage of the technology for a variety of reasons.

Computers in the library

Many schools have computerised their school libraries. Current technologies can be employed to computerise the library's card-index system, to provide students with access to laserdisks and CD-ROM, and to provide students with conduits to information stored beyond the school. The Smith Report found that a number of schools had computerised their card-catalogue system but had used a diverse range of incompatible software, making the transfer of information between libraries difficult; some schools had invested in more sophisticated forms of information such as CD-ROM; but very few school libraries were connected to the Internet (Smith 1994: 19).

Computers and multimedia

The term multimedia is used to refer to the integration of several types of media such as text, graphics, sound, animation and motion video. All these media forms are presented and sequenced under computer control. Sophisticated forms of multimedia require considerable computing power, speed and storage, but the construction of multimedia, the application of multimedia and the use of multimedia for classroom presentations has certainly fired the imagination of many educators.

The Smith Report found that multimedia had not had much of an impact on schools because few schools had the equipment to offer full multimedia capabilities to students (Smith 1994: 24–5). The DEETYA Report (1996), however, indicated that this situation was changing. Of the forty-five case studies presented, seventeen were either utilising CD-ROM material authored by someone else or requiring students to author their own multimedia presentations, however humble.

Exploiting multimedia authored by someone else or engaging students, and perhaps teachers, in creating their own multimedia material is where the real power of multimedia lies. However, in an attempt to take advantage of what multimedia seems to be offering, the Victorian Education Department has been trialling, in some schools, CCC Successmaker, an integrated learning system produced by the Computer Curriculum Corporation of Los Angeles.

Integrated learning systems run on microcomputer networks with large capacity hard drives as file servers. They combine a computer-managed instruction system with a large set of interrelated computer-based instruction programmes. The programme gathers, stores and generates reports on student progress; the teacher can set up a class roster and specify which lessons students may study; individual learning routes can be mapped by the student or teacher; and many systems include diagnostic and prescriptive capabilities (Merrill 1992: 235).

Successmaker offers interactive multimedia-based lessons in mathematics, reading, writing, language and science at all levels from Preparatory to Year 10. It is being trialled in a number of primary and secondary schools, where the package is delivered on networked computers in a laboratory setting (DSE 1994).

Computers and the Internet

The Internet is a worldwide information network, often described as a network of networks (Neely 1995: 10). Through the Internet, universities, libraries, research establishments, news and business corporations, and government departments are linked via a network of computers.

Many secondary colleges and primary schools across the nation have become involved with the Internet through projects such as Oz Projects, which delivers a wide range of programmes to schools, including CSIRO Scientists Online, Murder Under the Microscope, Postcards from Oz, Virtual Field Trips, Project Atmosphere Australia, Travel Buddies and Where in Australia?; the International Education and Resource Network (I*EARN), which encourages students to collaborate on global projects; Global Lab, which connects students from over twenty countries for collaboration on projects such as the Global Ultra Violet Radiation and Stratospheric Ozone Project; and Internet services such as Schools NET, Pegasus, Nexus and Keylink.

Schools are also publishing their own World Wide Web pages and use the electronic-mail facilities of the Internet to correspond with students in other states and countries, and teachers are using the e-mail, newsgroup and forum facilities of the World Web Wide for professional development activities.

Computers and Telematics

In Victoria computers are also used as part of the Telematics programme. Telematics involves the use of a number of interactive communication technologies to connect students and teachers for the purposes of sharing resources and delivering curriculum. The technologies involved are audiographics, which involves the use of telephone, facsimile machines and computers; Interactive Television by satellite; video conferencing; broadcast television; computer conferencing; and interactive multimedia.

The use of Telematics is increasing. During the latter half of 1993 seventy-six Victorian classes were using audiographics, mainly in the areas of LOTE and for the Victorian Certificate of Education; and a majority of schools are now connected to the Interactive Television Network. The current tactic is to use a variety of communication media including audio, fax, computer, interactive television, print and face-to-face meetings to create productive learning environments (Smith 1994: 26).

There are many examples of individual schools and teachers who have come to grips with the technology and have been able to develop and implement innovative, exciting and creative computers in education programmes, but for many there is still confusion and apprehension. There is also anxiety about the future.

Future trends

The technological revolution has moved with astonishing speed, is growing at an exponential rate and is far from finished. Under such circumstances, making predictions about the future can be problematic. However, in the near future four main trends appear to be poised to make a significant impact.

Multimedia

Multimedia is the buzzword of the 1990s. As demonstrated by the DEETYA report (1996), the trend towards the use of multimedia and student authoring of multimedia in the classroom is gathering pace. CD-ROM technology, with its capacity to store vast amounts of text, graphics, sounds and video, is now commonplace in many homes. New CD-ROM products are coming on to the market every day, and the technology is becoming cheaper and more sophisticated. This trend is likely to continue and the quality of CD-ROM titles and multimedia authoring tools is likely to improve. In the future schools will be able to offer students sophisticated access to vast amounts of information. The information will be presented in creative and interesting ways, and students will be able not only to interact with the presentations, but also to create their own sophisticated multimedia to further enhance and enrich teaching and learning. Many advocates are predicting that multimedia technology will have a dramatic effect on education. However, the impact of multimedia on teaching and learning is going to depend on cost, quality and appropriate use.

At the heart of the issue of convincing schools to invest in multimedia will be the quality of the software and the type of learning environment it supports. At present the Australian market is flooded with American titles of varying quality. What is needed, however, is Australian software that reflects our culture and supports a constructivist teaching and learning environment. As the Australian market is small, it may be, as the Smith Report suggests, that 'various entities – State and Federal agencies, universities, schools, technology developers, theorists and instructional designers – will

185

need to develop programmes suited to Australia's schooling culture' (Smith 1994: 55).

Supplying a quality multimedia product, however, is no guarantee that it will be used appropriately. This is where quality professional development is paramount in demonstrating to teachers how the multimedia products can be used effectively and how some of the pitfalls – such as allowing the products to usurp the role of the teacher or to replace the computers in education programme – can be avoided.

There is no doubt that multimedia is an exciting medium, and it will offer teachers a powerful tool to create interesting and challenging learning environments. However, this will depend on the quality of the software and the teacher's ability to employ multimedia appropriately. Above all, it will depend on the industry's ability to deliver multimedia at a reasonable price.

Integrated Learning Systems

An extension of the multimedia market is the Integrated Learning System (ILS). Although ILSs are relatively new in Australia, they have been in use in the US for many years and debate about their effectiveness has been divided. Schools thinking of investing in ILSs need to be aware of the relevant issues before they make a commitment.

First, schools should determine whether the ILS supports the type of learning and teaching environment that they are aiming to achieve. Early use of ILSs was based on a behavioural view of learning, and some systems tended to be no more than sophisticated drill and practice machines. If schools accept a constructivist view of the learner such systems would be inappropriate.

Second, there is a danger that some teachers will allow the machine to take over some aspects of their role and, as a consequence, some subjects may be neglected. It would not be too difficult to imagine, for instance, a teacher who is not too confident in science neglecting certain topics because they are covered by the machine.

Third, there is the problem of content. Many of the ILSs are American. The literature, history, customs, geography, politics and so on will not be appropriate for Australian students. It is unlikely that totally Australian systems will be produced. Some overseas companies will offer to adapt their material, but this may prove to be an unsatisfactory compromise.

Fourth, there is the problem, as mentioned earlier, of software hegemony. One of the tenets of self-managing schools is the notion of schools developing distinctive programmes for their students. Overuse and dependence on the ILS to teach certain subjects means that the software is driving the curriculum. Perhaps a better approach would be for schools to say, 'This is the curriculum we have developed. Is there a place for the ILS in helping us to deliver it?'

Finally, there is a real danger that the ILS will usurp the computers in education programme. If a school pours a vast amount of cash into an ILS computer laboratory, two problems arise. First, the lab will probably only be used to run the ILS, so that little time will be left for other computing activities, and, second, little money will be left for hardware and software in the classroom. Lack of support for computers in the classroom could be construed by teachers reluctant to embrace the technology as diminishing, or even eliminating, their role in the computers in education programme.

The likely trend is that ILS will grow in sophistication with the growth of multimedia. Along with this growth will come increased demand fuelled by clever marketing and, as in the early 1980s with regard to microcomputers, a groundswell of support from the community, which will be anxious about children missing out. Evidence will be produced claiming increases in test scores as a direct result of using an ILS, and there will be strong competition among rival suppliers of ILS products, leading to a reduction in price.

However, the purchase of ILSs will still require substantial funds and heavy investment in computers with multimedia capacity. Individual schools will struggle to raise finance for the systems without the help of the central authorities and vigorous fundraising. Schools will need to be sure that their investment will yield a high return. This means scrutinising the research on the use of ILSs critically and determining how an ILS will aid in establishing the desired teaching and learning environment.

The Internet

There are some who rank the construction of the Internet right up there with the construction of the pyramids – one of humankind's greatest achievements. Potentially, the Internet means that students will have available to them vast amounts of data on various topics which can be viewed on the screen or downloaded for later perusal; they will be able to communicate with other students and various experts all around the world; they will be able to participate in collaborative research projects; they will be able to participate in local and worldwide forums; and they will be able to publish their work for all to see. This may very well be so, but there are some major issues connected to the use of the Internet which schools need to deal with.

First, there is the issue of appropriate use, or using the power of the Internet for an authentic purpose. The hyperbole surrounding a new and exciting technology can sometimes overshadow the primary objectives. Schools spending money on connecting classrooms to the Internet need to consider within what instructional framework students will have access. Integrating access into an enquiry-learning strategy that develops information-handling and problem-solving skills would be preferable to an ad hoc, 'gee whiz' approach which teaches how to connect and how to navigate, but not why.

Second, there is the issue of censorship. The Internet was constructed in order to facilitate a free flow of information between the inhabitants of the planet. Unfortunately, this free flow of information includes provocative topics such as pornography, racism, violence, terrorism and sexism. Schools will have to develop policy on this aspect of Internet use. Enforcing censorship is extremely difficult at present as software which restricts access has its weaknesses. Some schools have opted against censorship and concentrate on educating students to use information technologies, including the Internet, in a moral and ethical way. Whatever position schools take, this aspect of the Internet is likely to be very controversial and widely debated. Already, the media have published a number of articles which highlight the problem.

Finally, there is the issue of cost. Connection fees, infrastructure costs, access to expert knowledge and professional development will not be cheap. Meeting the cost of surfing the Internet will be very difficult for some schools. Already, the gulf between information-rich schools and information-poor schools is widening and becoming a real social-justice issue. How quickly the Internet becomes a reality for all schools will depend on the ability of schools to install communications infrastructure, purchase the necessary hardware and put the personnel with the expert knowledge in place. There is a lot of hyperbole about the Internet at present from the media and politicians, but the day all classrooms in the state have immediate access to the Internet is a long way off.

Open learning

The arrival in the classroom and, to some extent the home, of multimedia, the Internet, Integrated Learning Systems and other technologies such as mobile phones, facsimile machines, video conferencing and interactive television means students will have greater control over what, when, where and how they learn. New information technologies will provide greater flexibility in the delivery of programmes and expand opportunities for students to participate in new and different learning environments.

This trend, to give students more control over their learning, is referred to as open learning. Technological advances will enable schools to participate more fully in the spirit of open learning, thus enhancing student learning and understanding (Smith 1994: 15).

Issues for schools

There are four major issues facing schools over the next few years. The first considers the ways in which computers might enhance student learning; the second considers the professional development required to ensure that teachers are well prepared to utilise these new possibilities; the third considers the resources available to schools to implement computer-enhanced learning; and this leads to the fourth, a consideration of equity and access.

Computers and learning

One of the major findings of the Smith Report was that the time was right for merging constructivist learning theories with the technology (Smith 1994: 38). A more extensive review of the literature by the authors would have revealed that this notion of a merger has been pursued vigorously by many people involved in research and at the level of practice for a number of years (Romeo 1993, 1996).

Nevertheless, it is a cogent reminder that at the essence of the debate is the use of technology to improve learning. Self-managing schools must first decide just what sort of teaching and learning environment they wish to create, and then think about how the technology will help them to achieve their goals.

If this type of approach is not adopted some real pitfalls await the unwary. First, there is the danger of techno-romanticism (Underwood and Underwood 1990). This happens when a fascination with the technology clouds pedagogical thinking. The romanticism is fuelled by the computer companies, the politicians and the media, who want to believe that the technology by itself will make learning easier, or cheaper, or more efficient. Stakeholders can guard against techno-romanticism by making sure that the introduction of new technologies is underpinned by solid research and supported by a valid set of instructional strategies.

Second, there is the danger of software hegemony. This occurs when software developers and authors usurp the role of the educator, drive the educational agenda and begin determining the curriculum, when software is produced with little or no input from educators, introduced to the market and vigorously advertised as a panacea. It is easy to be seduced and fascinated by technological wizardry, but educators need to be critical of software and systems that promote teaching and learning environments contrary to the school's stated teaching/learning policy. Greater pressure needs to be placed on software developers to produce quality products that involve educators in the development process and reflect a constructivist learning philosophy.

Professional development

The exploitation of new technologies for educational purposes will rely on teachers participating in quality professional-development activities to upgrade their knowledge and skills. Such participation will depend on whether relevant and worthwhile activities are available, and on the self-managing school's ability to pay.

The delivery of professional development for computers in education in the past has met with only moderate success, and a number of activities currently offered tend to focus on developing computer literacy skills and proficiency in a particular software application. Teachers need basic computer literacy skills, but of equal importance is the need for opportunities to learn and practise the pedagogy of using computers in the classroom. This means paying attention to how professional development is delivered, as well as to its content.

Delivering relevant and worthwhile professional development requires that organisers embrace the research on teacher training and development. The 1988 report of the In-service Teacher Education Project (DEET 1988) outlines the principles of good professional development practice which should underpin quality programmes. The principles include recognising:

- the fact that teachers are adult learners who need to apply and critically evaluate new practices in their own contexts;
- the contribution that both innovation-focused and action-research delivery modes make to teacher learning;
- the importance of setting, focus, leadership and support structures;
- the importance of joint planning and collaborative control;
- the importance of critically applying the results of educational research.

If schools and the central authorities are serious about professional development they should be looking for programmes which embody these principles.

Determining the content of professional development means seeking out experts in the field and helping them to develop programmes that expose teachers to the latest research and thinking on the use of computers in the classroom. Simply training teachers and pre-service teachers to use a computer and particular pieces of application software is not enough; they need to be familiar with the research literature, have the opportunity to develop appropriate instructional strategies and encounter situations where they can practice and reflect on the pedagogy of using computers in the classroom.

Resources

Investment in technology is expensive, yet already the world community has spent billions of dollars endeavouring to make the computers in education dream a reality. As we move into the self-managing paradigm, educators and administrators at the local level will be faced with the prospect of deciding how diminishing education funds will be spent. All stakeholders will need to be aware of the major issues in order to make informed decisions.

Much of the hardware and software accumulated by schools is coming to the end of its working life. New, more powerful and more sophisticated machines are needed to take advantage of new technologies such as multimedia and the Internet. Complicating the resource problem is the fact that in most primary schools there is only one computer per classroom, leaving little time for computing across the curriculum.

Decisions will have to be made on the upgrading of machines, the number of machines to purchase and where within the school the machines will be located. These are decisions that cannot be made lightly as they will require substantial funds. There will be pressure on all concerned to make informed decisions, to divert funds from other ventures and to raise extra capital. Where the money comes from and how it is spent will be significant issues for self-managing schools.

There is a danger, because of a lack of knowledge and the costs involved, that schools will move away from the more difficult, but potentially more rewarding, aspects of learning with computers and opt for soft solutions such as installing an ILS lab and calling that the computers in education programme. Ensuring that schools spend their budgets appropriately is a real dilemma for the central authorities. On the one hand, there is a policy of autonomy and, on the other, there is the challenge of ensuring that schools make appropriate decisions.

Developing quality professional-development programmes which offer innovative and creative delivery modes and expose teachers to the latest research and thinking is also an expensive exercise. It will be up to the central authorities not only to provide the necessary funding but also to make sure that quality programmes are offered. They can do this by developing their own programmes or by turning to university education faculties.

Even with a good supply of quality programmes there is always the danger that the self-managing school, under increasing financial pressure, will view professional development as a luxury it just cannot afford or can afford only in certain areas. This is another example of the dilemma of school autonomy. How does the central authority ensure that the autonomous school finances relevant and worthwhile professional-development activities?

Access and equity

This issue of equity and access applies to information technologies in general. Some students in some schools have access to superior hardware and software, including access to multimedia, are able to connect to the Internet and use its resources for an authentic purpose, and have access to teachers who have superior training and knowledge in the area; yet some students struggle even to lay a finger on a keyboard. Even in the information-rich schools it may well be that some groups do not, for a variety of reasons, have equal access to the technology.

In the past, governments have endeavoured to remedy such problems with initiatives like the disadvantaged schools programme and affirmative action. If the imbalance between the information-poor and the information-rich schools is to be redressed, then schemes financed by the federal and state governments will be necessary, and they will be expensive. Failure to tackle the problem may not only have social implications but may also have an impact on the country's economic future.

Conclusion

This chapter has endeavoured to show that the introduction of computers into classrooms has had a mixed impact. Some schools and individual teachers have seen the potential and grasped the initiative; some have taken the initiative but seem to be going in the wrong direction; some have invested heavily in hardware and software and are unsure what direction to take; and some are totally confused and anxious about the future.

How is the self-managing primary school to make sense of it all? The first important step is the development of the school charter. It is this document which should establish a school's teaching and learning philosophy. The next step is to develop a curriculum based on this philosophy and to sort out the role computer technology will play.

As the preceding discourse has demonstrated, this is by no means an easy task, but it does not mean reinventing the wheel. A lot of good research on merging contemporary learning theories and new information technologies has already been done, and a great deal of effort has gone into developing innovative and creative instructional strategies. The challenge is to get the knowledge across to teachers and provide them with the professional development, the infrastructure and the opportunity to experiment, investigate and further research the possibilities.

References

Alder, K. and Guss, L. (1985) *Directory of Victoria's Major and Minor Project Schools*, Moorabbin, Victoria: State Computer Education Centre, Education Department of Victoria.

Allitt, P. and Hellier, Y. (1987) *Changing Teacher Practice*, Moorabbin, Victoria: Victoria State Computer Education Centre/Ministry of Education.

Caldwell, B. (1994) 'Resourcing the transformation of school education', *Education News*, 1 December: 10–13.

DEET (Department of Employment, Education and Training) (1988) *Teachers Learning: Improving Australian Schools Through Inservice Teacher Training and Development*, Canberra: Australian Government Publishing Service.

DEETYA (Department of Employment, Education, Training and Youth Affairs) (1996) *Gateways: Information Technology and the Learning Process: A Collection of Teacher Practice from Australian Schools*, Tuggeranong, ACT: ACT

Department of Education and Training and Children's, Youth and Family Services Bureau.

DSE (Directorate of School Education) (1993) *Schools of the Future: Preliminary Paper*, Melbourne: Directorate of School Education, Victoria.

—— (1994) 'An Australian first in classroom technology launched', *Education News*, 2 June: 1.

Merrill, P. (1992) *Computers in Education*, Boston, MA: Allyn & Bacon.

Ministry of Education (1985) *The School Curriculum and Organisation Framework P-12*, Melbourne: Ministry of Education, Schools Division, Victoria.

Ministry of Education and Training (1991) *What Do You Think? Report of the Inclusive Computing Project*, Melbourne: Education Shop, Ministry of Education and Training, Victoria.

NACCS (National Advisory Committee on Computers in Schools) (1983) *Teaching, Learning and Computers: Report of the NACCS*, Woden, ACT: Commonwealth Schools Commission.

—— (1985) *Teaching, Learning and Computers in Primary Schools: A Report Prepared by the NACCS*, Canberra, ACT: Commonwealth Schools Commission.

Neely, M. (1995) *Australian Beginners' Guide to the Internet*, Kiama, NSW: Southern Media Services.

Print, M. (1991) *Curriculum Development and Design*, 3rd edn, Sydney: Allen & Unwin.

Romeo, G. I. (1993) 'Computers and the integrated curriculum: can I do that in my classroom?', in G. Ferres and A. McDougall *Can I Really Do That in My Classroom: Using Computers in Innovative Ways* (CEGV Conference Proceedings), Richmond, Victoria: Computing in Education Group of Victoria (CEGV).

—— (1996) 'Developing an instructional strategy for the integration of the computer into the primary curriculum: an action research case study', unpublished PhD thesis, Faculty of Education, Monash University, Melbourne.

Ryan, M. and Grimmett, G. (1991) *The Queensland Sunrise Centre: A Report of the First Year*, Hawthorn: Australian Council for Educational Research.

Smith, R. (1994) *Technologies for Enhanced Learning*, Melbourne: Directorate of School Education, Victoria.

Underwood, G. and Underwood, J. (1990) *Computers and Learning: Helping Children Acquire Thinking Skills*, Oxford: Blackwell.

Walker, R. (1991) 'The development of educational computing policy in the Victorian school system 1976–1985', *Australian Journal of Education* 35(3): 292–313.

Software

Hypercard	Claris Corporation
Lego/Logo	Logo Computer Systems (LCSI)
LogoWriter	Logo Computer Systems (LCSI)
Microworlds	Logo Computer Systems (LCSI)

Internet resources

CSIRO Scientists Online   rjd@adl.dmt.csiro.au

Global Lab   http://www.dar.csiro.au
International Education and Resource Network (I*EARN)
    http://www.igc.apc.org/iearn/
Keylink   http://www.igc.apc.org/iearn/
Murder Under the Microscope   bronwyn.stuckey@tafensw.edu.au
Nexus   http://www.nexus.edu.au
Oz Projects   http://www.nexus.edu.au/ozprojects/
Pegasus   http://www.igc.apc.org/iearn/
Postcards from Oz
    http://owl.qut.edu.au/common-cgi-bin/oz-projects/PFOTEACHERS/
Project Atmosphere Australia   paa@peg.apc.org
Schools NET   http://www.schnet.edu.au/
Stratospheric Ozone Project   http://www.dar.csiro.au
The Global Ultra Violet Radiation   http://www.dar.csiro.au
TravelBuddies
    http://owl.qut.edu.au/common-cgi-bin/oz-projects/TRAVELBUDDIES
Virtual Field Trips
    http://owl.qut.edu.au/common-cgi-bin/oz-projects/VFTTEACHERS/
Where in Australia?   dthomas@ecn.net.au

10

EFFECTIVE RESOURCE ALLOCATION IN THE PRIMARY SCHOOL

Tony Townsend

Introduction

The past two decades have seen substantial changes in the level of resources allocated to Australian primary schools, to the formulae by which resources have been allocated to schools and to the powers given to the school community on how it will allocate the resources it has within the school. Prior to 1973 there was very little flexibility in resource allocation, with staffing and school maintenance costs centralised and with any alterations or extensions to the school controlled by public works departments. What little school-based funding there was was controlled by the principal on the advice of school committees. Additional funds were raised for school use by Mother's Clubs, Parent–Teachers' Associations and the like, and, in the case of funding new buildings, funds raised locally were usually matched by the government.

The Karmel Report of 1973 first promoted the idea of school communities becoming more involved in the decisions related to education and the 1970s saw the beginning of schools becoming more responsible for the expenditure of their funds. The introduction of school councils saw the start of greater responsibility for overseeing the school-based proportions of government funds and for advising government on extensions or new school buildings; this became more methodical after the Effective Resource Allocation in Schools Project (Caldwell and Misko 1984) tried to establish a better understanding of the way in which the resources allocated to schools, and in schools, might affect the level of effectiveness of those schools. The authors' conclusion was that the development of a corporate planning strategy, together with the development of a programme-budgeting approach to policy-making, if implemented carefully, might lead to more generally effective schools. Programme budgeting asked teachers to incorporate a consideration of cost into their curriculum and policy decisions, and to make priorities on which programmes and activities should run within the limitations of the school's budget.

This method of resource allocation was trialled in schools in Victoria and Tasmania in the mid-1980s and resulted in a new way of viewing the management of schools (Caldwell and Spinks 1988). The decade of the 1990s has also seen Australia fall into line with other countries to embrace the market approach to financing schools. Swanson and King argue:

> To ensure that both individual and societal demands for schooling are met, decisions about the provision of education are made in both the public and private sectors. Decisions in the public sector are made through political processes by governments, whereas decisions in the private sector are made by individuals using market mechanisms.
>
> (Swanson and King 1991: 5)

Thus, the model of self-management proposed by Caldwell and Spinks, which has been very influential in the shaping of decentralisation activity within Australia, promoted the concept of the School Global Budget, which emerged in Victoria's Schools of the Future, where schools are directly allocated 'more than 90 per cent of Victoria's school education budget' (Caldwell 1996). It could be argued that Schools of the Future takes the issue of resource allocation almost to its logical limit.

Critical issues in resource allocation

There are three main issues that need to be considered when one discusses resource allocation in primary education. The first considers the total quantum of funds available to schools, both from the government and from other sources, and the means by which the government ensures that all students have an equal chance of receiving a quality education; the second considers decisions about how this total quantum of funds is distributed to schools; and the third considers the way individual schools allocate the resources they have to programmes that will promote the best outcomes for students within the school. Each of these issues is critical to the development of primary schools because evidence is starting to emerge that the way resources have been allocated in the past might not have been as effective as we might have liked.

Resource allocation has two central concerns, namely efficiency and equity. In the first instance, it is critical that we have an efficient use of resources so that we get the best value for the money being allocated to education, particularly when there are so many others in the community demanding services that require government funding. In the second instance, it is important that the money be used in such a way as to give every student in the school system an equal chance of succeeding.

However, sometimes the notions of efficiency and equity can be in conflict with each other. Some would argue that the most efficient use of resources occurs when those most capable are allocated higher proportions of resources to ensure that they achieve their full potential. Others would argue that an equitable allocation of funds means that those most disadvantaged should receive higher levels of funding to try and bring them up to the levels of those with family or social advantages.

It could be argued that in a devolved system the education authority and the school have responsibilities for both efficiency and equity, but that these will be implemented differently at each level. Perhaps the major concern at the central level is to ensure equity across the system (which may mean differential distribution of funds to schools with different circumstances) and to monitor the efficiency of resource allocation at the school (to check that the money has been spent in accordance with its goals). On the other hand, the major concern at the school level is to ensure efficiency of resource allocation (so that appropriate funds go to the various curriculum and administrative programmes) and to monitor equity within the school (by making sure that all students experience success in these programmes).

Government support for education: the size of the Australian cake

As a nation, Australia does not spend a great deal of public money on educating its population. In 1992 Australia ranked fifteenth out of seventeen OECD countries in terms of government spending on education as a proportion of GDP (Marginson *et al.* 1995: 22). Recently this proportion has further declined, but the bottom may not yet have been reached. The Institute of Public Affairs went so far as to suggest that a further A$1.4 billion could be saved if all states reduced their per-pupil allocation to that of Queensland (then the lowest-spending state) and that such a reduction would have no effect on student outcomes (Clare and Johnson 1993: 64).

Perhaps the most critical issue related to funding that has emerged in the past decade has been the move towards the marketisation and privatisation of education; the former argues that parents have a right to send their child to the school of their choice, and the latter suggests that families should increase their contribution to the cost of education, even within the government school system.

There has always been an element of privatisation in education in Australia, but this has recently moved into the realm of public schooling as well. About one-third of children in Australia attend private (or non-government) schools, a very high percentage in world terms. In all cases since 1963, non-government schools have received some funding from both the Commonwealth and state governments but top this up with additional funds raised by charging parents fees. These fees might be quite low in some of the denominational schools but can be in excess of A$10,000 per year for students in the more prestigious private schools. However, up to 90 per cent of costs (for the poorer, low-fee-paying denominational schools) and an average of about 70 per cent of the cost of sending a child to non-government schools is supplied by the Commonwealth and state governments. In 1994/5, the Commonwealth and state governments combined provided an average of A\$3,117 for each student in government schools and A\$2,307 for each student in non-government schools (Senate Employment, Education and Training References Committee 1997: 27).

However, recent decisions by the newly elected Commonwealth government push the privatisation issue even more. It has reduced the per-capita funding for education, particularly in government schools, even further than had the previous government, and at the end of 1996 it introduced a number of changes that will potentially have a dramatic effect on funding public education. It established what was called the Enrolment Benchmark Adjustment (EBA). A benchmark of 29.4 per cent was set as the national percentage of students enrolled in non-government schools, although each state varied from this figure slightly. Under the scheme a total of A\$1,712.50 would be deducted from expenditure on government schools for every new student who enrols in a non-government school. The Australian Schools Lobby reports that 'The Federal government justifies the cut of \$1712.50 per student with the argument that state governments "save" twice that amount each time a student moves from a government to a non-government school' (Australian Schools Lobby 1996: 3). Table 10.1 indicates the changing proportions of government and non-government students which would have effected Commonwealth funding of government schools in Victoria had the scheme applied for 1995/6.

Since the percentage of students in non-government schools increased by 0.23 percentage points from 1995 to 1996, this would have become the base figure for the calculations. The A\$1,712.50 is deducted for 0.23 per cent of the 782,712 students in the state (i.e. 1,800 students). Thus the state of Victoria would receive 1,800 × A\$1,712.50, or A\$3,082,500, less from the Commonwealth under the EBA scheme despite having 2,720 additional students. At a time when several state governments are severely cutting education budgets themselves, this decision makes the funding levels of government schools even lower than they were before.

This reduction in spending becomes more dramatic if the percentage of state government budgets spent on education is considered. Between 1988/9

Table 10.1 Victorian students in government and non-government schools

	Students in government schools	Students in non-government schools	Totals	% in non-government schools
1995	519,804	256,143	775,947	33.01
1996	522,524	260,188	782,712	33.24

and 1994/5 the average state government expenditure per student decreased in total by 5.8 per cent, from A$2,868 to A$2,700 (in 1988/9 prices) per student (Senate Employment, Education and Training References Committee 1997: 27). These reductions vary from state to state, with, at one end of the scale, South Australia and the Northern Territory increasing school expenditure by 12 per cent and 10 per cent and, at the other end of the scale, a 5 per cent and 7 per cent real cut in per-student expenditure in Victoria and Tasmania despite a total increase in budget income of 28 per cent and 17 per cent respectively (Marginson, *et al.* 1995: 25–9).

This is borne out, at least in Victoria, by successive government Yearbooks. In 1980/1, the last year of the previous Liberal government, the recurrent expenditure on primary and secondary education was 31.4 per cent of the state recurrent expenditure. By 1985/6 this had dropped to 27.3 per cent, and it dropped further, to 23 per cent, by 1991/2, the last year of the Victorian Labor government. By 1994/5, after two years of the new Liberal government, the proportion spent on primary and secondary schools dropped to 14.5 per cent of the state budget. This is a 54 per cent reduction in the proportion of resources spent on education during a period when the number of students in primary and secondary schools in Victoria fell by just 12 per cent.

Victoria has been the state to suffer most from funding reductions over the past few years. Whereas on average across Australia government expenditure on schools increased by around 12.5 per cent (from A$4,265 to A$4,784 per pupil) from 1992/3 to 1994/5, Victoria suffered a decline of about 12 per cent (from A$5,070 to A$4,434 per pupil). This suggests that governments around the country – but in particular the Victorian government – have accepted the premise that too much money has been spent on education and that productivity has not matched the expenditure. These reductions led *Education Nation* to suggest that:

> The shortsighted and sometimes parochial behaviour of State governments in relation to funding government schools and the absence of an effective national financial plan for Australian schools [are] placing Australia's long term skill base and social cohesion at risk. . . . The major losers in this situation are, of course, the students and the standard of living they will be able to pass on to their children and grandchildren.
>
> (Marginson *et al.* 1995: 36)

However, there is further evidence that government funding is no longer enough for schools to operate their programmes, even at a minimal level. Parents are taking more and more responsibility for funding the education of their children, despite the rhetoric that government education is free. A study of 640 low-income families conducted by the Smith Family in four

Australian states, Queensland, South Australia, New South Wales and Victoria found that primary-school parents paid up to A$2,002 per year to meet annual education expenses, including uniforms, excursions, fees and the like (Griffith 1997: 38).

A study conducted by the Victorian Opposition (Harland 1997) which consolidated the non-salary income and expenditure of 237 Victorian schools, including 167 primary schools, found that, on average, A$387 per primary student was raised locally for direct school costs, through income streams such as fees, equipment and materials, camps, excursions and through fundraising activities. This represented about 32 per cent of the non-teacher-salary component of the school's income. This percentage of funds raised locally substantially agreed with the earlier findings of Townsend (1995), who also indicated that the actual raising of funds varied dramatically from school to school. The primary school most capable of raising funds locally was able to raise more than A$250,000 per year, compared to less than A$2,000 per year for the one least capable.

Specific examples provided evidence of how the reliance on locally raised funds created inequalities for children. Of two small rural primary schools in different regions (97 and 93 students), one predicted that it could raise an average A$316 per pupil per year locally and the second only A$43. Since staffing allocations and other factors would provide approximately the same grant from the government, one school would have an additional A$26,000 to spend on school projects. Similarly, of two larger suburban schools (564 and 588 students), one indicated that it could raise an average of A$359 per pupil per year and the second A$33. Again, if other factors were roughly equal, one school had A$180,000 more to allocate per year than the other. The ability to purchase extra computers, library books and the like varied greatly from one school to the other.

The evidence suggests (see, for example, Brotherhood of St Laurence 1996) that the restructuring activity has allowed some schools to increase their capabilities when it comes to raising funds, but for others the struggle is becoming more and more difficult. It has probably always been the case that levels of local funding differ because of the socio-economic area in which the school is located, but now that there are diminishing government funds the reliance on locally raised funds to provide a quality programme is much greater.

The balance of evidence suggests that the vast majority of schools are struggling to raise sufficient funds to compensate for the decrease in government funding. Local fundraising is no longer for 'extras', but is now being used on curriculum and other programmes central to the schools' operations. The report *Not a Level Playing Field* argued:

> The retreat of governments from their responsibilities to provide an adequate school education is apparent in a number of ways. The evidence indicates:

- an apparent decline in the level of government funding in recent years,
- that privately raised funds are making an increased contribution to the total expenditure on school education, a contribution that at the local level of school operating costs is nothing less than crucial, and
- that schools have come to rely on privately raised funds to provide essentials, not just extras.

Cumulatively, the evidence before the Committee is compelling. The level of government funding for schools is inadequate.
(Senate Employment, Education and Training References Committee 1997: 24–5)

Given all the responsibility of the other things that schools are designed to do, spending countless hours on fundraising may take away some of the energy that might be directed at students. Townsend argued that the issue of finance for schools is critical to long-term development. He cautioned that:

The potential for a class system of schools with three classes of school emerges: the wealthy, high fee paying, private school; the well-off, moderate to high fee paying, government (or Catholic) school and the under-resourced school that charges little or no fees because parents have no means of paying.
(Townsend 1996b: 191)

Education, like a number of other social services, now seems to be seen by governments as a cost to society rather than an investment in the future, a view which does not bode well for the children of tomorrow.

Internationally, the set of studies which allowed governments to argue the case that they could increase the quality of student outcomes and simultaneously decrease the expenditure on education has been the set of production-function research. There had been universal agreement on the need for improvement in student outcomes, but far less agreement on how this might be achieved. The production-function studies attempted to derive a model that described the relationship between educational inputs and outcomes. The most influential studies were those conducted by Eric Hanushek. Some educators had argued that to improve the outcomes of students more money was required by the school system. Hanushek's studies led to a conclusion that there was little consistent relationship between educational expenditure and pupil achievement (Hanushek 1986: 1161). However, a recent re-analysis of Hanushek's data used more sophisticated analysis mechanisms and concluded that there was:

strong support for at least some positive effects of resource inputs
and little support for the existence of negative effects . . . the pattern
of effects is most persuasive for global resource variables (PPE
[per-pupil expenditure] and teacher experience), the median effects
are positive for most resource variables.

(Hedges *et al.* 1994: 13)

In *Education Nation*, a report developed under the auspices of the
Australian Education Union, the authors argue:

In a changing complex world, **Education Nation** has one simple
message: *public education is central to the future*. A nation that is
committed to the advancement of its own education systems, properly resourced and organised, on a national basis – an **Education
Nation** – will be best positioned for the challenges ahead.

(Marginson *et al.* 1995: 6)

McGaw (1994) argued that many of the recent restructuring activities
indicate a lack of faith in the impact of resources which resulted from a lack
of any systematic research to indicate the benefits of increased resources in
the 1970s and 1980s. He suggested that:

what critics who first claimed that standards were falling now
demand, in the face of evidence that they have not fallen, is that standards should be rising as a consequence of increased funding and in
response to increasing social and economic demands on education.

(McGaw 1997: 6)

However, despite the fact that there is no specific evidence relating financial inputs to student outcomes, the last decade in Australia has seen
considerable evidence of the development of at least cost-effectiveness and,
arguably, an improvement in the educational effectiveness of schooling in
Australia. Australian schools today are what Ashenden calls 'high quality
and modest cost' (Ashenden 1994: 3) when compared with other systems
and our own systems of the past. Government school retention rates to Year
12 more than doubled from 1981 (28.5 per cent) to 1993 (73.8 per cent)
(Marginson *et al.* 1995: 15) and the number of Year 12 graduates going on
to tertiary education jumped 97 per cent in the five years from 1986 to 1991.
These data included a dramatic improvement for students from low socio-
economic groups as well, and retention rates to Year 12 for this group
improved from 39 per cent in 1985 to 65 per cent in 1992. This overall
improvement has come at a time when educational budgets for schools were
largely static, despite the greater recognition and financial support for
students with disabilities, special programmes for students with learning

disabilities, and student welfare and counselling, not to mention increased administrative responsibilities being given to schools.

Cutting the cake: allocating resources to schools

Despite Tickell's concern that 'the debate over vouchers is both long-running and divisive . . . the term provokes such hostility and suspicion that a government seeking to establish self-managing schools would be wise to renounce any intention of introducing vouchers' (Tickell 1995: 20), the notion of resources following students is certainly not a new idea. As far back as the late 1960s, Illich proposed a 'learning web' with the notion of an 'edu-credit' where 'each citizen would be given a basic credit with which to acquire fundamental skills' (Illich 1973: 92).

Recent research into vouchers and school choice presented by Terry Moe from Stanford University and Richard Elmore from Harvard at the 1996 American Education Research Association conference in New York (cited in Henry 1996) has done nothing to resolve the debate. The Harvard study found that 'parents participating in choice programs in Detroit, Milwaukee, St. Louis, San Antonio and Montgomery County, Maryland, are better educated, have higher achieving children and are more involved in their youngsters' schooling than parents whose children remain behind in neighbourhood schools' (*ibid.*: 1), and the Stanford study found that 'parents who use vouchers are highly satisfied with the schools they have chosen and believe the shift from public to private has been beneficial' (*ibid.*). Of course, there is no inherent contradiction in these two findings, but they do suggest that choice and vouchers may help to increase the gap between those parents able to make appropriate choices (and have them funded) and those parents who, because of their own previous educational disadvantage, make the wrong choice or who fail to choose at all.

However, it could be argued that, in Australia, there is a government ideology that has instigated the cutbacks as part of a move to make the user pay – that is, to privatise education. The ideology of choice and the market has been brought to bear. More than a decade ago Hedley Beare considered the impact of perhaps the most pervasive force in recent times on education:

> Education's corporate image has now become a matter of survival.
> So if your school wants customers and resources in the next few
> years, you had better proclaim how good it is, how competitive are
> its services, how excellent its staff, and you had better not advertise
> its deficiencies. You had better use its resources – capital, monetary,
> personnel – in ways that will maximize profits. Over the next
> decade, only successful, positive, confident, client-oriented schools
> will have a right to survive, or be rewarded with improved resources.
> (Beare 1982: 17)

The rhetoric says that one could choose a school just as easily as one could choose a car. However, in the real world, choice is limited to the people who have resources. The poor have as much chance of choosing to send their child to a high-fee-paying school (either government or non-government) as they have of choosing a Rolls-Royce as their preferred means of transport. The truth is that some people will send their child to the nearest school and will use public transport, or walk, not because they want to, but because they have neither the resources nor the understanding not to do so. The only way that the choice issue and the social-justice issue can be reconciled is if all schools provide equal value, but in different areas of human knowledge. Choice becomes a matter of what one wants to learn rather than how well one will be taught it.

In Australia, the most advanced mechanism for allocating funds to schools is the School Global Budget, part of Victoria's Schools of the Future, and it is worthwhile spending a little time describing it as one means of promoting student-focused resource allocation.

The School Global Budget

Based on the Edmonton, Alberta, model identified by Caldwell (1993: 63–4) as the 'best practice' example of School Global Budgeting, this funding model identifies a series of principles which should underpin any allocation of resources to schools. They are:

- the pre-eminence of educational considerations (the relative weighting of chosen factors should be based on educational considerations);
- fairness (schools with the same mix of learning needs should receive the same total resources);
- transparency (the basis for allocations should be clear and readily understandable);
- subsidiarity (decisions should be made centrally only if they cannot be made locally);
- accountability (a school which has received resources because of a certain student mix should be accountable for the use of resources, including student outcomes);
- strategic implementation (new funding arrangements should be implemented progressively to eliminate dramatic change in a short period of time).

(Education Committee 1994)

Two further principles were added in 1996:

- effectiveness (relativities among allocations should reflect knowledge about school and classroom effectiveness);

- efficiency (allocations should reflect knowledge about the most cost-effective ways of achieving desired school outcomes).

(Education Committee 1996)

There are two major issues to consider when funds are allocated to schools. The first is the unit of funding to be allocated to children in each year-level of the school, which makes up the basic grant, and the second is a consideration of the individual characteristics of the students to provide additional weighting to those who might be considered in some way disadvantaged. Consequently, the funding model consists of two components: a core component, based on each schools' student population, and an indexed component, based on the special learning characteristics of those students. The School Global Budget for Schools of the Future included six components:

- core funding, which would comprise at least 80 per cent of the total budget;
- additional funding for students:
  - with disabilities and/or impairments;
  - identified as being at educational risk (special learning needs);
  - from non-English-speaking backgrounds;
  - in isolated or rural areas;
  - additional funding for priority programmes.

Core funding

Core funding includes funds for *leadership and teaching* (teaching staff and professional development), *teaching support* (non-teaching staff and school operations), *premises* costs (contract cleaning, grounds costs, building allowances, utilities, maintenance and minor works) and *on-costs* (work cover, superannuation, payroll tax).

The argument about efficiency and equity might be considered in terms of the core resourcing of primary and secondary schools. There are disagreements about the base rate for a primary student compared to that of a secondary student. Some argue that high levels of resources should flow to primary students to ensure that the basic curriculum is well covered and well learned. Others feel that secondary students should attract more funds because of the level of support required for learning at more complex levels and using more complex equipment. At its most simple when the overall level of government funding is limited the issue is whether it should be directed mostly to the early years of schooling, when everyone attends, in the attempt to ensure that everyone has strong basic skills by the end of primary school, or whether it should be directed towards secondary education and, more specifically, the final years of school, when a smaller proportion of people attend, but when learning is more complex and expensive.

A recent meta-analysis of the international literature (Mortimore 1995) indicated that effective distribution of resources to primary schools needs to become more sophisticated. He reviewed research on the relationship between class size and student outcomes from the United Kingdom, the United States and Canada, and has recognised, as do Slavin *et al.* (1994) in the USA, that the issue of class size, in itself, will not make a substantial difference to student achievement. In addition, the research so far has shown that the costs of reducing class sizes are high in comparison to the improvements gained.

In 1996 California implemented a system whereby the state provided additional resources to schools which agreed to lower class sizes in the junior school to twenty or below. The cost was about US$800 per student (of which the state provided US$650), a per-student increase of 15–20 per cent of the total funds allocated. Mortimore argues for the possibility of using the money on other programmes, such as reading recovery or individual tuition, which may be likely to have 'better pay-offs' than reducing class sizes. However, the balance of evidence led Mortimore to conclude that 'the evidence justifies, wherever possible, putting reception and Year 1 pupils in smaller classes, even if this means paying for this with larger classes for older pupils' (Mortimore 1995: 11).

In general, the allocation of funds to education increases progressively as the level of study becomes more complex. Thus kindergarten children are funded at lower levels than primary children, who in turn are funded less than secondary children. This continues into tertiary education, where technical and further education (TAFE) and college students attract less funding than university students. This caused the Australian Primary Principals' Association (APPA) to instigate a national campaign called Funding Justice for Primary School Children (APPA 1995: np). They identified 'enormous national inequities . . . between the funding received by tertiary students and primary school students in Australia' and sought an increase in funding at the primary level, while identifying a commitment to 'seeking that no reductions in the dollars allocated to per capita funding for secondary students' (*ibid.*) should be instituted. Presumably, this meant that resources would be reallocated from tertiary education to primary education, since it was unlikely in the existing climate that additional resources would emerge. The difficulties of having school education funded by state governments and tertiary education funded mainly by the Commonwealth were an additional complication.

Until the mid-1990s primary-school children were allocated about 40 per cent less resources than secondary-school children, but recent work by the Education Committee in Victoria (Education Committee 1996) suggests that there are three distinct stages of schooling and that each stage, and each grade within each stage, must be funded differently, based upon the needs of the students at that level. The current and proposed funding structures are:

	Current	Proposed
Prep Grade	1.0	0.9
Grade 1	1.0	0.9+
Grade 2	1.0	0.75+
Grade 3	1.0	0.75
Grade 4	1.0	0.75
Grade 5	1.0	0.9
Grade 6	1.0	0.9+
Grade 7	1.4	1.05
Grade 8	1.4	1.05+
Grade 9	1.4	1.12
Grade 10	1.4	1.12
Grade 11	1.4	1.34
Grade 12	1.4	1.49

(Education Committee 1996: 56)

The first stage of schooling is the junior years, Preparatory to Year 4. During this time the child moves 'from the culture of the home into the culture of school learning' (Eyers 1993; cited in Education Committee 1996: 27), where the key learning task is that of literacy, which is seen 'not just as a set of skills to be mastered but as a mental functioning which actually structures and organises specifically literate ways of thinking' (Raban-Bisby 1995; cited in Education Committee 1996: 28). Research by Raban-Bisby (1995) and Dyer (1992) has indicated that students who 'fail to develop literacy by year three fall further behind as they progress through school' (Education Committee 1996: 28); this led the committee to conclude that substantial resources should be allocated to the junior years to enable a structured literacy programme for all students, one-to-one tutoring for those who fall behind and home–community support programmes, all supported by a programme coordinator.

The Education Committee proposed substantial changes to teaching and learning that will have particular effect on the education of primary-school children, rather than secondary children. Yet, despite substantial and incontrovertible arguments made for allocating resources to the early years of schooling to ensure that each child has the academic background to succeed in secondary school, we find that the proposed funding formula leaves the first three years of school comparatively worse off in relation to the final two years of school than they were before. If we take the average allocation in the first three years of school and the last two years of school we find that in proportional terms the allocation to the first three years will fall from its current 71.4 per cent to 61.3 per cent of the allocation to the last two years of school in the proposed scheme.

This is a shift of resources away from the years when everybody can benefit to the years when comparatively few people are left. This appears to oppose the *efficiency* principle that the Education Committee added in 1996. One would have to argue whether or not spending the highest proportion of funds on the smallest number of people was more cost-efficient (the Committee's description of *efficiency*) than spending high levels of funding to ensure that more people stayed in school longer.

The second stage of schooling is that of young adolescents, the middle school years 5–8. The committee took into account a number of research findings which, among other things, indicated that students in these years would:

- be more diverse . . . due to uneven development;
- value security and safe limits at the same time as having room for independence;
- need to make sense of themselves while developing an understanding of the social and political world.

(Education Committee 1996: 34)

The middle school has become one of the areas of concern in the past decade as it is at this time that students are making the choice of whether they will complete school or drop out. The committee found that it was necessary to improve management of the transition from primary to secondary school, including changing the way the upper years of primary school were handled. To do this, the committee recommended that the student allowances for these years 'should be essentially the same for years 6 and 7, and generally similar for years 5–8' (Education Committee 1996: 39).

It is interesting that the Education Committee seems to have given no consideration to the possibility that the levels of alienation identified as being a characteristic of the middle years might be closely related to the success or otherwise of the student in the early years of schooling. It has been argued (Mortimore 1995), but not yet proven, that resources redirected from the later years to the early years might ensure that all students succeed in their quest for literacy and numeracy. If, in fact, this could be shown to be true the levels of alienation that accompany lack of success in upper primary and lower secondary school might drop substantially, thus lowering the need for the support systems later on. There is much anecdotal evidence suggesting that the students who drop out of secondary school and the students who struggle with literacy (and other things) in the early years are the same group. The primary school might be the best place to address this problem, but it can only do this if adequate resources are provided.

Once the issue of resource allocation for the core areas of school operations is determined, a second consideration is that of equity for individuals. For instance, what should the resource allocation differences be for a 'basic' Year 3 student, a Year 3 student who cannot speak English, a Year 3 student from a very poor family or a rural area and a Year 3 student with severe physical or intellectual disabilities?

Disabilities and impairments

As indicated above, the Victorian education system has gone some way in considering the indexation required to overcome various types of disadvantage. Students suffering from various types of disability or impairment are funded at one of six levels, ranging up to A$25,200 per student for severe disabilities (Education Victoria 1996: di. 2). This funding enables the employment of integration teachers and teacher aides, paramedical or interpreter staff and transportation costs. The specific level of disability support is determined using a questionnaire. However, one concern that has emerged is that some parents and teachers believe students have sometimes been rated at a level insufficient to cover the level of services they require.

English as a second language (ESL)

Additional funding for ESL students is based upon the year-level in which the student is enrolled and the length of time the student has been in an Australian school. Seven levels of funding are available, ranging from (in 1997) A$245 for primary-school students who have been in school for more than three years up to A$3,495 per student for secondary students who have been in school for less than one year. Schools must reach a threshold of A$10,000 (for primary) or A$18,000 (for secondary) before any funding is made available (Education Victoria 1996: esl. 2). The threshold has created some difficulties for some smaller primary schools because more than thirty students within the category are required before any funding is provided.

Rurality and isolation

Schools outside Melbourne and the major provincial cities with enrolments of less than 200 (primary) or 500 (secondary) are eligible for additional funding to employ extra staff. Schools may also be eligible for an isolation grant, the level of which depends on the school's distance from Melbourne, its distance from the nearest major provincial centre and its distance from the nearest equivalent school that does not receive a rural grant.

Special learning needs (SLN)

Perhaps the most important of the additional grants in terms of the equity issue, and the one most commented on by educational commentators, is the additional support for students with special learning needs. The 1997 *Schools Global Budget Guide* identifies SLN funding as being for 'those students whose readiness to learn is impaired for a range of reasons including prior educational experiences and family or other personal circumstances' (Education Victoria 1996: sl. 1). Hind and Caldwell identify the view of the committee charged with the development of the mechanism for resource allocation with respect to 'students at risk' thus:

> The committee's view was that the most important issue is the determination of the most appropriate way to target funds for programs in support of such needs. An index of need was judged as offering the most potential for inclusion in the School Global Budget.
>
> (Hind and Caldwell 1995: 11–12)

For students with special learning needs, an index was developed, based on the following student characteristics:

- proportion of students receiving the Educational Maintenance Allowance (EMA) or Austudy;
- proportion of students who transfer into the school other than at the beginning of the year;
- proportion of students who are Koorie (aboriginal);
- proportion of students who mainly speak a language other than English at home;
- measure of family status;
- measure of occupational status.

> (Education Committee 1996: sl. 2)

Each of the above measures was weighted and an index threshold that will achieve a 40 per cent coverage of Victorian students was set. In 1997 all schools which fit within the SLN index received a minimum of A$267 per student in addition to its core grant. Schools which had students who were considered the most disadvantaged received a maximum of A$345 per student (Education Victoria 1996: sl. 3). In addition, because of the identified concern for literacy, all schools with Preparatory to Year 6 enrolments received A$20 per pupil to assist them in planning activities designed for early literacy success.

The Schools Global Budget in the Victorian education system demonstrates how complex the issue of identifying the exact value of each student is. It is obvious that the Victorian government has made some attempt to ensure that the educational budget is allocated in a way that is fair to all students. One may argue with the specific index for each of the identified components of the budget, but one must give credit for the detailed analysis that has led to the final product.

However, Tickell expressed some reservations about the use of a weighted student resource allocation of funds by suggesting that any *per capita* allocation to students categorised as disadvantaged is unlikely to be effective as the funding is spread too thin' (Tickell 1995: 21–2). Other concerns included 'whether or not the quality of compensatory programmes is taken into account and whether or not schools are required to apply the resources to the students identified by the index' (*ibid.*: 22). It could be argued that the index identified is the fairest of any such indexes in the world, that is, it can seriously be considered 'world's best practice'; however, that simply brings us back to the issue of how much money is made available for distribution under this category. Since the maximum allocation for SLN in 1997 is less than 8 per cent of the average per-student allocation (A$4,434) by the Victorian government in 1995, the question of how much difference this amount might make to the most severely disadvantaged students is yet to be answered.

In other words, it does not matter whether the division of the cake is fair; if the size of the cake means that there is not enough to go around there are going to be problems.

Eating the cake: allocating resources within schools

Once the school has received its resources for the year, from government, from local fundraising and from other sources, it has then to allocate those resources within the school in such a way that they promote the best learning opportunities for the students. It becomes obvious that to do this properly the school must give a great deal of thought to activities, policies and programmes related to student learning, and the administrative supports that will enable them to succeed. Thus resource allocation within the school becomes part of the planning process.

Two models are instructive in describing the process of connecting resource allocation within the process of school development. The first is the model proposed by Caldwell and Spinks (1992) which combined a 3–5-year management strategy with an annual management cycle. This model became the blueprint for the Victorian Schools of the Future. The management strategy includes the development of a school charter containing policies, priorities and a development plan which, in the Victorian case, is reviewed every three years. This contains the overall structure which guides the development of yearly programmes, within a management cycle that moves through the following stages:

- annual priority setting;
- curriculum design;
- curriculum delivery;
- resource allocation;
- learning and teaching;
- evaluation and review.

A second model, proposed by Townsend (1994), might be considered by schools that wish to incorporate broader community activities within the cycle. In this model, schools will consider each of the following:

- identification of community needs;
- development of a school vision;
- development of general school goals;
- development of school policies.

These roughly equate with the Caldwell and Spinks longer-term management strategy. In addition, schools will consider the following:

- development of specific curriculum (and community) objectives;
- consideration of process issues (leadership, involvement, resource allocation, communication, school ethos and environment);
- programme development (curriculum and community);
- planning for specific classroom (or community) activities;
- programme and process evaluation.

These equate with the Caldwell and Spinks management cycle, but incorporate concerns for the broader community as well.

In both instances, the people involved in the decision-making strategies will be different at different stages, with a general trend of having wider involvement (of parents, teachers, community) at the policy stages, and greater teacher involvement and less parent involvement as the process becomes more practical and specific. These two models provide some understanding of the cyclic nature of planning an ongoing school programme and the position that resource allocation within the school might have.

Conclusion

In the past decade the funding of education at all levels has fallen substantially. Governments are much more likely to target particular outcomes they wish to achieve, such as literacy and numeracy, and to provide specific funding directed towards those outcomes. It is clear that the idea of increased government funding in the future is more of a dream than a possibility, although Caldwell argues that, 'Except where it is inextricably linked with excessively zealous efforts to achieve greater efficiency, it is difficult to see the trend to self-managing schools as an economic rationalist plot' (Caldwell 1995: 187).

However, it is interesting to compare government decisions about education in Western countries with those in Asia over the past decade. Almost invariably, the movement towards decentralisation in the West (for example Australia, New Zealand, the United Kingdom, the United States) has been accompanied by a diminishing funding base. On the other hand, many of

212

the Asian countries (Thailand, Vietnam, Malaysia, Hong Kong, to name just a few) have embarked on a similar course of decentralisation, but with increasing government funding. It seems strange that, although these are the very countries that Australians have been called on to be competitive with, our governments have decided that education must play its role, but must do it with less money.

The impact of funding reductions, the movement towards a market approach to education, and the use of sponsorship from business and industry have not been shown to be successful in school systems in other parts of the world. It is admitted that some schools have thrived under the new way of doing things, but many more schools have struggled to maintain their programmes. In the end, it does not matter how equitably resources are distributed, nor how well they are allocated in the school; if the amount of resources available to education in total is insufficient, students will suffer. The problem is that we might not know how much for another decade or so.

References

APPA (1995) 'Funding justice for primary school children', Melbourne: Australian Primary Principals' Association (photocopy).

Ashenden, D. (1994) *Australian Schooling: Two Futures*, Melbourne: National Industry Education Foundation.

Australian Schools Lobby (1996) 'The enrolment benchmark adjustment', *Skip* 1(1): 2–3.

Beare, H. (1982) 'Education's corporate image', *Unicorn* 8(1).

Brotherhood of St Laurence (1996) 'What is happening to "free" public education? Low income families experiences of primary and secondary education', *Changing Pressures Bulletin, No. 3*, Melbourne: Brotherhood of St Laurence.

Caldwell, B. (1993) *Decentralising the Management of Australia's Schools*, Melbourne: National Industry Education Foundation.

—— (1995) 'The provision of education and the allocation of resources', in C. Evers and J. Chapman (eds) *Educational Administration: An Australian Perspective*, Sydney: Allen & Unwin.

—— (1996) 'A *Gestalt* for the re-engineering of school education for the knowledge society', paper presented at the UNESCO ACEID (Asian Centre for Educational Innovation and Development) Conference, Bangkok, December.

Caldwell, B. and Misko, J. (1984) 'School-based budgeting: a financial strategy for meeting the needs of students', *Educational Administration Review* 2(1): 29–59.

Caldwell, B. and Spinks, J. (1988) *The Self-managing School*, London: Falmer Press.

—— (1992) *Leading the Self-managing School*, London: Falmer Press.

Clare, R. and Johnson, K (1993) *Education and Training in the 1990s*, Economic Planning Advisory Council (EPAC), Canberra: Australian Government Publishing Service.

Dyer, T. (1992) 'Reading recovery: a cost effectiveness and educational outcomes analysis', *ERS Spectrum* 10: 10–19.

Education Committee (1994) *The School Global Budget in Victoria: Matching*

Resources to Learning Needs in Schools of the Future, Melbourne: Directorate of School Education.

—— (1996) 'Consultation paper: the stages of schooling in core funding', Melbourne: Directorate of School Education (photocopy).

Education Victoria (1996) *Guide to the 1997 School Global Budget*, Melbourne: Department of Education.

Eyers, V. (1993) *The Education of Young Adolescents in South Australian Government Schools: Report of the Junior Secondary Review*, Adelaide: Education Department of South Australia.

Griffith, C. (1997) 'Schools punish poor', in *Brisbane Sunday Mail*, 6 April: 38.

Hanushek, E. (1986) 'The economics of schooling: production and efficiency in public schools', *Journal of Economic Literature* 24: 1141–77.

Harland, P. (1997) 'School budget study' (photocopy); available from the South Pacific Centre for School and Community Development, Monash University, Victoria.

Hedges, L. V., Laine, R. D. and Greenwald, R. (1994) 'Does money matter? A meta-analysis of studies of the effects of differential school inputs on student outcomes', *Educational Researcher*, April: 5–14.

Henry, T. (1996) 'Are school tax vouchers worthwhile?', *USA Today*, 11 April: 1.

Hind, I. W. and Caldwell, B. J. (1995) 'Resource allocation and outcomes in the radical transformation of Victoria's Schools of the Future', paper presented at the International Congress for School Effectiveness, Leeuwarden, the Netherlands, January.

Illich, I. (1973) *Deschooling Society*, Harmondsworth: Penguin.

Karmel, P. (1973) *Schools in Australia: Report of the Interim Committee for the Australian Schools Commission*, Canberra: Australian Government Publishing Service.

McGaw, B. (1994) 'Quality, equality and the outcomes of schooling: key issues', keynote presentation at the 7th Annual Conference of the International Congress for School Effectiveness and Improvement, Melbourne, Australia, January.

—— (1997) 'Quality and equality in education: central issues in the restructuring of education', in T. Townsend (ed.) *Restructuring and Quality: Issues for Tomorrow's Schools*, London and New York: Routledge.

Marginson, S., Martin, R. and Williamson, J. (1995) *Creating an Education Nation for the Year 2000*, Melbourne: Australian Education Union.

Mortimore, P. (1995) 'The class size conundrum', *Education*, 1 September: 10–11.

Raban-Bisby, B. (1995) *Early Childhood Years: Problem of Resource?* Dean's Lecture Series, Melbourne: University of Melbourne.

Senate Employment, Education and Training References Committee (1997) *Not a Level Playground: The Private and Commercial Funding of Schools*, Canberra: Senate Printing Unit.

Slavin, R., Karweit, N. and Wasik, B. (1994) *Preventing Early School Failure*, Boston, MA: Allyn & Bacon.

Swanson, A. D. and King, R. A. (1991) *School Finance: Its Economics and Politics*, New York and London: Longman.

Tickell, G. (1995) *Decentralising the Management of Australia's Schools*, vol. II, Melbourne: National Industry Education Foundation.

Townsend, T. (1994) *Effective Schooling for the Community*, London and New York: Routledge.

—— (1995) 'Schools of the future are gaining acceptance, but still have some way to go' (available from the South Pacific Centre for School and Community Development, Monash University, Victoria).

—— (1996a) 'Matching the goals of Schools of the Future with the demographic characteristics of their local communities', unpublished research project funded by the Australian Research Council.

—— (1996b) 'The self-managing school: miracle or myth?', *Leading and Managing* 2(3): 171–94.

11

THE EDUCATION MARKET

The view from the school

Lindsay Fitzclarence and Jane Kenway with Janine Collier

The new lexicon

The choices made by the 'consumers' of education will increasingly shape the viability of schools and their programmes. In this chapter we will examine what these developments mean for key participants in the marketisation of education: students and principals. Before moving to a specific consideration of the experiences and attitudes of a range of principals and students, we need to set the scene with some background analysis of the changing context in which schools, and their participants, are positioned.

The market: context and imperatives

In recent years the language used to describe the processes of education has produced some new themes. Wexler asserts that 'The language of education is the language of restructured, post-Fordist, post-industrial work' (Wexler 1993/4: 178). Schools are to be managed as small businesses; students and parents are the clients of these small businesses, and principals are the managers. Principals as managers are, in turn, exhorted to develop schools which recognise the importance of the client, respond to client needs, and provide a service and a product.

In line with these developments, schools advertise their 'product' to attract more clients. Slogans such as 'Give your daughter a competitive edge' and 'Essential skills for a technological age' appear as part of the advertising used to market particular schools. In turn, schools are encouraged to develop new relationships with media and marketing personnel to find ways to promote themselves to the buying public. Seminars on 'Marketing your School' and 'Positive Publicity' are advertised as professional development activities for teachers. Townsend (1994), in describing the developments leading to 'free-market public education' within Victoria, Australia, focuses on a recent development called the Schools of the Future policy (1993) and, in particular, the role of the school charter. He notes:

> The prospectus for the new education market [is] school charters. Telling of past achievements and glowing hopes for the next three years, they are a key selling point in attracting parents and pupils to the million-dollar businesses that are our schools.
>
> (Townsend 1994: 22)

As Townsend correctly observes, education has become part of the wider processes of cash transactions. The public is encouraged to expect 'value for the education dollar'. Indeed, as Edwards has argued, 'the real issue in schools is getting *better* value for the education dollar' (Edwards 1993). The change highlights the emergence of a new language for the education enterprise (see Table 11.1). Let us consider this new lexicon more closely.

Table 11.1 The new language for the education enterprise

Market language	Educational language
client	student
consumer	parent
customer	community
product	student
enterprise	school
total quality management	school improvement plan
manager	principal
line manager	principal who does what he or she is told by those above
product shelf life	up-to-date or out-of-date curriculum
choice	something exercised by the people with the best resources
value-added school	school improvement
user pays	devolving educational costs to private individuals or groups
downsize	sack teachers
outsource	privatise education
niche marketing	selective provision of education
image	school profile
image audit	compare your school profile with that of another school education culture
market culture	assessment and evaluation
performance indicators	payment by results
performance pay	

The linguistic mapping represented here has emerged from a general cultural shift in which global markets have framed many of the activities of nation-states. Throughout many industrialised nations there is tangible evidence of a policy shift designed to privilege the role of the autonomous competitive school (ACS). Examples of the general language to describe this trend include:

The USA	site-based management
The UK	local management of schools
Australia	the self-managing school
New Zealand	tomorrow's schools

Some examples of the specific policy documents which act to bring the ACS into concrete educational practice in Australia include:

New South Wales	Schools Renewal (1989)
Western Australia	Better Schools (1987)
Victoria	Schools of the Future (1993)

Such policy developments are visible expressions of a remaking of the identity of public education. The public system, unlike the private one, has a long history of being removed from direct contact with wider market forces and logics, but this has now changed (Kenway et al. 1993). The exclusive funding arrangements that tied individual schools to centralised control have been broken down. In their place is an endorsement for schools to develop a quasi-corporate identity.

Policy-makers and politicians have been key players in shaping the new education landscape by imposing principles of 'micro-economic reform' on schools as if schools were like any other industry in the marketplace. Government policy now directs a much closer connection between schools and the economy. For schools struggling with the changed circumstances this has become a dominant consideration, and if market logic is used to describe what is happening it can be seen that there will be, as in all market relations, unequal forms of adaptation. Also, as in any market economy, the attitudes of students and parents (the 'clients') will increasingly influence the practices of teachers and school administrators (the 'vendors').

Currently in Australian education there are two primary driving political forces: one is centralising and the other is decentralising. The former is mainly concerned with curriculum and the latter with management. The master discourse is economics and, to put it crudely, financial anorexia. Education is to cost the state less, hence the devolutionary imperative. It is also to serve the economy more, hence the centralising and vocationalising curriculum imperative. The inherent, and apparently contradictory, link between centralising and decentralising political forces raises a number of points. The first is that one side of the agenda cannot be adequately under-stood without the other, and it will be interesting to observe the power plays between and within the state and the market, given the development of the market imperative. The second point is that public institutions, including education, are being told by senior management to adopt a market model. This is not a grass-roots imperative. The model includes the development of internal markets, competition, buying and selling within the state sector. It includes state and private forms of collaboration: school/industry links are an obvious example here. The model also involves contracting out. This involves passing over the activities of the state to private providers – the 'outsourcing' of professional development, for example. This allows the government to 'downsize'.

The autonomous, competitive school is a site in which all these tendencies come together. In this new market environment schools are expected to develop a market identity, to adopt marketing techniques, manners, morals and language. Schools, as marketing institutions, are implicitly expected to compete with each other for scarce state dollars, for scarce private dollars from anywhere (parents, business), and for community loyalty and support. In short, they are expected to attract customers and investors.

According to marketing experts, in order for institutions to attract both they have to be 'well packaged'. Packaging is partly about marketing a product and an image to those outside the institution, and this, the marketing experts argue, must not be haphazard. It requires careful plan-ning, which involves operational 'mission' statements, a long-term focus, the development of appropriate financial, organisational, personnel and techno-logical infrastructures, the recruitment of experts, if possible, and market research. Packaging for the market is also about being strategic: it is about developing a 'product/market mix' which allows the institution to gain a 'differential advantage'. This means making decisions about which aspects of the 'product' to promote and which to discard because of their lack of marketability. Second, it means making decisions about which 'segments' of the market to 'target' for research, publicity and investment. It means keeping a constant eye on 'the opposition' in order to assess relative strengths and weaknesses, and having an eye to the future and seizing new market opportunities before others do. From the point of view of policy-makers and educational marketers, either schools will 'shape up' or parents will 'ship out'. 'Good' schools will survive and 'bad' schools will sink. Also, because of the different needs of different groups the argument is that consumer power will ensure diversity.

How are students positioned?

The idea of students as clients/consumers is a conceptual development of recent times. Traditionally, students have been discursively framed by a number of dominant sociological and psychological discourses, in which they are represented as individuals, an organism passing through predetermined stages, an object of instruction, a necessary, educational fantasy around which has been built a huge infrastructure of teacher education, professional development and educational policy. Redefining the student as a consumer maps on to a wider redefinition of childhood in terms of consumption. For example, McNeal notes:

> Children are seen by many producers and retailers as a ready market for a variety of goods and services. In this sense children are viewed as having needs, having money to spend on items that satisfy their needs, and having a willingness to spend money.
>
> (McNeal 1987: 5)

The framework of analysis offered by McNeal, despite a caveat that little is known about the consumer socialisation process, highlights a number of socialisation agents. Parents, peers, teachers and business, including advertising, stores and products, are listed (*ibid.*: 15–23). The dual process of consumer socialisation associated with the listed agents involves intentional instruction and incidental learning. This is a conventional framework drawn from conservative developments within sociology and psychology, and is, in effect, a mapping of the same discourses that traditionally position the student as learner and compliant school attender on to the concept of the student as consumer.

The dramatic social developments of recent times, such as the end of Cold War divisions and a proliferation of market associations at the international level, have opened the way for not only a new form of global politics but also a fundamental reconsideration of many of the dominant theoretical frameworks that act to order different social institutions, including education. In a celebration of this trend, the conservative New Right policy analyst Francis Fukuyama notes that 'liberal principles in economics – the "free market" – have spread, and have succeeded in producing unprecedented levels of material prosperity. . . . A liberal revolution in economic thinking has sometimes preceded, sometimes followed, the move toward political freedom around the globe' (Fukuyama 1992: xiv). One aspect of the changes noted by Fukuyama has been a reconsideration of the nature of the child. For example, the idea that children pass through school and on to a linear pathway to full adult status no longer works conceptually or in reality. That is, the boundaries between childhood and adulthood are no longer clearly marked. Chambers quotes Robert Elms, a writer for the fashionable youth magazine *The Face*, saying: 'nobody is a teenager any more because everybody is' (quoted in Chambers 1987: 2). On the one hand, structural unemployment relegates many would-be independent adults to a state of extended financial dependency. On the other hand, mass media developments have created a whole cohort of pseudo sophisticates, prompting Guber and Berry to assert that 'kids are worldly' (Guber and Berry 1993: 14). In part, this worldliness comes from access to the mass media and, something that marketing consultants have been quick to realise, a direct engagement in marketing activity by virtue of a form of disposable income. These patterns raise many questions for those who act *in loco parentis*.

We have studied the marketisation process with a dual focus:[1] principals as key players, and students and their parents as clients who define themselves as active consumers. In the following sections of this chapter we will examine some reactions by principals and students to the changing context of schooling and offer some critical interpretation of the perspectives outlined. In conclusion we will raise some general considerations that need to be addressed.

The principals' perspectives

Schools as markets

Since the 1980s, following political moves to deregulate the economy and in concert with new technological developments such as the extension of computer networking, many new marketing developments have been made possible. Trading in commodities has proliferated in many areas of society as the marketing imperative has taken hold, and schools, with their communities of parents and students, have emerged as ready-made markets for eager entrepreneurs. The following aspect of our analysis examines this process from the perspective of the school's 'gatekeeper', the principal.

From a marketing point of view the most common way into a school is across the principal's desk. Over a two-month period in Term 1 of 1994 the project team arranged for the principal of a primary school to put in a box rather than a bin all the mail of a commercial or business nature that came over his desk. The team was interested in the amount and kinds of commercial approaches that schools are now experiencing. The number of brochures and the amount of promotional material received in this period were astounding. The box contained 105 separate items of mail. This volume of mail adds to the already significant non-commercial correspondence with which a principal has to deal.

Principals seem to have a number of different ways of dealing with the printed material that comes across their desk. Many use the distinguishing logos on the envelopes to determine action. This often means that a significant proportion of advertising material is discarded unopened. Some material is passed on to the most appropriate person. At least one principal spoken to opened all mail addressed to 'The Principal' and kept the staff informed by means of a daily 'spread it round' bulletin. The amount of time spent on sorting daily mail ranged from five to thirty minutes. For those principals who processed all of their mail, working out what to do with it was often not straightforward, as a categorisation of the mail sample collected showed. This categorisation also highlighted a number of the implications of marketisation for changes in education:

Publishers – book, computer software	24
Stationery suppliers – classroom, office, etc.	21
Equipment – playground, office, etc.	16
Educational programmes and resources	14
Excursions, camps, etc.	11
Professional development programmes	3
Newsletters	3
Community service	2
Fundraising activities	11

The first three categories were expected. These were the usual brochures and catalogues that form a traditional part of any school's incoming mail, although the volume of even this 'routine' mail was surprising. What was of particular interest were the flyers and promotional materials offering fundraising activities, programmes and/or resources, which were many and various. Fundraising activities ranged from the usual chocolates and lollies to the more unusual offers of direct-mail shopping and raffle tickets provided by Vic Football; while programmes and resources covered everything from student motivation to sport and environmental education.

More interesting are the links across the categories: the newsletter containing the sports equipment competition, the fun-run programme offering an opportunity both to raise money and to provide a community service, the book publisher inviting schools to 'earn' a computer and the margarine company promoting book grants in return for bar codes. These companies appear to be responding to the financial crises facing many schools by developing promotional activities which offer the opportunity of obtaining expensive resources.

Some of this type of promotion has been offered to schools for years, but its quantity was surprising. In just two months there were eight offers to the school either to raise money or to 'earn' equipment. All schemes required student involvement, in the collection of dockets, food wrappers or bar codes, in the purchase of particular products or in their participation in sporting activities. Obviously, schools are selective in their support of these schemes, but in an era in which funding for education generally continues to decline, the schemes that are now being 'binned' by many principals may become more acceptable. As more and more schools take up these kinds of fundraising activities the schemes take on a kind of acceptability among schools.

The developments outlined here highlight an emergent symbiotic relationship between schools and commercial enterprises. 'Cash-strapped' schools are primed to look for ways to generate a budget surplus and suddenly encounter a plethora of commercial possibilities. Business houses eager to find a niche market and to promote loyal consumer support have targeted schools as part of their commercial strategy. The data we have outlined here suggest that the range of developments is increasing and is likely to continue to do so.

Marketing schools

> My entrepreneurial dream is that some day somebody from the
> 'other side of the river' is going to walk in here and say 'I want
> to send my child to your school'.

These are the words of a principal, and in many ways they represent the changed circumstances that principals and their staff now encounter. Schools and those within them have become the targets of wider market forces. Parents and students, as clients, make critical choices about what schools have to offer. Principals are the key personnel in the market operations of schools, but reactions to the marketisation trend are not uniform. The extended interviews conducted with a number of principals supported a typology of marketing positions. At one extreme there is the vigorous educational entrepreneur, while at the other is the cautious resister. Between these two there is a range of positions which might best be described as ambivalent. Whatever their response, few principals see any way of avoiding the marketisation process.

The vigorous educational entrepreneur

Q: What sort of strategies do you use to promote the school to the public?
A: We have done a lot of promotion because you have to with a new school to try to get community confidence. We had a lot of public meetings, a very detailed information booklet. We have, we think, a very good newsletter that goes home fortnightly. We've done a lot of work in making parents welcome into the place.

I will show you the newsletter. . . . This is a marketing thing that we have tried, using ads. This has been printed commercially, plus the ads have been printed commercially. We did things like we made sure we purchased a high-quality laser printer and things like that. . . .

The idea of the pamphlet is then to go to business houses, some of the bigger companies around. We will go and visit them. Send a brochure out, visit them and then have a list of twenty-five things ranging from a couple of hundred dollars to $5,000 that they might like to donate. You know, 'If you put $200 in we'll put your name up some-where.' We are thinking about having a sponsors' board. . . .

We pay for a cleaner but do a lot of it ourselves. . . . It's done by parents on a roster. . . . There are forty-eight families involved and they clean the school. We have just got this loose arrangement with the cleaner that we'll just ring up and say, 'Well, how much?' So we think that will raise $11,000 this year and $18,000 next.

Q: The future. Where do you see it all going?

A: I think it is going to have a significant impact on schools in the sense that we will all be competing. We will be competing for students. . . . Electricians don't get together to find out how much people are paying for safety switches, so schools won't get together. Collegiate groups of principals will no longer exist, in my view. . . .

I have got a plan in place when the new principal is appointed at X, that we do something about it. Because we will kill 'em, if they want to compete, we will kill 'em.

The cautious resister 1

Q: Do you have a planned promotional thing to sell your school to the community?

A: We aren't yet into high-profile marketing. . . . I find it's against my philosophy to go out and push Y as against other places. I don't find it easy at all. I am gearing myself up to do it because it is a necessary evil. But I don't agree with it on a philosophical basis, the idea of state schools competing against each other for kids, at all. Because that's what it becomes, and it has become nasty in a couple of other areas.

But most of our promotion in that sense has been all very subtle and low key. In a lot of ways we have relied very heavily on just simply the good name of the school and the things that we have done.

The cautious resister 2

Q: How do you feel about billboards in your front yard?

A: No!

Q: How would your school council feel?

A: I don't think that they would agree either. . . . We are on about educa-tion here; we are not about providing services as such.

Q: How do you see the future going, then?

A: I worry about the future. Schools of the Future is certainly exciting in many aspects because it is going to allow us to become very creative and entrepreneurial, but I just hope that everyone maintains the theme of promoting the system rather than competing or comparing with neigh-bouring schools. That's my biggest worry. It depends on your personality also. I'm not the type of person to go out and compete aggressively because I believe that that doesn't work anyway. I believe that the talk down at the front gate is where you win or lose. . . .

These are particularly difficult times for principals. Just about everything that was solid about the role of the principal and about schools has melted into air and, accordingly, there are many different ways in which principals are responding to the new identities being offered to them. On the one hand, there is an unquestioned celebration of the changes, while, on the other, there is a deep uncertainty about the new imperatives. Many do not like what is happening but feel that there is not much option but to 'go with the flow'. Many are simply trying to survive, which implies that they are struggling to maintain the viability of their school and staff.

Can schools be marketed in a socially and educationally responsible manner?

In thinking about this question a work by Hugh Emy, *From the Free Market to the Social Market* (1993), is quite useful. Emy wants to attach alternative social and moral values to the free-market agenda and wants the institutions of the state to promote these values. He calls this a social market. Broadly, he recognises that people do need to be protected from the unintended consequences and excesses of the free market, that the market must rest on ethical as well as economic principles, and that economic security and cultural integrity can go hand in hand. The social market respects human dignity and the right of every person to have a fully human existence. It also encourages the principle of solidarity. At all levels of society, people are encouraged to see themselves as partners in a common enterprise; businesses are encouraged to collaborate and to develop a strong ethic of public service. Individual responsibility goes hand in hand with collective responsibility.

Within the range of interviews we have conducted with principals there is evidence that some schools have been operating within the framework of a social market as suggested by Emy. Rather than embrace the marketing possibilities in a fully independent and hyper-competitive manner, some principals have continued to work as members of a team and have acted out of a belief in the importance of promoting the system of public education rather than simply promoting individual schools.

Through the eyes and ears of students

The broad purpose behind commerce in schooling is the production of generations of children who are active consumers. At the same time, marketing experts have identified the child and youth market as the site of 'big bucks' (see, for example, Molnar 1994). With these general marketing considerations in mind, we talked to students about the things that mattered to them about their schools and their sense of future. In specific terms, the following excerpts explore issues about marketing within their current school and considerations about what they would see as desirable in the choice of a secondary school.

Schools as Markets

Grades 3 and 4

Q: Here is a newspaper photo of a classroom. There is a television, video recorder and computer supplied by the Coles docket competition. There are hockey sticks from a sports competition that Pizza Hut ran, footballs from a Hungry Jacks competition and cricket gear from a Western Star competition. What do you think about having a classroom like that?

A: It would be awesome . . . because at our school we have all the sports equipment in the room over there and we get to borrow it every morning, but by the time I get to school and go the sports room and I want to borrow skipping ropes, they have closed. So that would be all right because you would get the sports equipment in your room and you can take it out every playtime.

Q: What sort of competitions would you like to be involved in?

A: Coles.

Q: Why is Coles the best?

A: Because it has the most.

A: And the computers are better than the sports equipment, and the television is good as well because computers teach you more than a basketball can. And a television can teach you more than a football can teach you.

Q: So what prizes would you like to see?

A: I reckon, for the school, lots of computers. At least three for each room because you can have a group on each computer, because you can't have the whole grade on one computer.

Grades 5 and 6

Q: How would feel if this was your classroom and you were wearing these caps and all the equipment in your classroom came from being in competitions?

A: Pretty good!

Q: Why?

A: Because they have got all good stuff and they could use it whenever they like.

A: I would feel lucky to get it.

Q: How would you feel about having to wear a cap advertising Pizza Hut?
A: We are not allowed to.
A: It's all right when you get them for free, though.
A: If you get them for free it's all right.

These responses are offered for their symbolic value. Throughout our interviews at primary and secondary level there was an inherent acceptance of marketing as a basic feature of everyday life. The response that 'if it's free it's okay' is a statement about the understanding of commodity values: a tangible return for minimal input means there is some basic value in the exchange. The idea that computers have more value than footballs is an extension of the same point. In terms of basic exchange-value computers are signifiers of a high-value commodity because they are linked to the high-status employment of the high-tech industries and because of their central role in providing entertainment. In this sense the Coles/Apple computers for dockets competition taps into a well-established set of understandings and values about links between education and the maximum value zones of the emergent global information-based economy. Our data suggest that even at a young age students have definite ideas about these links.

Choice of secondary school

Grades 3 and 4

Q: What sorts of things would make you think, 'Wow, I love this school, I want to come here'?
A: I'd look at the work that they do.
A: I would look at the yard and think if it was clean enough and if they have got enough equipment.
A: Science stuff and science toys.
A: I would look for friends, making friends.

Grades 5 and 6

Q: What would attract you to the school and make you think that you would like to come here?
A: The programmes and facilities.
Q: What sort of facilities would you be looking for?
A: The sports area and arts area.
A: The principal, what they talk about, what they've got; and the teachers, whether they are nice or not, and whether the school is big or small, so that you don't get lost.
Q: Has anybody decided which school they are going to?
A: I decided to go to Z because they have got everything set out, like there is a big hallway and they have got what is down that hallway, like it says

'technology and maths'. It's a smaller school and you won't get lost. And they've got tennis courts and basketball courts and a big gym, and they've got good stuff.

Q: Is there anything in particular you are interested in now in primary school that you would like to follow on with?

A: Technology . . . computers, using your brain.

A: A caring community: if you can't cope with school they care for you, like they understand what you're going through.

The responses noted suggest that major recurring themes emerge from discussions with children about desirable features of school life. There is a consistent focus on the significance of computer technology. Such a focus should come as no surprise as these students are the 'Nintendo generation'. Wark explains this term by noting of video games that 'They are the first digital media technology socialising a generation on a mass scale, world-wide – the vast majority of games players are aged 12–17' (Wark 1994: 22).

Growing up with computers and video games sets certain parameters to expectations. Children passing through today's schools are increasingly likely to think in terms of working with information technologies rather than working in the manual-skills sector of the economy. At the same time, Hugh Mackay (1993) makes it clear that young people are being educated during a period of massive social uncertainty and redefinition. The anxiety generated by social and political change is registered in some of the concerns about schools being secure and safe environments. Accordingly, how schools 'appear' (friendly/safe/pleasant compared to hostile/unsafe/alien) is likely to be fundamental to the choice factor.

While some studies have examined marketing education from the perspective of the parent (see, for example, David 1992), little work has been done, from within mainstream education, on generating understandings from the perspective of students as active consumers. In our opinion, this is a serious omission because it leaves many education scholars outside a discourse which is being increasingly taken up by market researchers who have recognised schools and students as components of a large market.

Conclusion

Much has been written about the arrival of an information age, the extended market relations of transnational corporations and new trading blocs of nations. Policy analysts, social commentators and economic advisers have contributed to this level of analysis. Writers such as Barry Jones (1990) make clear reference to the increasing significance of education as part of the value-added component of a knowledge-based economy. This analysis, from a global perspective, is generally blind to or assumes stereotypical local impacts, and is largely responsible for the plethora of educational policies and practices of the 1980s and 1990s that have tamely fallen into line with the dominant market logics. The new marketised global/local articulations, now largely unmediated by intervening medium-level structures, make the local (the educational consumer or student) a highly significant site for critical study and analysis.

There is a need to detail the types of high-tech multimedia experiences with which students are most familiar. Schools and teacher-education programmes have generally been slow to make the break from chalk and talk, from print-based modes of teaching, and where they have the response has typically been reactive and often ill-informed. Unless more proactive responses to the changed circumstances for educational practice can be developed, these institutions will be at risk in an information-based economy where formal education increasingly competes with the entertainment sector of the economy. These issues become crucial concerns for principals in the new market environment we have described in this chapter.

Within the different stories we have recounted there is a warrant for proclaiming that 'the markets must be controlled' (Cox 1995: 79). As a theorist of contemporary public policy, Cox has come to the conclusion that the social costs of the dominant marketisation ideology are far too great. Her thesis is that the current preoccupation with economic management and growth have subverted the fundamental social aspect she calls 'social capital' (*ibid.*: 14–26), a concept designed to specify 'the processes between people which establish networks, norms and social trust, and facilitate co-ordination and co-operation for mutual benefit' (*ibid.*: 15). These processes, together, act as the social glue which unites people around common goals and therefore fosters a general, public sense of identity. When social institutions are turned over to market forces they act to propagate social competition and personal greed, and as such become institutional agents of social disharmony. By their very nature, markets are predatory, acting in competition with one another, and, by implication, their associated institutions are forced to behave in an avaricious manner. To combat the destructive aspects of this trend, so Cox's argument goes, there is a need for public institutions which actively re-assert a sense of the common good and therefore foster essential trust in vital public processes. Schools, recognised as vital public institutions, are important for generating a sense of belonging, inclusiveness and civic responsibility, which are the necessary ingredients of safe, stable democracies. In an era of increasing social complexity schools are uniquely placed to help develop the skills and attitudes needed for maintaining social cohesion and goodwill, as expressed in practices of caring and sharing, at all levels of society. These ideals do not belong to a market lexicon; they are drawn from communal practices which have stood the test of time and which are in need of reinstatement at this point in our social history. In our opinion, education, generally, is required to make a contribution towards the development of a robust public sphere and therefore help stem the tide of destruction effected by the dominant ideology of marketisation.

Note

1   All data referred to in this chapter come from the *Marketing Education in the Information Age* (1993–4) and the *Consuming Education: Contemporary Education Through the Eyes of Students* (1995) research projects, which were funded by the Australian Research Council. The investigators for these projects were Associate Professor Jane Kenway, Dr Lindsay Fitzclarence and Dr Chris Bigum, with research assistants Janine Collier and Karen Tregenza, Deakin University, Geelong.

The *Marketing Education* research project was designed to explore the different manifestations of the marketisation of education. This involved gathering data in order to compile representations, dubbed 'cameos'. Alongside this process a number of principals were interviewed in order to investigate their reactions to the marketisation trend.

The *Consuming Education* research project focused specifically on student reactions. One component consisted of a series of short interviews with government secondary-school students. Another component involved a longitudinal series of interviews with a smaller number of students, exploring expressions of educational consumption that might be considered 'second nature' for students.

References

Chambers, I. (1987) 'Maps for the metropolis: a possible guide to the postmodern', *Cultural Studies* 1(1).

Cox, E. (1995) *A Truly Civil Society: 1995 Boyer Lectures*, Sydney: ABC Publications.

David, M., West, A. and Ribbens, J. (1994) *Mother's Intuition? Choosing Secondary Schools*, London and Washington, DC: Falmer Press.

Department of Education (1989) *Schools Renewal: A Strategy to Revitalise Schools Within the New South Wales State Education System*, Milsons Point, NSW: Department of Education.

Directorate of School Education (1993) *Schools of the Future: A Preliminary Paper*, Melbourne: Directorate of School Education.

Edwards, P. (1993) 'Getting down to the business of quality education', *The Age*, 19 October: 13.

Emy, H. (1993) *From the Free Market to the Social Market*, Sydney: Pluto Press.

Fukuyama, F. (1992) *The End of History and the Last Man*, New York: Free Press.

Guber, S. and Berry, J. (1993) *Marketing to and Through Kids*, New York: McGraw-Hill.

Jones, B. (1990) *Sleepers Wake! Technology and the Future of Work*, Melbourne: Oxford University Press.

Kenway, J., Bigum, C., Fitzclarence, L. with Collier, J. (1993) 'Marketing education in the 1990s: an introductory essay', *Australian Universities' Review* 36(2): 2–6.

Mackay, H. (1993) *Reinventing Australia*, Sydney: Angus & Robertson.

McNeal, J. (1987) *Children as Consumers*, Lexington, MA: Lexington Books.

Ministry of Education (1987) *Better Schools in Western Australia: A Programme for Improvement*, Perth: Ministry of Education.

Molnar, A. (1994) 'An "Apple" for the teacher', *Changing Education* 1(1): 14–16.

Townsend, T. (1994) 'Slow evolution of education leads to Schools of the Future', *The Age*, 19 July: 22.

Wark, M. (1994) 'The video game as an emergent media form', *Media Information Australia* 71, February: 21–30.

Wexler, P. (1993) 'Educational corporatism and counterposes', *Arena Journal* 2: 175–94.

Part IV

AFTERWORD

12

THE PRIMARY SCHOOL OF THE FUTURE

Third world or third millennium?

Tony Townsend

Introduction

As we have seen in the chapters of this book, primary schools and the people within them have had to respond to an astonishing array of changes in a very short period of time. There have been changes to curriculum, to technology, to funding, to accountability and management strategies, all of which have been implemented by the centre as a means of promoting 'devolution'. The education profession has had to put up with a range of personal and professional attacks. In Victoria, successive ministers of education have made substantial attacks on teacher unions, then individual teachers, principals' associations and, most recently, teacher educators. None of these attacks has been substantiated by evidence of any kind and they could be compared with what Barber, in the United Kingdom, called 'free-market Stalinism' (Barber 1996: 55). The model that he used to describe the policy process under free-market Stalinism included aspects such as 'invent a daft idea', 'invent a mythical problem which the daft idea is intended to solve', 'place some articles in the middle-brow tabloids about how serious the mythical problem is' and 'propose the daft idea as a solution' (*ibid.*: 59). He even provided a specific example, which might sound familiar to Australian teachers.

> A particular policy example might help explain the cycle. The Centre for Policy Studies [CPS] had consistently advocated that educating teachers in universities caused problems. Instead, the CPS argued, consistent with its market approach, schools should train the teachers they need when they need them. Over a long period, stories appeared from time to time in papers friendly to the government (such as the *Mail on Sunday* and the *Daily Express*) about either the poor quality or the political extremism to be found in

university departments of education. In March 1993, John Patten announced that the training of teachers wholly in schools would be piloted from September 1993. In June – *three months before the pilots began* – a government circular stated that because the new scheme was so popular it was likely to be extended. In December 1993, after a handful of pilot schemes had been running for only three months, legislation was introduced making it possible to extend this scheme nationally. The teaching profession had little or no input at any stage in this process.

(Barber 1996: 58–9)

In many respects one would expect the primary school to be a place secure from massive change. After all, the need to impart basic skills in a caring and nurturing environment, as the first step in a child's education, is hardly likely to change much. And yet it has. Not so much in specifically what has to be taught, but in the way it has been taught and the conditions in which the teaching occurs. The changes have had different impacts. Some people have seen them as a means of rapid development within the school and others seem to have kept their heads down and hoped that it would all go away. Townsend characterised these differing responses in the following way:

People currently involved in restructuring efforts could be considered as analogous to the surfer catching a wave breaking on the shore. They might remember the time when the sea was smooth, but now are faced with all sorts of upheavals that a breaking wave brings. Some will catch the wave and pick up speed towards the future, others will be dumped, and yet others will miss the wave altogether and be relegated to the thoughts of the past.

(Townsend 1997: 225)

However, thoughts of the past will not serve us well into the future. The seas of education may never be smooth again. Already, in Victoria, just four years after the implementation of Schools of the Future, the next wave has already hit. 'Schools of the Third Millennium', 'Successful Schools' and 'Building on Schools of the Future' are now the terminology of the future. Schools of the Future are already things of the past.

This has caused a further wave of instability, as school communities ponder the minister's recent announcement that there will be further change but without giving any indication of how this change might been instituted. Will there be further staff cuts? Will technology take over? Will social-justice issues be further eroded? The instability generated by uncertainty has probably lowered staff morale, staff motivation and staff performance as teachers become more concerned about their own future than their students' present.

Yet predicting the future is a risky business. Not only are there possible futures, probable futures and preferred futures, but the prediction itself might make one or other of the possible futures a self-fulfilling prophecy. If we predict good things and work towards attaining them the prediction is more likely to come true. If we predict bad things we work towards preventing them from happening, and the prediction may then be way off.

One of the exciting developments of technology in education is the ability to 'conference' without 'holding a conference'. The Australian Council for Educational Administration, in the middle of 1997, held its first virtual conference. A group of people provided a range of papers, which were all placed on the Internet. Participants in the conference were given access to the site, were able to download the papers and comment on those that they wanted to through e-mail. This conference, and the formal one which preceded it, provided a range of opinions about what the future held for schools, ranging from the statement that 'the formal education system could be said to be in its last throes' (Spender 1997: 1) to the belief that 'the most probable state of schools in 2007 is that they will be much the same as they are now' (White 1997: 1).

However, a look at past predictions may help us to see towards the future a little bit better. If predictions made in the past have been fairly accurate we might have some confidence about predicting what might happen in the future. In 1979 I was part of a group of people who made some predictions about the world and the teacher's role in it for the year 2000 as part of the *Submission of the State College of Victoria at Frankston to the Teacher Education Inquiry* (State College of Victoria at Frankston 1979) to both Commonwealth and state inquiries into teacher education. Some of our predictions seem now to have been pretty accurate and others were way off the mark. Here are some which were pretty accurate:

- The proportions of people in the higher age groups of the population will have increased.
- The type of population in the future will change from a predominantly European origin towards a more Asian/European background, with the consequent alterations in cultural and religious patterns.
- The development of automation will result in job elimination.
- Work will have to be invented to give people a feeling of social usefulness.
- Some people will not be employed for the whole of their lifetime.
- Economic factors will be the most important ones considered when decisions are made about education and welfare.
- Children will break away from the traditional family grouping and form other groupings.
- The significant increase in the quantity and quality of information will create an information elite.

- Skills other than the three Rs will be regarded as basic.
- The expertise needed to fulfil the needs of 'learning groups' will not be that possessed by teachers as trained in the 1970s.

Some which might be considered way off the mark are:

- The inequality in the distribution of goods and services will have diminished.
- There will be a shift in the need for money as a personal resource.

There were other scenarios where, although we are not there yet, we are well on the way:

- The nominal hours per week of work will have decreased to 28–32 hours.
- Work and occupational role will no longer determine so directly the lifestyles of individuals.
- As fuel becomes scarce there will be less mobility in terms of travel from home to work or entertainment, with a consequential increase in the importance of local community facilities.
- Students in small or isolated institutions will have the same access to information as students in large educational institutions.
- The basic organisational module in educational institutions will be 'learning groups', not classrooms.

Generally speaking, the responsibilities that teachers now have were fairly accurately predicted as well. Some of the teacher responsibilities which are now normal expectations within the teaching task but were not as evident in the 1970s include:

- To assess the educational needs of individual learners and to prescribe appropriate learning programmes to meet these needs.
- To update one's own knowledge and expertise continually to maximise the effectiveness of the learning experience.
- To develop the personal and professional attitudes necessary for work as a member of a team.
- To establish appropriate relationships with a growing body of para-professionals and support staff.
- To work cooperatively with other professionals to produce teaching strategies appropriate to the achievement of instructional objectives.
- To develop a commitment to the concept of lifelong learning and one's own involvement with all sections of the community.
- To assess the educational needs of the community and to determine appropriate responses to those needs.

- To participate with others in the community in a wide range of educational decision-making.
- To adopt strategies for coping with the stress of a changing society and new roles and interpersonal relationships with students, colleagues, para-professionals and parents.
- To utilise research findings and other means of furthering professional growth.

In overview, perhaps two key things emerge with hindsight: first, the world that we had predicted was to be a kinder, more caring place than the one that has in fact emerged; second, the impact of changing technology on schools, and decisions made about schools, has been far greater than we predicted.

The loss of the 'caring' community

We believed that the technological changes of the future would enable more people to share what was available, such as work, money and resources. In fact the opposite is true, as some of the information in Chapter 4 will confirm. In what Mike Hough (1997) calls a 'paradox', the hours of work have intensified for some at the expense of others. The employers of unskilled and semi-skilled workers have found that it is cheaper to employ the people you already have for longer hours (especially with the impending demise of overtime rates) than to take on new staff. Professionals such as teachers, on a fixed income, have found themselves being asked to do much more, simply because there are fewer people around to share increasing numbers of tasks. What we have found is that there are substantially increasing profits for companies and increased salaries for the executives that run them, because there are fewer people being asked to do more and more with little or no additional recompense.

We are now finding that community services (health, welfare, education) are being asked to operate under the same business principles. Yet, as Hughes argued:

> We may be tempted to ask why we should use a business concept in the reform of education. Business has not been uniformly successful, even in surviving. Of the top 100 firms on the business magazine Fortune list of 1970, one third had gone out of business by 1990.
>
> (Hughes 1996: 1)

Are we to accept the possibility that one-third of our schools will not be in existence in twenty years' time? What are the implications of this for communities and individual students? One difference between business and education is that if one car company goes out of business there is another model that we can buy. We might have to go a little further to get it, but we only have to go once. But what happens if a school goes out of business? Either it will be replaced by a school of another type (privatisation) or we will have to send our children to another school further away, not just for a single visit to purchase, but every day for the rest of the child's schooling.

Already, rural Australia is crying out about the demise of its communities. Large banks have left town, leaving just automatic teller machines (ATMs) or a couple of hours' drive to the nearest bank; hospitals and schools have been shut down by governments on the basis that they are too small to be 'economic'. So the local teacher can no longer coach the town football team, the ATM cannot open the bowling for the town cricket team, and the nursing and teaching staff no longer organise the local art show. Losing these services diminishes us all, yet governments and big business seem to turn a deaf ear to anything that does not pay its way.

At the same time as the majority of the general population are becoming comparatively poorer, state governments take money away from hospitals and schools, yet fight over grands prix and big-budget musicals that, in the end, cost rather than make the taxpayer money. The question hangs in the air: how many of the 70 per cent of Australian families (mum, dad, two kids in school) who now have a family income less than the average weekly wage could actually afford to take the family to the Australian Grand Prix or *Sunset Boulevard* or *Miss Saigon*? Is this not an example of the richest in our community getting things to do at the expense of public health and education for the majority? If this trend continues, where will it end?

Technology: the unstoppable force

The second factor which comes from the 1979 predictions is that we seriously underestimated the pervasiveness of computer technology. We believed that teachers would have to deal with the technology, but not in the myriad ways in which Geoff Romeo indicated in Chapter 9.

Bill Gates argued that we have seriously overestimated the extent to which technology will develop over the next five years but have seriously underestimated its development over the next fifty. We now need to deal with the possibility that at some time in the not too distant future we will have virtual classrooms, with students plugging their helmet and gloves into their computer at home to become virtually surrounded by their classmates and the teacher. Or we could have students walking out of their front door on to the plains of Africa or the ice of Antarctica. Such a development is no more or less feasible than the Internet would have been to the scientists of the 1940s, who would walk for five minutes to get from one end of their computer to the other.

It appears that technology has its own version of Zeno's paradox. (This

Greek philosopher suggested that if you took half of a pile of sand, then repeatedly took half of what was left, you would never actually have no sand left.) Technological change has increased rapidly, as was pointed out in 1970 by Alvin Toffler in *Future Shock*, and it continues to speed up. We think that it must slow down some time soon, but it never does. We might be getting closer and closer to the limits of human ingenuity but we are not there yet, and possibly we never will be.

It almost seems as if it takes humans about a hundred years or so to work through a manual way of doing things to the 'powered' approach. There were just over a hundred years between balloon flight and *Kittyhawk*, just over a hundred years between the wire telegraph and radio. Look at where flight and communications are today, less than a hundred years after that first major step.

Education may well just be entering its powered phase. As for both flight and communication, there were about a hundred years between Australian education being made 'free, compulsory and secular' (1872 in Victoria, 1875 in Queensland and South Australia, later in other states) and the Karmel Report of 1973, described by Caldwell as 'arguably one of the most influential documents in school education in the last twenty-five years' (Caldwell 1993: 3). Since that time, less than a single generation has seen, among other things, the movement from a debate about community involvement in educational decision-making to the formalised practice of it.

One wonders what Plato, who was concerned about the introduction of writing because he suggested that once thoughts hit the paper they would leave the mind, would think of the new technologies in education. Could it be that the advent of new 'whiz-bang' methods of computer-aided learning will see the demise of more pedestrian forms of information collection, such as listening to teachers or reading books, as students demand that they be entertained while they learn? It may well be that technology is more critical to the future of Australian education than we think. It might mean the difference between Australia maintaining its position as a first-world nation and becoming more like one from the third world.

Improving our competitiveness: third world or third millennium?

In term of both population and economics we are a small nation and, as such, uncompetitive in many areas. These factors lead to Australia's inability to compete internationally, particularly in areas economic. Yet the government and economists are arguing that we should be able to compete. Since we can no longer rely on our natural resources to maintain our living standards, there are only two ways of increasing our influence in the world. The first relates to becoming more competitive in terms of our manufacturing base and the second involves becoming 'world's best' in terms of knowledge production and dissemination.

The third-world option

Maintaining first-world living standards for all is incompatible with manu-facturing goods at third-world prices. To accomplish first-world living standards for some means having a majority of the population working for third-world wages, and reducing welfare benefits for those who do not work, thus ensuring that a small proportion of the population can maintain its first-world standards. This is a similar situation to that in many third-world countries now. Millions of people work for pennies to keep a comparative few in luxury. Australia, among other nations, has complained about the human rights issues that exist in some of these countries, yet it could be suggested that things such as the 'Accord', which restricted wage growth for more than a decade, together with recent changes to labour laws, the concept of youth wages (despite these young people having 'adult' expenses), together with the attacks on the welfare system, have opened up the possi-bility of this happening here.

The data contained in Chapter 4 demonstrates the growing number of people who are struggling financially and a considerable widening of the gap between rich and poor, and might lead to the suggestion that Australia could be considered to be moving towards a third-world economy that would see many Australians marginalised so that a few can live in the manner they think they deserve. Those who have opted for this view see 'service' industries as the work of the future. The comparatively few high-income earners would employ others to do their cooking, cleaning and other menial tasks, presumably for considerably less pay. The growth in service-industry workers suggests that this is already an option some have taken, but this does not capture any more of the global wealth. It simply redistributes the wealth already in Australia, and this will lead to a rapid decline in the living conditions of many people. If this track is pursued, many Australians will have cause for concern.

The third-millennium option

However, there is an alternative view, if we care to pursue it. The second way to promote Australia's position in the world economy and capture more of its wealth is to sell ourselves at the top end rather than the bottom, not by manufacturing and selling goods, but by producing and disseminating knowledge. If it ensures that it focuses on the future and moves towards what will be economically productive in that future, a small country such as Australia can offer high-quality services in the knowledge area to all parts of the world. A number of the current 'Tiger' nations show that this is true. High technology is the way of the future and the Internet is the new world market. If we can produce something which is both the best in the world and something the world needs, then the opportunities are enormous.

Australia has always been able to develop technologies of use to the world, from the stump-jump plough to the wine cask, from the black box used on every airline in the world to the bionic ear. A recent instance of Australia's ability to do this is the use of nanotechnology to promote new medical capabilities. Using an Australian product, the nanomachine, it is now possible to detect the equivalent of a cube of sugar in a volume of water the size of Sydney Harbour, and this has potentially changed the whole area of detecting illness in humans. O'Neill (1997) describes the new skills required by scientists not only to develop such breakthroughs but also to keep ahead of the opposition in such developments, to maintain the competitive edge on other countries. For almost a decade, scientists, who live and die by publishing what they have learned, had to commit to secrecy so that other people would not find out what they knew.

Let us take an educational example of the third-millennium view of development. If a group of teachers in a particular school has what might be considered to be world's best practice in terms of teaching mathematics, or music, or science, a method which is both student-proof and teacher-proof, to the extent that it could guarantee success, why could it not be packaged and made available to others worldwide? The literacy work of Robert Slavin with 'Success for All' and Marie Clay with 'Reading Recovery' are early instances of what can be done.

If we could develop such things in Australia (and some already have), both the school (as publisher) and the individual teacher (as author) would benefit, in terms of money and reputation. If a school was known to have the best maths teaching in the world, could it market this to international students, either in person or through flexible delivery? Could we not encourage our students to be entrepreneurial in this way? What do we need to teach them for this to happen? Could not this skill base be equally marketable? Clusters of schools, each with their own particular strengths, could be serving their local community directly, utilising the best practice they can find from all around the country, and would compete internationally instead of with each other.

However, we might also want to go one step further, by producing an educational system which promotes these types of skills – vision, entrepreneurship, high-level development capabilities, teamwork – not in just a few of our students, but in most of them. We would not only be able to sell our products, but also the educational system that developed the people who made them. An alternative view to the third-world solution to our current economic problems is possible, but only if we accept that all people in the future must be capable, skilled and self-motivating. In order for this to happen we need to change our focus from the past and present towards the future, and we need to change our education system to match that future. However, the recent fall in Asian currencies demonstrated clearly that no level of technological expertise, in itself, can guarantee ongoing success. The focus on the economy must also be balanced by an ongoing concern for developing values such as honesty, integrity and concern for others. Without these, those in power may move countries to the brink of ruin.

The past and, generally speaking, the present education system – namely, primary and junior secondary schools for all, senior secondary schools for some and university for a few – served society well in the industrial age. If the world of the factory and other unskilled jobs required people who undertook rote, repetitive tasks and were required to be punctual and submissive, the school years from 5 to 16 provided this. Those who were to be middle-level professionals completed school and perhaps went to do practical and theoretical training for specific tasks (teachers, nurses). The movers and shakers of society went on to university.

The evidence suggests that technology will continue to change, that government funding will continue to be a problem, that the social and employment needs of students will continue to change. However, if the reform must continue at the speed currently indicated, perhaps we should be reviewing not just schools but the underlying purpose of schools as well. Let us start with what we might consider to be the underlying goals of education. It could be argued that all the specific objectives we might have for an education system can be consolidated into two all-encompassing goals:

- To pass on the traditions, knowledge and attitudes held by the society from one generation to the next.
- To help the individual develop the skills, attitudes and knowledge necessary for him or her to survive within that society over the course of a lifetime.

Having identified what the purpose of the education system of the future might be we can then ask ourselves two complementary questions:

- What does the society of the future need for its population?
- What skills does the individual need in the future?

Perhaps, for the first time in history, the needs of society and the needs of the individual might be identical. The following list is a start, rather than being definitive:

- a strong skill capability in literacy, numeracy and computer literacy;
- cultural, artistic and human sensitivities;
- the ability to change work as work changes;
- the ability to learn and relearn;
- the ability to make decisions, individually and in groups;
- the ability to use leisure time profitably;
- the ability to make maximum use of diminishing resources;

- a commitment to work with others to improve the community;
- the ability to use technology as a means to an end.

Many of these items promote community living as well as individual development. As governments decrease their commitment to many of the services previously seen as their responsibility, local communities will have to generate ways in which they do these things themselves. A number of recent activities, from safety houses, to neighbourhood watch, to hospice programmes, to neighbourhood houses and community learning centres, are early examples of this move. Using the responses to the questions about what both society and the individual might require in the future as a basis, we might now ask ourselves how the education system of the future might be different from schools as they are now and how primary schools fit within that system. Table 12.1 is an attempt to provide such a comparison.

If we look at the two lists in Table 12.1 we can ask ourselves where the gaps are in the current system that need to be addressed in order to move to

Table 12.1 The changing nature of the role of the school

Characteristics of schools in the late 1990s	*Characteristics of education in the year 2010*
Everyone must attend a formal education programme for a certain minimum amount of time	People have access to learning 24 hours a day, 365 days a year
Everyone must learn a common 'core' content of knowledge	Everyone must understand the learning process and have strong learning skills
The information to be learned must be graded in a specific way and must be learned in that order	Information is accessed according to the learner's capability
What is to be taught, when it is to be taught and how it is to be taught should all be determined by a professional person	What is to be taught, when it is to be taught and how it is to be taught will all be determined by the learner
When a person leaves formal education he or she is fully prepared for society and life	A person does not have to be in formal education to interact with learning networks
Important learning can only occur in formal learning facilities	Important learning is that determined by the learner and can be learned anywhere
The terms 'education' and 'school' mean almost the same thing	The term 'school' may have disappeared from the language
The more formal education you have, the more successful you will be	The more learning you have, the more successful you will be
Once you leave school you enter the 'real world'	'School' is only one gateway to the 'real world'

the new system. How do we make the new system one that responds to the third-millennium rather than the third-world response to the current economic situation? We might now argue, as Minzey (1981) has, that in the past educational change has been similar to rearranging the toys in the toy box, when what we really needed was a whole new box. If so, what might that box look like? Beare poses a similar question:

> If, as an educational planner, you were presented with a greenfields site on which a new town or suburb was to be built to accommodate dwellings for approximately 22,000 people, what schools or educational buildings would you offer the developer?
>
> (Beare 1997: 1)

Beare argues that there are some things that you would *not* have, including:

- the egg-crate classrooms and long corridors;
- the notion of set class groups based on age-grade structures;
- the division of the school day into standard slabs of time;
- the linear curriculum parcelled into step-by-step gradations;
- the parcelling of human knowledge into predetermined boxes called 'subjects';
- the division of staff by subject specialisation;
- the allocation of most school tasks to the person called 'teacher';
- the assumption that learning takes place in a place called 'school';
- the artificial walls that barricade school from home and community;
- the notion of a stand-alone school isolated from other schools;
- the notion of a school system bounded by a locality such as a state (or even country);
- the limitation of 'formal schooling' to twelve years and between the ages of 5 and 18.

> (Beare 1997: 2–4)

If we accept his arguments about what schools in the future should not be, we have some indication of the task facing primary-school communities, teachers and parents, on the one hand, and governments and educational policy-makers, on the other. One of the difficulties we have is that we are not establishing a system from scratch. We already have schools and they have been in existence for a century and a quarter.

But perhaps what we need to do is to turn the clock back a little, to wonder what we might do if schools did not currently exist. Some changes that might be predicted, particularly if we see a future where schools are something like they are now, include extending the range of the school's activities. This might include extending the school hours from the current less than 15 per cent of the year to something over 50 per cent, extending the school clientele from the current 20 per cent of the population to the whole population, or both. It does not seem cost-effective to have a publicly owned building, with a range of facilities that might be used by all members of the community, shut for the majority of each day and on more than one-third of the days in a year.

Promoting a range of inexpensive, relevant programmes to community members outside school hours seems to be one way in which the school might increase its base of community support, provide a much more cost-effective use of public plant and funding, and perhaps raise some additional funds which might extend the range of school programmes. If society is going to continue to change, even at its current rate, the need for retraining and for local support services (health, welfare, safety) will continue to escalate. Rather than these services being spread all over town, schools could be redesigned to incorporate them so they would be readily available to all families.

If these things are to come to pass, there are particular issues that primary schools need to address. For a start, primary schools will need to embrace the new technologies with all their power of learning. This will mean adjusting the curriculum, providing for professional development of staff and even diverting resources from one area to another to ensure that students have the best chance of gaining the skills required to take charge of the future. It will mean intensifying efforts to ensure that every student is literate and numerate, for without these skills the technology is simply another toy. It may mean extending the school day and the school year, because if these aspects of the curriculum are intensified we must also have time for development of the social, cultural and personal skills that make us human.

Second, primary schools are not geared to provide service and resources to the whole community, so partnerships will need to be established. Primary schools will need to become partners with other primary schools to offer a range of options in a collaborative rather than competitive way, to share both expert teachers and the broader administrative load. They will need to become partners with secondary schools to provide their parents with access to adult learning facilities. They will need to become partners with other agencies, so that the school building can become a one-stop shopping centre for people to find the services they need.

But perhaps most critical of all, primary schools must establish partnerships with their local community – not just parents, but all within the community; otherwise, given the third-world scenario, there is a real danger that primary schools, particularly government primary schools, will dispense literacy and numeracy skills only, with the rest being overtaken by various forms of technology. Unless whole communities see the value of schools (and, remember, parents with school-age children are now a minority group), governments seeking 'savings' will provide only what they see as absolutely necessary. Everything else will become 'user pays'.

An understanding of the need for these partnerships and the initial impetus towards their development must come from school leaders, principals, teachers and parents. It will not be a matter of training leaders for the future, but of having school and community leaders taking charge now so that the possible future is also the preferable future. We could argue that, in these days of rapid and substantial change, not to have some vision of the future is to promote decline.

Primary education has played a major role in the development of Australian society. In Chapter 2 Brian Caldwell talks of 'heroes'. We have conquered the challenge of moving from a quality education system for a *few* people (Hedley Beare's 'pre-industrial' metaphor) to a quality education system for *most* people. Our challenge now is to move from having a quality education system for *most* people to having a quality education system for *all* people.

The most critical challenge for those making decisions about education at this time, at whatever level they are being made, is the one addressed by adapting Judy Codding's final words at the recent Successful Schools conference in Victoria: 'The best guide I had as a high school principal was to try to do for the 2,500 students I had responsibility for in my school, what I would want done for my own three children' (Codding 1997: 17). We might now suggest that the best guide we, as educators, have for improving the quality of education provision for school communities throughout the country is to consider what we would want done for our own families.

In my view, the best education that we can hope for, for our students, for our families and for Australia, is one that is local (i.e. in my community) and global (i.e. one which provides access to the knowledge resources of the whole world). It is grounded in the community in which I live but opens up a world of possibilities. It is educative and it is social. It provides me with the skills that I need now and gives me access to those I will need later. I am linked to my education at all times of the day and no matter where I am in the world. My school-age children, the rest of my family, my neighbours and my friends can all participate with me. We would want the best school to be my local school. In short, this new institution has become a community facility which is sometimes used for the education of children, and has replaced the school, which was not a community facility, but was only sometimes used for the education of children.

References

Barber, M. (1996) *The Learning Game*, London: Victor Gollancz.

Beare, H. (1997) 'Designing a break-the-mould school for the future', paper presented at the virtual conference of the Australian Council for Educational Administration, Hawthorn.

Caldwell, B. (1993) *Decentralising the Management of Australia's Schools*, Melbourne: National Industry Education Forum.

Codding, J. (1997) 'Designing highly effective programs for successful schools', keynote presentation at the Successful Schools Conference, Melbourne, 3 June.

Hough, M. (1997) '"Paradox": a way of approaching schooling in the context of a post-industrial society', paper presented at the virtual conference of the Australian Council for Educational Administration, Hawthorn.

Hughes, P. (1996) 'Vision and realisation: re-engineering in the context of UNESCO's vision: a prospective on re-engineering education for change', paper presented at the UNESCO ACEID (Asian Centre for Educational Innovation and Development) Conference, Bangkok, December.

Minzey, J. D. (1981) 'Community education and community schools', address at the State College of Victoria, Frankston, Australia, May.

O'Neill, H. (1997) 'Secret science', *Australian Weekend Review*, 21–22 June: Features/5.

Spender, D. (1997) 'From the factory system to portfolio living: access, equity and self promotion in the 21st century', keynote paper presented at the annual conference of the Australian Council for Educational Administration, Canberra, October.

State College of Victoria at Frankston (1979) *Submission of the State College of Victoria at Frankston to the Teacher Education Inquiry*, Frankston: State College of Victoria at Frankston.

Toffler, A. (1970) *Future Shock*, London: Pan.

Townsend, T. (1997) 'Afterword: problems and possibilities', in T. Townsend (ed.) *Restructuring and Quality: Issues for Tomorrow's Schools*, London: Routledge.

White, R. (1997) 'Schools in 2007', paper presented at the virtual conference of the Australian Council for Educational Administration, Hawthorn.

INDEX